BODIES OF SOUND

To all who ride the boogie and share the beat of love.

Bodies of Sound

Studies Across Popular Music and Dance

Edited by

SHERRIL DODDS
Temple University, USA

SUSAN C. COOK
University of Wisconsin-Madison, USA

ASHGATE

Published by
Ashgate Publishing Limited
Wey Court East
Union Road
Farnham
Surrey, GU9 7PT
England

Ashgate Publishing Company
110 Cherry Street
Suite 3-1
Burlington, VT 05401-3818
USA

www.ashgate.com

British Library Cataloguing in Publication Data
Bodies of sound : studies across popular music and dance.
 – (Ashgate popular and folk music series)
 1. Music and dance – History – 19th century. 2. Music and dance – History – 20th century. 3. Music and dance – History – 21st century.
 I. Series II. Dodds, Sherril, 1967– III. Cook, Susan C.
 306.4'84'09–dc23

The Library of Congress has cataloged the printed edition as follows:
Bodies of sound : studies across popular music and dance / edited by Sherril Dodds and Susan C. Cook.
     p. cm.—(Ashgate popular and folk music series)
  Includes bibliographical references and index.
  ISBN 978-1-4094-4517-3 (hardcover)—ISBN 978-1-4094-4518-0 (ebook) 1. Popular music—History and criticism. 2. Dance—History. I. Dodds, Sherril, 1967– II. Cook, Susan C.
  ML3470.B66 2013
  781.6409—dc23

2012033537

ISBN 9781409445173 (hbk)
ISBN 9781409445180 (ebk – PDF)
ISBN 9781472402165 (ebk – ePUB)

Printed and bound in Great Britain
by MPG PRINTGROUP

Contents

List of Figures and Table

Table

List of Music Examples

Notes on Contributors

Joanna Bosse, Assistant Professor at Michigan State University, is an ethnomusicologist and dance ethnographer. She has conducted fieldwork in dancehalls in the Midwestern US, studying the performance of couple dances like salsa, swing, ballroom and country two-step. In addition to the relationship between music and dance, her work on popular culture involves the dynamics of affinity groups, cross-cultural encounters, and amateur performance. Her research on whiteness, race and performance appears in *The Journal of American Folklore*, *Dance Research Journal* and elsewhere.

Theresa Jill Buckland is Professor of Performing Arts at De Montfort University, Leicester, England where she supervises research students in dance ethnography and dance history. Theresa is editor of *Dance in the Field: Theory, Methods and Issues in Dance Ethnography* (1999) and *Dancing from Past to Present: Nation, Culture, Identities* (2006), and author of *Society Dancing: Fashionable Bodies in England, 1870-1920* (2011). She is Vice-Chair of the International Council for Traditional Music Study Group on Ethnochoreology.

Susan C. Cook is Professor of Music at the University of Wisconsin-Madison. Her teaching and research focus on contemporary and American musics of all kinds and demonstrate her abiding interest in dance and cultural studies. Her publications include *Opera for a New Republic* (1988), *Cecilia Reclaimed: Feminist Perspectives on Gender and Music* (1994, edited with Judy Tsou) and essays in *The Cambridge History of Twentieth-Century Music* (2004), *The Garland Encyclopedia of World Music* (1998-2002), *The Arts of the Prima Donna in the Long Nineteenth Century* (2012) and *Contemporary Theatre Review*.

Sherril Dodds is Professor and Chair of the Dance Department at Temple University. Her publications include two monographs, *Dance on Screen: Genres and Media from Hollywood to Experimental Art* (2001) and *Dancing on the Canon: Embodiments of Value in Popular Dance* (2011). She sits on the Editorial Boards of Congress on Research in Dance and Society of Dance History Scholars, and is co-founder of the research network PoP MOVES.

Rachel Duerden lectures in Dance at Manchester Metropolitan University and her research interest focuses on dance–music relationships in choreography. Her book, *The Choreography of Antony Tudor: Focus on Four Ballets*, was published in 2003. More recently, her interest in dance–music relationships has drawn her to the choreography of Mark Morris, and she has published articles on his work in *Dance Chronicle* and *Dance Research*.

Simon Featherstone is a Principal Lecturer in Drama at De Montfort University. He is the author of *Postcolonial Cultures* (2005) and *Englishness: Twentieth-Century Popular Culture and the Forming of English Identity* (2009), and has also published on nineteenth-century music-hall performance, transatlantic blackface minstrelsy and twentieth-century poetry.

Anne Margrete Fiskvik has worked as a professional dancer and choreographer and since 2000 she has pursued an academic career. Her main research areas are: Early Dance History, Norwegian Theatre Dance History, Choreomusical Analysis and Practice(s) in Theatre Dance and in Popular Dance and Music Cultures. She currently works as 'Førsteamanuensis' (Assistant Professor) at the Department for Musicology and Dance Studies, NTNU.

Joanna Hall is a Principal Lecturer in Dance Studies at Kingston University, London. She completed her PhD in Dance Studies at the University of Surrey, supported by an Arts and Humanities Research Council Award. Her research interests include the popular dance practices of musical and club cultures, and the relationship between dance and cultural identities. She is a member of the PoP (Performances of the Popular) MOVES research committee, presents at conferences internationally and has contributed to *Decentring Dancing Texts: the Challenge of Interpreting Dances* (2008).

Chih-Chieh Liu is a Post-Doctoral Fellow in the Department of Music, University of Hong Kong. With interdisciplinary training across the fields of dance (PhD, University of Surrey), children's literature (MA, University of Reading), anthropology and history (BA Dual Hons, National Taiwan University), she has a particular research interest in the nexus between translation and corporeality in Asian popular culture. She has presented her work internationally, and is currently pursuing publications on the (re)production of the body, the processes of (mis) translation and issues concerning (dis)synchronization.

Jeff Packman has a PhD in Ethnomusicology from University of California, Berkeley. He teaches in the divisions of Performance and History/Culture at the University of Toronto's Faculty of Music. With support from Fulbright and Canada's Social Sciences and Humanities Research Council, he has conducted extensive fieldwork in Bahia, Brazil, since 2002. His research on professional music-making, cultural politics, and discourses of race and socio-economic class in Bahia's capital, Salvador, has appeared in journals including *Ethnomusicology*, *Black Music Research Journal* and *Latin American Music Review*.

Clare Parfitt-Brown is a Senior Lecturer in Dance at the University of Chichester. Her research focuses on the cultural histories of popular dance practices. She has co-authored the books *Planning Your PhD* and *Completing Your PhD*, and published articles in *Research in Dance Education* and the *International Journal of Performance Arts and Digital Media*. Her research has been presented at conferences in the United States, France, South Korea and the UK.

Danielle Robinson is an Associate Professor of Dance at York University in Toronto, Canada, where she is cross-appointed with the graduate programmes in Theatre Studies and Communication and Culture. Her scholarly work on the intercultural movement of African Diasporic popular dance forms has been published in *Dance Theatre Journal* (UK), *Dance Research Journal* (USA), *Dance Chronicle* (USA), *Dance Research* (UK), and *Research in Dance Education* (UK). From 2011 to 2012 she was a Leverhulme Trust Visiting Fellow at the University of Chichester (UK).

Laura Robinson is an AHRC-funded PhD candidate at the University of Surrey whose research focuses on the re-presentation of male street dance crews in UK televised talent show competitions. Laura holds a Master's degree in Dance Histories, Cultures and Practices from the University of Surrey, and was awarded the Janet Lansdale Prize for outstanding Masters Dissertation on male burlesque striptease. Laura currently lectures at the University of Surrey and the London Studio Centre.

Bonnie Rowell was a Principal Lecturer in Dance Studies at Roehampton University London before her recent retirement. Her particular interest is in dance analysis, contemporary choreography and philosophy. Publications include a monograph, *Dance Umbrella: The First 21 Years* (2000), and chapter contributions to various anthologies including *Dance, Education and Philosophy* (1999), *Europe Dancing* (2000), *Dancing off the Page* (2007) and *Contemporary Choreography: A Critical Reader* (2009).

Catherine Tackley (née Parsonage) is Senior Lecturer in Music at The Open University. Her first book, *The Evolution of Jazz in Britain, 1880-1935*, was published by Ashgate in 2005 and she has recently completed a monograph on Benny Goodman's 1938 Carnegie Hall Concert for the 'Studies in Recorded Jazz' series of Oxford University Press. She is a co-editor of the *Jazz Research Journal* (Equinox). Catherine is currently Musical Director of Dr Jazz and the Cheshire Cats Big Band.

General Editor's Preface

The upheaval that occurred in musicology during the last two decades of the twentieth century has created a new urgency for the study of popular music alongside the development of new critical and theoretical models. A relativistic outlook has replaced the universal perspective of modernism (the international ambitions of the 12-note style); the grand narrative of the evolution and dissolution of tonality has been challenged, and emphasis has shifted to cultural context, reception and subject position. Together, these have conspired to eat away at the status of canonical composers and categories of high and low in music. A need has arisen, also, to recognize and address the emergence of crossovers, mixed and new genres, to engage in debates concerning the vexed problem of what constitutes authenticity in music and to offer a critique of musical practice as the product of free, individual expression.

Popular musicology is now a vital and exciting area of scholarship, and the *Ashgate Popular and Folk Music Series* presents some of the best research in the field. Authors are concerned with locating musical practices, values and meanings in cultural context, and draw upon methodologies and theories developed in cultural studies, semiotics, poststructuralism, psychology and sociology. The series focuses on popular musics of the twentieth and twenty-first centuries. It is designed to embrace the world's popular musics from Acid Jazz to Zydeco, whether high tech or low tech, commercial or non-commercial, contemporary or traditional.

Professor Derek B. Scott
Professor of Critical Musicology
University of Leeds

Preface

The impetus for this collection arose from my encounter with two women whose friendship and intellect prompted serious conversation over the pervasive textual, social and mediated sites in which popular music and dance interact. The first, Dr Patricia Schmidt, occupied the office next to me at the University of Surrey. Although we belonged to different departments – Patty to *Music and Sound Recording* and myself to *Dance, Film and Theatre* – that had little interaction at the curriculum or research level, a fleeting chat revealed that she had worked on music fan engagement, while I had researched representations of dance, both within the genre of pop music video. A later and notably extended conversation allowed us to vent frustration at the neglect of the dancing body in popular music scholarship and, at the time, the somewhat scarce research on popular dance in general let alone its engagement with popular music. From this, an idea was born: *Popular Dance and Music Matters* (PDMM), an annual symposium from 2007 to 2009 that brought together approximately 30 Euro-American scholars willing to share their nascent ideas in response to the mutual exchange across the production and consumption of popular music and dance. Many of the presenters who participated in the symposia contributed to this volume and I am most grateful for their extended commitment to this developing field of enquiry.

While Patty decided to take a break from academic life to pursue other personal and professional goals, thanks to my second encounter – with Professor Susan C. Cook – I was able to realize this edited collection that I initially conceived with Patty. Susan and I served together on the Board of Directors for the Society of Dance History Scholars (SDHS) and over tea breaks we quickly came to realize a mutual interest in popular music and dance. Fortunately, we were given the opportunity to enjoy extended interactions about this topic through the *Popular, Social and Vernacular Dance Working Group*, which I founded at the SDHS annual conference in 2007 and continued to convene until 2010. With her musicology training and interdisciplinary interest in dance, Susan was an ideal co-editor for this volume and I sincerely thank her for the energy, passion and rigour that she has brought to this collaboration. Although we continue to be geographically remote, with Susan in Wisconsin and myself in Pennsylvania since I relocated to Temple University, the snatched beers after SDHS board meetings, the grainy skype conversations and the multiple email exchanges have all contributed to a great intellectual friendship.

In producing this volume, Susan and I would like to thank the following: the University of Surrey for supporting the *Popular Dance and Music Matters* symposia; Derek Scott, Editor for the Ashgate Popular and Folk Music Series, who offered generous feedback in response to our book proposal; Laura Macy, Senior Commissioning Editor for Music Studies at Ashgate, for welcoming our book proposal and for her professional guidance, as well as that of Sadie Copley-May and Mary Murphy who worked closely with us throughout the production process; Kelly Hiser, our graduate project assistant at the University of Wisconsin-Madison funded through the generosity of the Wisconsin Alumni Research Foundation, who has meticulously attended to referencing and bibliographic matter; Dr Patricia Schmidt for helping to initiate this work; and, finally, to our contributors who have been so receptive to our editorial feedback and have prompted Susan and myself to rethink the myriad ways in which we understand the interactions between popular dance and music.

Sherril Dodds

Introduction
Embodying Sound/Sounding Bodies

Sherril Dodds and Susan C. Cook

From the ragtime one-step of the early twentieth century to the contemporary practices of youth club cultures, popular dance and music are inextricably linked. While scholarly engagement with the historically marginalized 'popular' has grown across music and dance studies,[1] scholars have devoted less attention to the intrinsic and, we would argue, mutually constitutive relationship between popular music and dance.[2] This anthology therefore aims to reveal the intimate connections between bodies and sound in the production and reception of popular music and dance. The idea that neither the music nor the dance occupies a position in which one determines or dominates the other underpins our enquiry. Instead, we conceive a mobilization of meanings that come into play through the reciprocal exchange between popular music and dance. Furthermore, we seek to privilege the notion of embodiment as central to popular performance, whether through the codified posturing of singers, musicians and DJs in the moment of sound creation or in the way that dancers enact social identities and values through their corporeal response to the music. We therefore set out to explore how bodies are instrumental in the creation, transmission and reception of music, which we imagine as 'bodies of sound'.

Yet, conceptually and methodologically, our investigation into the tacit interactions across popular music and dance presents two significant research problems. First, scholars have frequently documented how the popular idiom represents an unstable phenomenon in terms of its definitions, values and

---

[1]   For an overview of the entry of 'the popular' into the academy, see Sherril Dodds, *Dancing on the Canon: Embodiments of Value in Popular Dance* (Basingstoke, 2011); and for a consideration of the neglect of the popular in musicology, see Susan Cook '"R-E-S-P-E-C-T (Find Out What It Means to Me)": Feminist Musicology and the Abject Popular', *Women and Music: A Journal of Gender and Culture*, 5 (2001): pp. 140-45.

[2]   Although a small selection of texts across dance studies (see Marshall and Jean Stearns, *Jazz Dance: The Story of American Vernacular Dance* (DaCapo, 1968); and Julie Malnig (ed.), *Ballroom, Boogie, Shimmy Sham, Shake: A Social and Popular Dance Reader* (Urbana and Chicago, 2009)) and popular music studies (see Simon Frith, Will Straw and John Street (eds), *The Cambridge Companion to Pop and Rock* (New York, 2001); and Andy Bennett, Barry Shank and Jason Toynbee (eds), *The Popular Music Studies Reader* (London and New York, 2006)) deals with related dance and music scenes, the reciprocal exchange between music and dance is rarely addressed.

concepts.[3] Therefore how do we consolidate our knowledge of a research field that is malleable, contentious and wilfully attracted to novelty and innovation? And secondly, given the pervasiveness of the popular, it can appear deceptively accessible and legible. In response, how might we query the popular through a critical lens that neither exoticizes its form nor reduces it to an expendable practice?

In answer to the first research problem, we recognize that, while popular music and dance occupy a global presence through their transnational mediations, their localized production and consumption occurs within conditions that are historically, politically, socially and economically circumscribed. Consequently, the specified meanings and values articulated through popular music and dance that are responsive to particular material circumstances ensure against a united and coherent definition of 'the popular'.[4] For this reason, we acknowledge that each essay in this volume might conceive popular music and dance differently and, instead, we focus on how our understanding of the popular is constituted, negotiated and challenged through the multiple sensual practices of moving and sounding bodies.[5] Equally, some contributors to the collection are less concerned with popular practices as such and, instead, consider how other cultural forms interact with and respond to the popular idiom.

Part of the attraction of studying the popular arises from these instabilities of 'knowing' and this intellectual aporia frequently forms key discussion areas within this collection. For example, while participants and producers of popular music and dance value adaption and modification, these aspirations for novelty are often undercut through discourses of tradition and authenticity. A similar tension can be observed in the way that the popular fluctuates between a hegemonic mode of representation and a liberalist perspective that is far more radical in the way that it conceives the social world. And while 'high art' often aspires to the popular's assumed capacity for access, inclusion and commercial gain, there comes a tipping point at which the popular is denigrated as 'appealing to the lowest common denominator' and 'selling out'. We therefore seek to embrace these polarities through exploring how popular music and dance negotiate such diametric concepts and values through their embodied practice.

Furthermore, we acknowledge that we bring to our scholarship values and assumptions that shape how we envision the popular. Thus our individual subjectivities can present difficulties for, if we adopt a relativist position of equivalence across all cultural forms, we self-consciously neutralize the passion and pleasures that we might normally invest in popular music and dance; and if

---

[3]   See Richard Middleton, *Studying Popular Music* (Milton Keynes, 1997); and Dominic Strinati, *An Introduction to Theories of Popular Culture* (London, 1995).

[4]   For an excellent overview of shifting definitions of 'the popular', see John Storey, *Inventing Popular Culture: From Folklore to Globalization* (Oxford, 2003).

[5]   As part of the instability of the category of 'the popular', we acknowledge that some authors use additional terminology, such as 'vernacular' or 'social', to describe dance forms that may be synonymous with or distinct from 'the popular'.

we commit to a reclaiming of the popular's marginal position in relation to 'high culture', this inverted value-judgement simply reinstates an 'art culture' versus 'popular culture' binary. Again, this collection adopts the position that there is no a priori knowledge of popular music and dance, but that any understanding of the popular emerges from the concomitant values of the researcher and those engaged in its practice. While the contributors to this volume occupy a range of relationships to the various subjects that they write about, our point of common ground lies in a commitment to the inclusion of the popular within all music and dance scholarship.

In relation to our second concern, how might we research an area of practice that has been intellectually marginalized, yet is so acutely well known as a site of pleasure, entertainment and escape? Given that the popular is elusive and contradictory in its meanings, values and definitions, we argue that it requires a range of critical methodologies that are cognizant of its distinctive modes of production, circulation, participation and consumption. In this collection, three primary approaches have come to dominate the research, historiography, ethnography and textual analysis, and each methodology is sensitive to the sources through which the popular articulates itself. Those essays that employ a historical lens draw upon archives that embody and document the everyday practices of the popular, such as general interest books, newspaper and magazine articles, internet sites, music scores, song lyrics and trade journals. Those scholars working within an ethnographic tradition are led directly to sites of popular production, such as music gigs, dance clubs, festivals and classes. And those researching mediated representations of the popular turn to Hollywood film musicals, pop music video, YouTube clips, television song contests and performance documentaries. In analysing these source materials, we bring expertise across musicology, dance analysis and cultural theory to make sense of how bodies produce, express and respond to sound within the field of popular culture. Within our collective scholarship, we recognize that the popular remains a locus of pleasure both for us and for its participants. Yet all of these essays reveal how popular music and dance are invested with complex and frequently troubled enunciations of gender, race, sexuality, nation and class. Therefore within this collection, the 'fun' of the popular demands serious contemplation.

We aim to provoke a wide-ranging, interdisciplinary and transatlantic conversation on the intrinsic relationship of popular music and dance and the collection includes scholarship from Asia, Europe and the United States, which explores topics from the nineteenth century through to the present day and engages with practices at local, national and transnational levels. We conceive this as an interdisciplinary project through which pressing matters of kinetic, sonic and culturally situated performance come to the fore. For the purposes of this volume, we attempt to make visible movement that might not be called 'dance', but which nevertheless falls into the range of actions, gestures and motilities that arise in the moment of sound creation. In summary, we seek to engage with the multiple sonic realities that co-exist with moving bodies. We therefore focus on how popular music and dance activate sensory experiences that reveal the pleasures of listening and responding, and how these sites of embodied sound raise questions of identity, value and politics.

The anthology is organized in four parts that examine different aspects of the popular idiom. While this structure highlights some clear thematic divisions, we wish to emphasize that many of the essays speak to ideas from other parts of the collection and are in dialogue with each other, and we would encourage the reader to take this into account when approaching the volume. In Part I, 'Constructing the Popular', the authors explore how categories of popular music and dance are constructed and de-stabilized, and their proclivity to appropriate and re-imagine cultural forms and meanings. Parfitt-Brown examines how different historical manifestations of the cancan produce a malleable understanding of the popular, from a dangerous revolutionary force through to a 'post-popular' construction; Dodds demonstrates how the band Bellowhead stages and reimagines folk music performance through a popular movement aesthetic that prompts an unsettling of cultural definitions and hierarchies; and Bosse focuses on how a ballroom dancing community delineates values and categories of the popular through perceived musical and dance competencies.

In Part II, 'Authenticity, Revival and Reinvention', the authors examine how popular forms produce and manipulate identities and meanings through their attraction to and departure from cultural traditions. Buckland details how the Boston of Edwardian England unsettled the Victorian values of order and uniformity, particularly through its novel approaches to space and time, thus appealing to the tastes of a younger and more socially mobile generation; Featherstone traces distinct approaches to the 'traditional English folk voice' from the 1950s to 1960s and how this responded to a broader cultural politics that engaged with new social and aesthetic formations; and Fiskvik analyses how the traditional Norwegian *Halling* borrows from the popular idiom to secure a favorable aesthetic and nationalist agenda as it is re-staged for concert audiences and a television song competition.

In Part III, '(Re)Framing Value', the authors interrogate how values are inscribed, silenced, rearticulated and capitalized through popular music and dance. Hall investigates how drum 'n' bass clubbers create a hierarchy of ambiguous and contradictory values situated within their articulations of gender, class and racial identities; Robinson and Packman explore how debates over notions of tradition and adaptation inform musical, movement, and evaluation practices during a samba competition in Bahia, Brazil; Duerden and Rowell identify how the film musical *West Side Story* employs vernacular music and dance to construct individual and community identities, but through inverting aesthetic and social hierarchies; and Cook excavates how the ragtime of the early twentieth century and its relationship to the recording industry produces tensions across race, class and gender through the constitutive interactions between dancing bodies and musical technologies.

Finally, in Part IV, 'Politics of the Popular', the authors read the popular as a site of political negotiation and transformation. Liu examines the 'performative translation' of dancing bodies as they are rapidly reinvented from the opening of a music concert by Taiwanese pop star Jolin Tsai through to the parodic fan performances of this event presented on YouTube; Robinson considers the shifting discourses of community and individuality across 1960s/70s Northern Soul and its contemporary practice, in conjunction with ideas of self and spectacle through its ageing subcultural membership; and Tackley traces how the live jazz music of the 1930s and the incorporation of jazz into 1980s DJ culture in Britain produced jazz dance as articulation of black British identities. In the Epilogue, we pause to reflect on how popular music and dance invite particular modes of 'engaging' and the issues that arise from the multiple sonic and embodied engagements that constitute this volume.

PART I
Constructing the Popular

Chapter 1

The Problem of Popularity:
The Cancan Between the French
and Digital Revolutions[1]

Clare Parfitt-Brown

Defining popular culture is a notoriously slippery business. British cultural studies theorist Stuart Hall writes, 'I have almost as many problems with "popular" as I have with "culture". When you put the two terms together, the difficulties can be pretty horrendous.'[2] This complexity is at least partly due to the fact that, as John Storey, another cultural studies scholar, has pointed out, popular culture has meant different things to different people at different times.[3] In *Inventing Popular Culture*, Storey explores a variety of nineteenth- and twentieth-century *intellectual* discourses about the popular. This chapter, however, is concerned with *physical* performances of the popular at different historical moments, contextualized in relation to the popular music that accompanied them, as well as wider political and social forces. My analysis focuses on a specific popular dance practice: the cancan. In considering what constitutes the cancan's popularity I examine three particular moments in the dance's history: the early cancan of the 1820s and 1830s performed by working-class dancers to quadrille music; the cancan at the Moulin Rouge of the 1890s performed by professional dancers to quadrilles played by the venue's orchestra; and the cancan danced to pop music of the late twentieth century in Baz Luhrmann's film *Moulin Rouge!* (2001). While much of the cancan's history is necessarily excluded by this selection, it nevertheless allows a comparison of three periods during which the dance's popularity was particularly visible. These snapshots reveal popularity as a distinctly malleable concept, in which various pasts, presents and futures are renegotiated in the moment of performance.

[1] Many thanks are due to my research assistant on part of this project, Dr Anna Davies, for her detailed translations of the primary sources from the 1830s and 1840s. I am also grateful to the University of Chichester for financial support for a period of research leave, research assistance, and illustration reproductions and permissions.
[2] Stuart Hall, 'Notes on Deconstructing "the popular"', in John Storey (ed.), *Cultural Theory and Popular Culture: A Reader* (London, 2006), pp. 477-87.
[3] John Storey, *Inventing Popular Culture: from Folklore to Globalization* (Oxford, 2003); John Storey, *Cultural Theory and Popular Culture: An Introduction* (London, 2006).

The Emergence of the Cancan: Deviations from Grace

The cancan emerged in working-class dance venues called *guinguettes* on the outskirts of Paris in the late 1820s. *Guinguettes* often had indoor and outdoor dance floors, and a small band of variable size consisting, for example, of a fiddle, clarinet, flageolet[4] and tambour or drum to provide the rhythm for the dancers.[5] The cancan was initially an improvised variation on the quadrille, a square dance performed in couples using steps influenced by ballet vocabulary and danced to rhythmic music in 2/4 or sometimes 6/8 time. Cancan improvisations often occurred in the final figure of the quadrille, danced to energetic music written for a *galop*. Throughout the nineteenth century these variations sometimes maintained the name 'quadrille', or even '*contredanse*' from which the quadrille was derived, but dancers, writers and courtroom judges often used the terms 'cancan' and '*chahut*' (uproar) to distinguish steps that deviated from the set figures, with the latter term designating wilder versions of the dance that broke social and legal codes of 'public decency' (the term 'cancan' will be used here to refer to both cancan and *chahut* variations, unless stated otherwise).[6]

The quadrille was danced by all classes,[7] but the form of the dance disseminated in dance manuals embodied the values of the post-revolutionary bourgeoisie through graceful bodily deportment, classical alignment of the body, control of the outer limbs from the centre, limited body contact and an emphasis on the male-female couple. During the 1820s, the quadrille's regular rhythm, composed for dancing rather than listening, and its simple walking steps, reduced in complexity from the intricate footwork of the *contredanse française*, led some bourgeois commentators to claim that the form had become uninteresting.[8] By 1826, however, working-class dancers, mostly male but also occasionally female, began introducing improvised variations that subverted the bourgeois ideals of the quadrille's set figures.[9] For example, the movement of isolated body parts, such as the legs, disrupted centralized control of the limbs. The power of dancing masters to control the bodies of the public by teaching set choreographies was also overturned by placing value on individual improvisation. Paul Smith (a

---

[4]   The flageolet is a woodwind instrument related to the recorder.

[5]   François Gasnault, *Guinguettes et Lorettes: Bals Publics à Paris au XIXe Siècle* (Paris, 1986), pp. 36-42.

[6]   For examples of primary sources that distinguish between 'cancan' and '*chahut*', see François-Joseph-Michel Noël and M. Carpentier, 'Chahut et Cancans', *Nouveau Dictionnaire des Origines, Inventions et Découvertes, dans les Arts, les Sciences, la Géographie, le Commerce, l'Agriculture, etc.* (vol. 2, Brussels, 1828), p. 17; *Le Semaine*, 18 October 1829, p. 2.

[7]   Maribeth Clark, 'The Quadrille as Embodied Musical Experience in 19th-Century Paris', *The Journal of Musicology*, 19/3 (2002): pp. 503-26.

[8]   Ibid.

[9]   Barlet makes reference to a trial as early as 20 Sept 1826. See Barlet, *Le Guide des Sergens de Ville, et Autres Préposés de l'Administration de la Police* (Paris, 1831), p. 33.

pseudonym for Désiré-Guillaume-Edouard Monnais), co-director of the Paris Opéra from 1839 to 1847, described these developments retrospectively in 1841, referring to the cancan as the *contredanse*:

> Each dancer set about improvising a kind of mimed dialogue, with very lively expression. Instead of dancing quite simply, with the most elegance and grace possible, with straight head, arms close to the body, and without departing from the catalogue of classical steps – the *assemblé*, the *six-sol*, the *entrechat* – they invented feet movements, arm movements, head movements; they attacked the status quo by dancing from all sides at once…. In a word, here the contredanse is a dramatic form where each person improvises, following his or her flair, expressing his or her individuality.[10]

Some of these improvisatory possibilities are shown in a series of sketches of the cancan by Quillenbois (a pseudonym for Charles Marie de Sarcus) published in 1845 (Figure 1.1, below).

The cancan improvisations seem to have been influenced by a variety of foreign dance forms that the working classes would have seen performed at the popular theatres of the Boulevard du Temple. A number of contemporary sources cite the influence of the Spanish *cachucha*,[11] performed by Spanish dance troupes touring France after 1825.[12] Other dances linked with the cancan include the Spanish *fandango*,[13] the Italian *tarantella* and *saltarello*,[14] the Polish *Cracovienne*[15] and the Haitian *chica*.[16] Foreign dance forms such as these appeared as exotic attractions in a wide range of popular theatrical productions in the first half of the nineteenth century, including romantic ballet-pantomimes and melodramas.[17]

These productions participated in the creation of what Petra Ten-Doesschate Chu describes as a new form of French popular culture built around the mass

---

[10] Paul Smith, 'Danses prohibées', *Revue et Gazette Musicale de Paris*, 8/21, February (1841): p. 114, translated by Anna Davies.

[11] Ibid., p. 113; Un Vilain Masque, *Physiologie de l'Opera, du Carnaval, du Cancan et de la Cachucha* (Paris, 1842), pp. 78-81; Théophile Gautier, *Histoire de l'Art Dramatique en France Depuis Vingt-cinq Ans* (vol. 1, Paris, 1858), p. 350.

[12] Gasnault, *Guinguettes et Lorettes*, pp. 50-51.

[13] *Courrier des Tribunaux*, 699, 18 March 1829, p. 671; Auguste Luchet, 'La Descente de la Courtille en 1833', *Paris, ou Le livre des cent-et-un* (Brussels, 1833), p. 42.

[14] Georges Matoré, 'Cancan et Chahut, Termes de Danse (1829-1845)', in Charles Bruneau (ed.), *Mélanges de Linguistique Française Offerts à M. Charles Bruneau* (Geneva, 1954), p. 178.

[15] Un Vilain Masque, *Physiologie*, pp. 79-80.

[16] Luchet, 'La Descente de la Courtille', p. 42.

[17] Marion Winter, *The Theatre of Marvels* (London, 1962); Lisa C. Arkin and Marion Smith, 'National Dance in the Romantic Ballet', in Lynn Garafola (ed.), *Rethinking the Sylph: New Perspectives on the Romantic Ballet* (Hanover, 1997).

CONSERVATOIRE DE DANSE MODERNE.

N.º 3.

Attention, Fifine, des mœurs dans la pose, si
c'est possible ! j'aperçois le père Lahire.

Deux bahuteuse et un étudiant pur sang.

l'Etudiant de 18.ᵉ année, a passé tous ses examens
à la Chaumière.—Il est bachelier ès-cancan. Le père
Lahire ose à peine moderer ses avant-bras.

Permets-moi de te serrer sur mon cœur
d'homme ! _ Tu me fais mal, Jobard.

C. Chez Aubert & Cᵐ Pl. de la Bourse, 23.

Imp. d'Aubert & Cᵉ

Figure 1.1   Illustrations by Quillenbois (Charles Marie de Sarcus) published in
               Le Conservatoire de la Danse Moderne (1845).

consumption of romantic historical literature and popular theatre.[18] Not satisfied with consuming foreign dances as spectacles, working-class dancers incorporated them into their own movement vocabularies and used them as inspiration for their own innovations. Perhaps these suburban dancers had recognized an opportunity to fashion a new, popular dancing body that undermined the hierarchy of taste performed in the bourgeois quadrille. This working-class corporeal rebellion can be interpreted in terms of changing notions of popular power in the wake of the French Revolution and its uncanny repetition in the Revolution of 1830.

The Convulsive, Contagious Cancan: Symptom of Popular Liberalism

When the cancan emerged in France in the late 1820s, economic depression and the gradual limitation of personal liberties under the conservative monarchy of Charles X (1824-30) fuelled calls for a return to the liberal rhetoric of the French Revolution of 1789.[19] Historian Roger Magraw argues that dissatisfied members of the bourgeoisie used the emerging liberal press to fan the flames of working-class unrest in an attempt to recruit workers as foot soldiers in a revolt against the Restoration Monarchy (1815-30).[20] The mobilized urban working classes took to the streets in July 1830 and overthrew the Bourbon Monarchy, only to find themselves subject to a new regime, the July Monarchy of King Louis-Philippe (1830-48). The new king aligned himself not with 'the people', but with the bourgeoisie, aiming, he claimed, 'to remain in a *juste milieu*, in an equal distance from the excesses of popular power and the abuses of royal power'.[21] According to Magraw, this precipitated, 'several years of popular disturbances, peaking in August 1830 and early 1832, in which workers and peasants tested the ability, and discovered the unwillingness, of the new regime to satisfy their grievances'.[22] These events gave the notion of 'the popular' a specific inflection; 'the people' were members of the working classes and *petite bourgeoisie* whose violent political power had been proven in 1789, but who remained disenfranchised. Popular culture therefore evoked the latent revolutionary potential of the masses, simmering beneath the surface of French society.

The cancan emerged in this volatile atmosphere of an incipient working-class consciousness enflamed by bourgeois and bohemian romantic political idealism.

---

[18] Petra Ten-Doesschate Chu, 'Pop Culture in the Making: The Romantic Craze for History', in Petra Ten-Doesschate Chu and Gabriel P. Weisberg (eds), *The Popularization of Images: Visual Culture under the July Monarchy* (Princeton, 1994).

[19] Arnold Hauser, *The Social History of Art. Volume III: Rococo, Classicism and Romanticism* (London, 1951); Roger Magraw, *France 1815-1914: The Bourgeois Century* (Oxford, 1983).

[20] Magraw, *France*, pp. 48-9.

[21] Cited in Guy Antonetti, *Louis-Philippe* (Paris, 2002), p. 713.

[22] Magraw, *France*, p. 49.

For many of those removed from working-class concerns, the body politic performed in the cancan was a dystopia. Louis Désiré Véron, director of the Paris Opéra from 1831 to 1835, wrote in his memoirs of 1856:

> After 1830 people's hearts took a long time to beat at a normal rhythm …
> Schoolchildren and the common people as one indulged in a bizarre, imaginative
> thrust to transform the way the French danced; out went the gradually developed,
> rounded and elegant movements of our forefathers, in came a frenetic, convulsive
> dance, indecent and respecting no-one, which became known appropriately
> enough as the *chahut* and which even gave birth to a new verb *chahuter* [to
> muck around].[23]

Véron portrays the cancan as a physical symptom of a disease that had infected the bodies of 'common people' during the revolution. This pathological model of the cancan resonates with the biological theories of historical regression that emerged in France in the wake of 1789, and were reinforced by each return to revolution in the nineteenth century. In the theory of degeneration, the lurching of French history between revolution, republic and monarchy was attributed to a hereditary disease in the bodies of its citizens and in the body of the French nation as a whole.[24] Later in the century, the historian Hippolyte Taine (1828-93) would identify this disease as popular liberalism, allowed to spread by France's gradual expansion of the electoral franchise.[25] For Véron, the cancan was a bodily expression of the pathological historical convulsions of French society, spread by contagious popular liberal attitudes.

As a symptom of social and physical disease, the cancan dancer's body quickly became a site for the reassertion of control and order over the national body politic by the French authorities. From at least 1829, inspectors policed the public balls,[26] charged with 'see[ing] that no indecent dance is practised there, such as the *chahut*, the *cancan*, etc.'.[27] Gasnault counts about 40 reports of trials for indecent dancing in the *Gazette des tribunaux* between 1829 and 1841, without a single acquittal, although he suspects that this may be a modest sample of the trials that

---

[23] Louis Désiré Véron, *Mémoires d'un Bourgeois de Paris* (Paris, 1856), p. 383, translated by Stan Bissinger.
[24] Daniel Pick, *Faces of Degeneration: A European Disorder, c. 1848-1918* (Cambridge, 1989).
[25] In 1814 the establishment of a constitutional monarchy in France had created an electoral franchise made up of men of property who paid more than 300 francs per year in tax. After the Revolution of 1830, the franchise expanded to include those who paid 200 francs per year, and the Revolution of 1848 brought universal male suffrage (Magraw, *France*, pp. 23, 49 and 120).
[26] *Journal des Dames et des Modes*, 5 December 1829, cited in Matoré, 'Cancan et chahut', p. 178.
[27] Barlet, *Guide*, p. 32, translated by Anna Davies.

actually took place.[28] The punishment for indecent dancing was three weeks' to three months' imprisonment.[29]

While *individual* cancan dancers were considered to pose a threat to public morality, in the atmosphere of increased working-class consciousness following the Revolution of 1830, the dancing *crowd* always held the latent threat of the cross-class revolutionary mob. At the public masked carnival balls of the 1830s, identities could be disguised and class distinctions submerged in mass quadrilles to the music of Philippe Musard, creating a prime opportunity for cancan improvisations.[30] Gasnault and Sarah Davies Cordova describe the French public's use of the cancan as a weapon against the prohibition of social dancing at the Paris Opéra balls that had been imposed by the Restoration Monarchy.[31] Gasnault reports that, on 5 January 1833, the crowd, dissatisfied with the ballet performance they were offered as entertainment, stormed the stage, demanding the *chahut*. This led to a 'danced riot',[32] which pitted the crowd's demands for corporeal freedom against the repressive measures of the police, who made several arrests. This incident dramatically demonstrated the potential of the cancan to operate as a vehicle for the bodily articulation, negotiation and expression of popular power in the 1830s, at a moment when France's history and future were under violent reconstruction.

The French Cancan: from the 'Common People' to the Nation

The cancan's associations with the revolutionary creation of liberal, cross-class alliances offered a potent symbol for an emerging republican nationalism in late nineteenth-century France. In his review of 1839, Théophile Gautier declared that, 'this dance ... will finish, in spite of the municipal guards, by becoming the national dance'.[33] Gautier's prediction was to come true after defeat in the Franco-Prussian war and the Paris Commune led to the establishment of the Third Republic (1871-1940). The Third Republic was founded on a shift away from the class concerns that had defined French politics since the Revolution, towards the

---

[28]   Gasnault, *Guinguettes et Lorettes*, p. 53.

[29]   Noël and Carpentier, 'Chahut et Cancans', p. 17; *Courrier des Tribunaux*, 699, 18 March 1829, p. 671.

[30]   Musard was a conductor and composer who had learnt his skills as a musician in the *guinguettes*, but gained fame for the galops that he composed and conducted for up to 90 musicians at concerts and theatre balls including the Paris Opéra. Gérard Streletski et al., 'Philippe Musard', *Oxford Music Online* [online] Available from: http://www. oxfordmusiconline.com/subscriber/article/grove/music/19390?q=philippe+musard&searc h=quick&pos=1&_start=1#firsthit [Accessed 27 October 2011].

[31]   Gasnault, *Guinguettes et Lorettes*; Sarah Davies Cordova, *Paris Dances: Textual Choreographies of the Nineteenth-Century Novel* (San Francisco, 1999), p. 139.

[32]   Cordova, *Paris Dances*, p. 139.

[33]   Gautier, *Histoire*, p. 350.

cultivation of cross-class alliances.[34] The cancan's associations with 'the people' and challenge to class boundaries were gradually appropriated by the bourgeois elites as a way to legitimize their position and unify support. The cancan came to symbolize a new French nationhood in which the French Revolution was celebrated as a source of national unity rather than class division.[35] The physical convulsions of the cancan, previously rejected as symptomatic of France's violent battle with the forces of popular liberalism, began to be accepted into the French republican body politic.

The new republicanism reworked the bohemian anti-bourgeois sentiment of the July Monarchy, leading to the reconstruction of a bohemian culture modelled on that of the 1830s and 1840s. After virtually disappearing in the 1870s following the decline and closure of the Opéra ball,[36] the revival of the political rhetoric of revolution and liberty led to the cancan's re-emergence in the 1880s. The working-class *guinguettes* of Montmartre, and new cabarets such as the Moulin Rouge established in the same area and designed to capitalize on their appeal, became the centre of an urban nightlife based on liberation from bourgeois morality and respectability. The Moulin Rouge's owner, Joseph Oller, and manager, Charles Zidler, re-established the cancan as its prime attraction. Félix Chaudoir composed quadrille music specifically for the venue, which may have accompanied the cancan, particularly when he conducted the orchestra in 1890.[37] Dancers and promoters often used the term 'quadrille naturaliste' in this period to align their performances with the earlier working-class version of the dance.[38] However, this was not a working-class rebellion as in the 1830s. Rather, it was an industry fuelled by a political rhetoric and bourgeois culture of revolutionary liberalism.

The Moulin Rouge opened in October 1889, and its publicity campaign was designed to attract the crowds drawn to Paris for the Exposition of 1889.[39] The

---

[34]   Magraw, *France*, p. 209.

[35]   See Pierre Nora, *Realms of Memory: The Construction of the French Past, vol. 3: Symbols*, trans. Arthur Goldhammer (New York, 1998), p. ix.

[36]   David Price, *Cancan!* (London, 1998), p. 62; Cordova, *Paris Dances*.

[37]   Chaudoir published several arrangements of quadrille music in 1890 (held in the Bibliothèque Nationale de France), one of which was titled *Le Moulin Rouge* and dedicated to Monsieur Zidler. Another, *Les Rieuses*, pictured the Moulin Rouge on the cover surrounded by portraits of four dancers. Jules Cheret's 1890 poster for the Moulin Rouge (also held in the Bibliothèque Nationale) announces that an orchestra of 50 musicians will be conducted by Mabille and Chaudoir. As Maribeth Clark (2002) notes, nineteenth-century French quadrille music has been spurned by musicologists as 'trivial' dance music, and thus little research has been published on the subject. This absence is particularly stark in literature on the Moulin Rouge, where writing on the cancan focuses on the visual spectacle, while musical research concentrates on the musical entertainments that took place in between cancan performances (such as Yvette Guilbert and Le Pétomane), rather than during them.

[38]   See Price, *Cancan!*, p. 3.

[39]   Howard G. Lay, 'Pictorial Acrobatics', in Gabriel P. Weisberg (ed.), *Montmartre and the Making of Mass Culture* (New Brunswick, 2001).

Exposition made visibly manifest the French government's attempt to regenerate the nation's morale and economy after its defeat in the Franco-Prussian war of 1871.[40] Six days after the opening of the Eiffel Tower had inaugurated the Exposition, a sketch of a cancan dancer by the artist Ferdinand Lunel was published on the cover of *Le Courrier Français*, a popular, liberal, socialist newspaper (Figure 1.2, below). Lunel positions the cancan dancer's raised leg parallel to the Tricolore-topped Eiffel Tower and a brightly lit street lamp, implying their analogous status as monuments to modern French nationhood in 1889, bringing the popular revolutionary energies of 1789, 1830 and 1848 into the electric-powered *fin de siècle*. The cancan becomes a spectacle of tamed working-class insubordination, harnessed and mass-produced to power the machine of modern, industrial France. The crowd that it attracts is not the revolutionary mob, but an audience of bourgeois spectators, willing to pay to indulge in a French fantasy of cross-class contact. The cancan's spectacle of popular liberalism would soon join the Eiffel Tower as a national symbol and prime tourist attraction.

At the Moulin Rouge the cancan was mass-produced through nightly performances and poster campaigns as a complex spectacle of femininity, masculinity, modernity, primitivity, nationality and class. Oller hired dancers such as La Goulue, Jane Avril and the male dancer Valentin le Désossé to perform the cancan on the dance floor, surrounded by the crowd. Their movements stylized the 'indecency' and working-class defiance of the early cancan into recognizable, spectacular motifs, such as high kicks and jump splits. These performances were complicated, though, by the identities of the performers, creating an atmosphere of cross-class transgression: Valentin le Désossé, a respectable notary's son who danced at the Moulin Rouge by night,[41] partnered La Goulue, who played with stereotypes of her working-class background by 'constantly search[ing] for the risqué gestures of the hand, the foot, the whole body'.[42] Class confusion also featured in the musical entertainments that appeared alongside the dances. American Studies scholar Larry Portis argues that the popularity of the singer Yvette Guilbert derived precisely from the class ambiguity of her performance, vocalized in her contrived upper-class diction and embodied in her costume: 'My black gloves were a symbol of elegance in a setting that was a bit vulgar.'[43] While Guilbert's voice signified affectation, Le Pétomane produced the opposite effect through his melodic farting, performed in formal attire for audiences comprising both tradespeople and royalty.[44] These performances converted the frisson of class

---

[40]Henri Brunschwig, *French Colonialism, 1871-1914: Myths and Realities* (London, 1966); Ly Y. Bui, *Plan of the Champ de Mars, Paris 1889* [online] (University of Maryland, 2005) Available from: http://hdl.handle.net/1903.1/308 [Accessed 23 April 2007].

[41]Jacques Pessis and Jacques Crépineau, *The Moulin Rouge* (Stroud, 1990), p. 34.

[42]Rodrigues cited in Price, *Cancan!*, p. 64.

[43]Guilbert cited in Larry Portis, *French Frenzies: A Social History of Pop Music in France* (College Station, TX, 2004), p. 41.

[44]Pessis and Crépineau, *The Moulin Rouge*, pp. 33 and 42.

Figure 1.2   Front cover of *Le Courrier Français*, 12 May 1889, by Ferdinand
              Lunel.

transgression into a liberal, 'French' popularity with both political and economic currency.

While French national identity solidified around previously marginalized republican symbols, such as Marianne[45] and the cancan, the growth of the French colonial empire between 1880 and 1895 brought a host of new, colonial dance practices into popular consciousness.[46] The Exposition of 1889 had profitably combined nationalist display with colonial spectacle, and the Moulin Rouge sought to appropriate and capitalize on this strategy. Oller transferred a giant model elephant from the Exposition to the cabaret's pleasure garden, and belly dancing performances took place inside its abdomen, while ballerinas performed on a stage next door.[47] As Zeynep Çelik and Leila Kinney have argued, belly dancing was incorporated into Parisian entertainment in the *fin de siècle* as a complement and counterpoint to existing Parisian conventions of female bodily display, such as the cancan.[48] As the cancan moved towards the centre of French identity, belly dancing occupied a tantalizing but threatening position on its colonial margins. Jules Lemaître (1853-1914), the French critic and dramatist, admitted that,

> the horrors of the belly dance revealed to me the decency of the can-can … the dance of the Orient is invading us, and that is why I do not fear sounding the alert, not as a moralist … but as a good Occidental … This invasion, if it continues, would be deplorable. Our dance is so superior to the other one by its grace, by its wit, by its decency! [The two forms of dance] truly express two different and even contrasting souls, two races, two civilizations.[49]

The cancan dancer, who performed in the main dance hall of the venue, occupied a space between the belly dancer and the ballerina. The independent mobility of her limbs opposed the centred control of classical ballet, rendering her 'primitive' in relation to ballet's civility. Indeed, several conservative commentators described the *fin-de-siècle* cancan as worse than the dances of 'savages'.[50] It also, however, symbolized a new body politic in which revolutionary energies were not divisive, but unifying. The cancan dancer's freedom of movement was juxtaposed with the apparently enslaved, foreign gyrations of the belly dancer who could

---

[45] Maurice Agulhon, *Marianne au Pouvoir: L'imagerie et la Symbolique Républicaines de 1880 à 1914* (Paris, 1989).

[46] See Magraw, *France*, p. 235.

[47] Marta Savigliano, *Tango and the Political Economy of Passion* (Boulder, CO, 1995), p. 96.

[48] Zeynep Çelik and Leila Kinney, 'Ethnography and Exhibitionism at the Expositions Universelles', *Assemblage*, 13, December (1990): pp. 34-59.

[49] Lemaître cited in Rae Beth Gordon, 'The White Savage in the Parisian Music Hall', *Fashion Theory: The Journal of Dress, Body and Culture*, 8/3 (2004): p. 269.

[50] Chadourne cited in Rae Beth Gordon, 'Natural Rhythm: La Parisienne Dances with Darwin: 1875-1910', *Modernism Modernity*, 10/4 (2003): pp. 631-2; Lily Grove, *Dancing* (London, 1907), p. 286.

be liberated only through civilizing French colonialism. Whereas the cancan had previously functioned as France's 'internal other', representing the threat of popular revolutionary energies to the French body politic, these energies now became incorporated into a newly constructed national culture of liberal gaiety, which the cancan symbolized. If the cancan's 'popular' status made it a dance of 'the people', then 'the people' had begun to shift from the working class to the nation.[51]

The Cancan Body as Palimpsest: from the Popular Past to the Post-popular

The documentary 'Nightclub of Your Dreams: The Making of *Moulin Rouge!*', a bonus feature on the *Moulin Rouge!* DVD,[52] begins with the sound of a coin dropping into a nickelodeon, followed by the frames of an early cancan film cranking up to speed, and then a montage of similar early films. The camera remains at a respectful distance, capturing dancers arranged in linear formations raising their legs, and sometimes their skirts, for the audience beyond the lens. These images segue into the *Moulin Rouge!* cancan. Bodies spinning, convulsing, struggling, embracing, kicking and fainting are rapidly intercut and overlaid with images of the film's protagonists. A single soundtrack – a music-hall-style version of David Bowie's *Diamond Dogs* (1974) – maintains the continuity between these cancan images, separated by a century. 'Diamond dogs' is the name for both the race of post-apocalyptic, sub-human scavengers in Bowie's lyrics, and the cancan dancers in *Moulin Rouge!*, who sell their bodies for jewels. By layering this track over the visual shift from the *fin-de-siècle* to the *fin-de-millennium* cancan, Thomas C. Grane, the director of the documentary, maps Bowie's vision of a future urban dystopia onto the relationship between the original Moulin Rouge and its future cinematic reincarnation. While Bowie depicts 'a sort of post-nuclear, technologically primitive hell, populated by tribes of proto-punks looting their way through the streets',[53] Grane renders *Moulin Rouge!* as a hyperbolic, post-digital-revolution version of the quaint grotesquerie of the *fin-de-siècle* cancan captured on early film. As the Moulin Rouge becomes *Moulin Rouge!*, a synthesized beat kicks in to fill out the tinny sound of the accordion and honky-tonk piano. Simultaneously, Grane infuses the black-and-white images with colour, replaces single-take scenes with frenzied editing, and fragments dancing bodies captured at a distance by a static camera into a whirl of camera angles and

---

[51]   For an expanded version of the argument presented in this and the previous two sections, see Clare Parfitt, 'Capturing the Cancan: Body Politics from the Enlightenment to Postmodernity' (PhD Thesis, London, 2008).

[52]   Thomas C. Grane, *The Nightclub of Your Dreams: The Making of 'Moulin Rouge'* [Documentary bonus feature on *Moulin Rouge!* DVD] (Twentieth Century Fox Film Corporation, 2001).

[53]   David Buckley, *David Bowie: The Complete Guide to his Music* (London, 2005).

close-ups. Here, turn-of-the-twentieth-century popular culture, already an industry for the production of national fantasies, is digitally remastered for entry into the global economy of twenty-first-century circuits of popularity.

Unlike the Moulin Rouge of the 1890s, *Moulin Rouge!* circulates its cancan imagery in a world where global technologies both promote and challenge national and ethnic identity claims. Luhrmann positions the film in relation to these politics:

> I believe we make universal stories for the world, but it has an Australian voice, and to maintain that voice you must be connected to your land. So the need to be in Australia motivated us to motivate [Twentieth Century] Fox to build a studio down there … For us, every single frame in Moulin Rouge, apart from those two pick-ups in Madrid, was created in Sydney, Australia, and it's set in Paris.[54]

This complex set of alignments places *Moulin Rouge!* between Luhrmann's universal claims for the film's mythic narrative, Hollywood finance, Parisian cultural history, Australian national identity and Aboriginal mythology of connection to the land. These affiliations form complex tensions when mapped onto the class and national politics of the *fin-de-siècle* cancan that *Moulin Rouge!* depicts, exemplified by the casting of Australian singer, dancer and actress Christine Anu as a cancan dancer. Media scholar Tara Brabazon argues that the presence in the film of Australian stars such as Anu, serves as a device for reclaiming the film's Australian-ness and resisting the globalizing force of American cinema.[55] However, Anu's performance of the cancan highlights further layers of meaning relating to her Torres Strait Island heritage, her involvement in Aboriginal politics, and her performance of femininity. The cancan's associations with class revolution, accompanied by the assertive, female, creole sexuality of the disco anthem *Lady Marmalade* (1974) sung by Anu and the other Diamond Dogs, can be read on Anu's body as Aboriginal and/or female empowerment. Her direct gaze at the camera evokes both the female dancers in early films who seduced their audience as if they were on stage, and contemporary female pop stars who assert their sexual power over consumers through their direct performance to camera in music videos. The relish with which she brazenly manipulates her skirts to reveal her legs and underwear, aligns her with contemporary neo-burlesque performers who re-embody archetypes of feminine sexuality, such as the cancan dancer. Yet the connotations of the *fin-de-siècle* cancan as a performance of female working-class primitivity for potential male clients, translated through lyrics attributed to a 1970s mixed-race New Orleans prostitute, simultaneously exoticize and marginalize her. This exoticization is reinforced by her cross-ethnic casting as

---

54   Luhrmann cited in Geoff Andrew, *Baz Luhrmann (II)* [online] (2001) Available from: http://film.guardian.co.uk/interview/interviewpages/0,6737,549699,00.html [Accessed 3 April 2003].

55   Tara Brabazon, *From Revolution to Revelation: Generation X, Popular Culture and Cultural Studies* (Aldershot and Burlington, VT, 2005).

'Arabia', a technique common in late nineteenth-century exotic performance and in Hollywood film musicals. Through this lens, Anu's performance is haunted by the modernist and colonialist fetishization of the bodies of racial and gendered others. Her embodiment of the cancan, therefore, conjures an array of historical identity politics, which play ambiguously on and with her contemporary body.

Anu's cancan performance can be considered in relation to film scholar Diane Sandars's argument that Australian musicals such as *Moulin Rouge!* constitute palimpsestic texts.[56] Luhrmann situates *Moulin Rouge!* as part of the Hollywood film musical tradition, while claiming to reinvent that tradition.[57] Indeed, Bazmark, Luhrmann's production company, collaborated on this and subsequent films with Twentieth Century Fox, a studio with a long history of film musical production.[58] However, Luhrmann cites Bollywood as a primary inspiration for *Moulin Rouge!*, and perhaps this hybridized cinematic form offered Luhrmann a way to position his film both inside and outside the Hollywood musical. Sandars complicates the picture further by defining *Moulin Rouge!* as an Australian film musical. Following film theorist Stuart Cunningham, she contends that, by grafting themselves onto the Hollywood musical tradition, Australian film musicals 'Australianize' their American predecessors. In this process, the Australian overlay transforms the meaning of the Hollywood musical text without erasing it completely. In the case of *Moulin Rouge!*, she argues that, by quoting a panoply of Australian and international popular music, from Anu and Kylie Minogue to Elton John and Madonna, Luhrmann pays tribute to the musical conventions of the Hollywood musical while simultaneously invoking 'a globally engaged Australian pop cultural identity'.[59] The film is therefore structured as a palimpsest, offering 'layered identifications' to a range of local and global audiences.[60] The same might be said of Anu's embodiment of the earlier dance 'text' of the cancan; her body becomes multiply palimpsestic, a site of encounter between the politics of the nineteenth-century cancan, 1970s disco and contemporary Australian popular music cultures.

This layering effect endows Anu's dancing body with currency in contemporary discourses of popularity. In *Moulin Rouge!*, the cancan operates within a global political economy of desire for the popular past, in which modernity's popular cultural sites of resistance are recirculated and consumed as a means of postmodern identity construction. Media scholar Philip Drake has outlined this context from a

[56] Diane Sandars, 'Highly Hybridic, Mostly Palimpsestic: Innovative Uses of Music Video in the Recent Australian Musicals, *Moulin Rouge* and *One Night the Moon*', paper presented at *What Lies Beneath*, Postgraduate Conference, 6 November 2003 [online] (University of Melbourne, 2003) Available from: http://www.ahcca.unimelb.edu.ac/events/conferences/WLB/sandars.htm [Accessed 25 May 2004].

[57] Luhrmann cited in Andrew, *Baz Luhrmann*.

[58] Pam Cook, 'Transnational Utopias: Baz Luhrmann and Australian Cinema', *Transnational Cinemas*, 1/1, January (2010): pp. 23-36.

[59] Sandars, 'Highly Hybridic'.

[60] Ibid.

cinematic viewpoint.[61] He argues that 1990s Hollywood cinema commercialized popular memory by cultivating 'retro aesthetics'.[62] The 'popular' status of *Moulin Rouge!* can be conceived in terms of 'the popularity of retro objects that are less about articulating a connectedness to a lost 'authentic' past than with consuming objects whose significance has become loaded with connotative markers of taste in the present'.[63] The cinematic exhibition of *Moulin Rouge!* was only the beginning of this process of converting the popular past into a consumable popular present. It continued through the release of the DVD in 2002, which included an array of bonus features allowing more interactive modes of consumption. Not only could viewers skip between chapters and listen to a range of commentaries by the production team, but they could become editors of the dance sequences by flicking between cameras in the 'multi-angle' view. Through the internet, appropriation of the film and the past popular cultures it references can be taken in creative directions by consumers, who then become producers. Fansites allow members to upload fanfiction and fanart (original fiction and art based on the narrative and imagery of the film), and on the popular video-sharing site *YouTube* sections of the film can be isolated for scrutiny, set to alternative or remixed music, or reworked through digital editing techniques to create individual versions of key scenes or trailer-like montages.

In these production and consumption strategies, popularity acquires new meaning. The appropriation of the popular past, whether through image technologies or live embodiment, becomes a means of positioning oneself not primarily in relation to national politics, as in *fin-de-siècle* popular culture, or primarily in relation to class, as in popular culture of the July Monarchy, but in relation to the modernist past itself. This self-positioning, like Anu's performance, is palimpsestic. It rehabilitates those aspects of modernity that constituted its internal 'other' – the cancan dancer, for example – while the reworking of these images positions the producer/consumer beyond modernity. The ambiguous doubleness of the resulting 'retro objects', their ghostly evocation of the past in the present, provides their currency and popularity.

The invocation of the popular past is clearly not a new phenomenon. The *fin-de-siècle* cancan was, as noted above, a revival of the popular culture of the July Monarchy, and many other popular cultures have referenced their own pasts. But only in the late twentieth and early twenty-first centuries has this self-referential tendency become the most distinctive feature of several live and mediated popular cultures.[64] Their performance of both continuity and discontinuity with the

---

[61] Philip Drake, '"Mortgaged to Music": New Retro Movies in 1990s Hollywood Cinema', in Paul Grainge (ed.), *Memory and Popular Film* (Manchester, 2003).
[62] Ibid., p. 197.
[63] Ibid., p. 190.
[64] An example from the realm of live performance is the revival, since the mid-1990s, of burlesque performance, particularly in London and New York. These parodic embodiments of feminine stereotypes of the past, often described as 'neo-burlesque', are

modernist past aligns them with postmodernism, suggesting that 'post-popular' might be an appropriate, if somewhat derivative, term for this type of popular practice.[65] But being derivative, and unashamedly so, is precisely what the post-popular is all about.

Popular Pasts, Presents and Futures

In this chapter, three moments in the history of the cancan have highlighted shifts in the notion of the popular from the 1830s to the turn of the millennium. In the cancan of the 1830s, the popular was inextricably linked to the rise of 'the people' as a potent political force, evident in the French Revolution and its violent political reverberations throughout the subsequent century. The cancan dancer embodied this challenge to elite authority, conceived by some as a medical and moral threat. The political connotations of the early cancan were revived in the *fin de siècle* as a symbol of the cross-class alliances that would cement the French Third Republic. Oller and Zidler reconceived the cancan's popularity as a revolutionary energy that could be harnessed for commercial purposes, while artists and critics recognized its potential as a national symbol. The release of the film *Moulin Rouge!* in 2001 reactivated the nineteenth-century connotations of the cancan in a new context of the global circulation of popular music and dance through mass digital media. The millennial cancan exemplifies a post-popular culture in which the popular past is re-embodied, reproduced and reconsumed as a means of self-positioning in relation to modernist, colonialist history. In all three instances, the popularity of the cancan body appears to lie in its capacity to mediate between particular pasts (revolutionary, class-dominated, or modernist) and particular futures (romantic socialist, liberal republican or post-popular), performing possibilities for the historical identity of the present. This is the source of the cancan's political potential and its danger. The post-popular continues this process, constructing the popular dancing body as a complex palimpsest, a site for negotiating past, present and future identity politics, within, against and beyond modernity.

---

attended by spectators who also participate in the performance of retro aesthetics through their clothing styles (see Clare Parfitt-Brown, 'Popular Past, Popular Present, Post-Popular?', *Conversations Across the Field of Dance Studies*, XXXI (2010): pp. 18-20).

[65]   English scholar Richard Burt has used the term 'post-popular' in relation to recent transformations in the popularization of Shakespeare in screen media. Post-popular culture, for Burt, is no longer opposed to elite culture and thus open to canonization in academic contexts. While mass media play a key role in both Burt's notion of the post-popular and that developed in this chapter, for Burt these transformations of popularity would appear to remove it from the popular realm, to de-popularize it as it were, whereas I am concerned with the recirculation of past popular cultures in new circuits of popularity. See Richard Burt, 'Shakespeare, "Glocalisation", Race and the Small Screens of Post-Popular Culture', in Richard Burt and Lynda E. Boose (eds), *Shakespeare, The Movie II: Popularizing the Plays on Film, TV, Video and DVD* (London, 2003).

Chapter 2

Bellowhead: Re-entering Folk through a Pop Movement Aesthetic

Sherril Dodds

Bellowhead set about doing something that, in their four years together, they have finessed into a fine art – taking a long forgotten text and subjecting it to the musical equivalent of a defibrillator, refusing to let up until the patient is dancing around the room with them.[1]

The manic pogo dancing to the Rochdale Coconut Dance suggests that big-band folk had become the new punk.[2]

These review extracts, which focus on live performances by the folk band Bellowhead, call attention both to a mobilization of folk music through a popular sensibility and to a capacity to express this sonic energy through dance. I suggest that this sense of 'movement' plays out across multiple levels, from the band's explosive musical performance and the audience's embodied reception, through to the dynamic and contested terrain of folk revivals and their shifting relationship to the popular music idiom.

Bellowhead is an 11-piece outfit that plays English folk music, which band member Jon Boden describes as 'the body of traditional English song and tunes from the eighteenth century up to the early twentieth century'.[3] Originally conceived by folk duo Jon Boden, who acts as lead vocalist and fiddle player, and John Spiers, who specializes in melodeon and concertina, Bellowhead also includes Andy Mellon, Justin Thurgur, Brendan Kelly and Gideon Juckes, who make up the brass section; Rachel McShane, Paul Sartin and Sam Sweeney, who primarily form a string section along with the occasional addition of bagpipes and oboe; drummer Pete Flood, who provides the backbeat, but also embellishes the sound with percussion such as frying pan and cutlery set; and Benji Kirkpatrick who contributes guitar, banjo, bouzouki and mandolin. While the source of the music resides in traditional folk tunes, their arrangements are variously described as referencing 'cabaret and music hall',[4] 'Sworfishtrombones-era Tom Waits',[5]

[1] Pete Paphides, 'Bellowhead', *The Times*, 4 November 2008, p. 16.
[2] Robin Deneslow, 'Bellowhead: Koko', *The Guardian*, 4 November 2008, p. 36.
[3] Jon Boden, Interview recorded at the BBC Folk Proms 2008.
[4] Pete Spencer, 'Band of Hope and Glory' *The Observer*, 14 September 2008, p. 77.
[5] Paphides, 'Bellowhead'.

'Brazilian influences'[6] and 'New Orleans jazz and a dash of Kurt Weill'.[7] Hence Bellowhead commits to a contemporary interpretation of traditional material and, as Hogkinson observes, 'this decision was heretical to more conservative members of the folk community concerned with maintaining the unchanging purity of tradition, but indicative of a looser, more confident attitude to folk music in its younger enthusiasts'.[8]

In this chapter, I begin with the premise that Bellowhead produces a musical shift through a popular sensibility. I seek to examine how dance acts as an agent for Bellowhead's popularization, recontextualization and revision of the codes and modalities of traditional English music,[9] and I explore this in relation to the movement aesthetics that the band members bring to their stage performances. From this, I wish to show how Bellowhead employs dance both as a pedagogic tool and as a commentary on the band's musical philosophy. I draw on scholarship in folk studies and popular music performance to explore the tensions that surround folk music and its revival performances, and I use both live and recorded stage shows by Bellowhead as case study material through which to situate these debates.[10]

Stasis and Exchange across Folk and Pop

The category of 'folk' appears to be less a coherent collection of music and dance forms than an aesthetic and ideological creation.[11] The two major English folk revivals of the late nineteenth to early twentieth century and of the mid-twentieth century illustrate how key stakeholders in a folk scene are required to construct a tradition in order to revive it.[12] In reference to the first English

---

[6]   Robin Denselow, 'Bellowhead: Royal Opera House' *The Guardian*, 28 February 2007, p. 38.

[7]   Deneslow, 'Bellowhead: Koko'.

[8]   Will Hodgkinson, 'Folk Has a New Sex Appeal', *The Guardian*, 19 September 2008, p. 13.

[9]   Much of this material concerning the history of English folk song and dance and the contested terrain of folk revivals aligns with Simon Featherstone's chapter in this volume.

[10]   For this chapter, I draw on field notes and observations from live gigs I attended at the Folk Proms (2008) in London, the Wychwood Festival (2009) in Cheltenham and the Sidmouth Folk Festival (2010), and from recordings of live performances at the Folk Proms (2008, BBC television) and *Bellowhead Live at Shepherds Bush Empire* (2007, DVD, produced and directed by Ed Cooper).

[11]   See Michael Brocken, *The British Folk Revival 1944-2002* (Aldershot, 2003); and Niall Mackinnon, *The British Folk Scene: Musical Performance and Social Identity* (Milton Keynes, 1993).

[12]   See Georgina Boyes, *The Imagined Village: Culture, Ideology and the English Folk Revival* (Leeds, 2001); Brocken, *The British Folk Revival*; and Mackinnon, *The British Folk Scene*.

folk revival, Sweers traces how folk collector Cecil Sharp produced a romantic idealization of a folk culture rooted in rural traditions; yet this preoccupation with agricultural communities and pastoral life was motivated by anxieties concerning late nineteenth-century industrialization and urbanization.[13] While the early twentieth-century revival presupposed an authentic folk culture that could be directly accessed, the music and dance forms were collected, recontextualized and recomposed for the purposes of public presentation.[14] As Brocken suggests, folk revivals are better understood as an articulation of the present rather than as an unmediated portal to the past.[15]

Similarly, the second folk revival of the mid-twentieth century was informed by the post-war rhetoric that espoused notions of nation and heritage, which proved a fertile ground for the revivalist interest in the preservation of English traditions.[16] The development of an English folk club scene ensured adherence to tradition through advocates such as folk singer Ewan MacColl, who insisted that performers must strictly pertain to the songs of their national origin, and through workshops to train singers in an 'authentic' English style.[17] Yet, as Brocken observes, this desire to produce a coherent and fixed tradition results in a musical parochialism and conservatism that lacks grounding in a historical reality.[18] The consequence of this self-conscious isolationism created a troubled relationship between folk and pop music.

Brocken describes how the dynamic between folk music and the notion of the popular play out in quite different ways across the first and second folk revivals.[19] In the early twentieth century, the desire to popularize folk traditions produced a paradox in the revivalist aim. To ensure that folk music and dance would be accessible to young, urban middle-class audiences, these 'traditional' forms were adapted and thus reinvented. In the second revival, the intent was to preserve the tradition in its 'authentic form'; yet this strategy placed folk within a cultural vacuum and promulgated the mythology of a pure and unchanging tradition. Consequently, there was no acknowledgement of folk's relationship to the popular and furthermore produced a division between the folk and popular idiom.

Sweers asserts that, while folk is conceived as a preindustrial form rooted in oral transmission, the popular arises from industrialization through its recorded production and mass dissemination.[20] Given that the English folk revival of the

---

[13] Britta Sweers, *Electric Folk: The Changing Face of English Traditional Music* (Oxford, 2005), p. 46.

[14] See Boyes, *The Imagined Village*; Brocken, *The British Folk Revival*; and Mackinnon, *The British Folk Scene*.

[15] Brocken, *The British Folk Revival*, p. x.

[16] Brocken, The British Folk Revival, p. 20.

[17] Mackinnon, The British Folk Scene, p. 28.

[18] Brocken, The British Folk Revival, p. 89.

[19] Brocken, *The British Folk Revival*.

[20] Sweers, *Electric Folk*, p. 21.

mid-twentieth century responded to the nationalist project of the post-war years, Brocken argues that folk culture serviced the notion of an imagined British community that was distinct from America and its associations with mass culture.[21] Whereas the new mass culture was deemed formulaic and manipulative, the folk tradition acted as a cultural repository of authenticity and truth. A further split between the two arises from their perceived relationship to the economy. While the folk community is driven by preservation and conservation, purveyors of the popular are motivated by commercial intent. Indeed, MacKinnon describes how the second revival folk scene was keen to keep folk out of the commercial music industry and under the control of the community itself.[22] Despite the anti-capitalist rhetoric, MacKinnon notes how folk clubs quickly commercialized themselves through booking professional singers for paying audiences. Stylistically, revival performers were also encouraged to adopt English accents and traditional arrangements as a strategy to distance folk from the contemporary sounds of syncopation, American accents and electric instrumentation that characterized the popular music of the 1950s and '60s.[23]

While some exponents of the English folk scene sought to maintain the aesthetic and ideological division between folk and pop, others moved to embrace the potential for creative development. Brocken recounts a bifurcation that occurred within the second folk revival across 'folk purists' and 'folk popularisers'.[24] This separation plays out though the emergence of 'folk rock' or 'electric folk' of the 1960s and '70s.[25] Sweers employs the term electric folk as 'a relatively broad expression encompassing a number of musical fusion styles that are based upon traditional material in various forms'.[26] Significantly, she suggests that electric folk is not simply the amplification of folk music through electrified instrumentation, but speaks more to an adaptation of traditional forms. Sweers asserts that the notion of 'going electric' runs in contradistinction to the values of a folk scene that privileged unaccompanied performances or traditional acoustic instrumentation. For Brocken, folk rock brought about an unsettling of fixed relations between folk and pop.[27] Folk rock called into question the revivalist philosophy of static preservation and instead focused on the composition of new material and a commitment to popularize the form.[28] Indeed, Bellowhead continues the ethos of the folk rock idiom with its fusion of folk material and popular music arrangements played out through the form of a 'big band sound'. In the following section I

---

21   Brocken, *The British Folk Revival*, p. 20.
22   Mackinnon, *The British Folk Scene*, p. 30.
23   Brocken, *The British Folk Revival*, p. 35.
24   Brocken, *The British Folk Revival*, pp. 84-5.
25   Bands that typified the 'folk-rock' idiom of this era were Fairport Convention, Steeleye Span and Pentangle.
26   Sweers, *Electric Folk*, p. 24.
27   Brocken, *The British Folk Revival*, p. 108.
28   Mackinnon, *The British Folk Scene*, pp. 63, 66.

move on to explore how Bellowhead utilizes dance and movement references to articulate to the audience its musical values and philosophy towards folk revival.

Dancing through the Boundaries of Folk and Pop

The significance of dance to understanding the sonic and performative enunciations of Bellowhead can not be underestimated. In musical terms, they are described as 'a rousing instrumental dance band'[29] and Spencer[30] asserts that 'live punters will affirm, the band can funk'. Indeed the extent to which movement constitutes a central component of the band's performance identity is highlighted in an interview with Boden and Sartin before their Proms performance (2008). The interviewer comments:

> I had no idea of the kind of visceral power of hearing you live or of experiencing you live. You obviously get people off their feet, you get the audience dancing.

A little further into the interview, Boden responds:

> that's what the music's for: it's dance music … So we wouldn't really be doing our jobs if we weren't enjoying it in the way it was designed to be enjoyed.

Thus both critics and the band perceive it as music to be danced to, and I aim to show how Bellowhead engenders this ethos through its live performance work.

The idea that Bellowhead can access cross-over audiences is evident as the band has moved beyond the folk club circuit to play at classical and popular music venues, such as the Royal Festival Hall and Shepherd's Bush Empire in London, and at outdoor pop music festivals. Yet even when they continue to play at traditional folk concerts, the audiences they attract are diverse. For instance, as a headline act at the Sidmouth Folk Festival in August 2010, while part of the audience consisted of middle-aged 'folkies' in cotton slacks, waterproof jackets and walking boots, a young, hip crowd was also identifiable in the form of a young woman in a wheelchair with a shock of pink and yellow hair and a goth-style girl with blue nail varnish and black corset.

The band also dresses in a playful mismatch of styles; at Sidmouth (2010), Boden came on stage in a silver lamé suit and his signature pink tie, Spiers wore white 'morris dance' trousers,[31] battered cord jacket and the straw hat of an 'English gent', and Sartin sported a knitted tanktop and leopard-skin trilby.

---

[29] Denselow, 'Bellowhead: Royal Opera House', p. 38.
[30] Spencer, 'Band of Hope and Glory', p. 77.
[31] Morris dance is traditionally conceived as a male ceremonial dance of the early 1800s, which is performed in a two-column formation. See John Forrest, 'Morris Dance', in Selma Jean Cohen (ed.), *The International Encyclopedia of Dance* (1998; Oxford, 2005

Such eclectic dress suggests a postmodern sensibility through the self-conscious juxtaposition of signifiers that enunciate the band's affiliations across popular and folk traditions. While Boden's flamboyant dress signals the spectacle of a Vegas-entertainer, Spiers's trousers are not only immediately recognizable to folk dance enthusiasts, but are also broadly embedded in the English cultural imagination in relation to the 'morris dance' teams, in their white shirts and trousers decorated with bells and ribbons, who perform at village greens and town squares.

It is the performance itself, however, that produces a distinct corporeal commentary on the band's musical identifications. Before looking at specific aspects of these embodied articulations, I begin with a snapshot description of a Bellowhead number from the Proms (2008).[32] Sartin introduces the *Sloe Gin* set as 'three dance tunes' and pauses before adding, 'that's a hint for those of you down in the arena'. Thus immediately, the band is clear in its direction to the audience to dance. As the musicians launch into an upbeat instrumental track, Boden, Kirkpatrick, Sartin and Sweeney execute a simple morris motif in unison,[33] characterized by a weighty spring hop from foot to foot with a rebound heel dig into the floor, while the brass section emphatically claps towards the auditorium as an invitation for the audience to participate. In response, the audience begins to whoop, and Spiers and Kirkpatrick feed off this energy as they respectively swing their melodeon and mandolin in time to the music, while expansively stepping from foot to foot as if to make a spectacle of their musicianship. On violins, Sartin, McShane and Sweeney repeatedly strike their bows into a succession of theatrical poses, while Spiers and Kirkpatrick jump kick from foot to foot in a ramshackle unison motif. As the second tune picks up pace, the audience now claps with little encouragement from the band and Boden plays wildly on his fiddle, with his head and torso beating out the tempo of the music, and Spiers and Kirkpatrick stamp their feet to visualize further the insistent duple metre rhythm. Kirkpatrick then faces the back to execute a mandolin solo, with legs astride and body thrown back in a deep lunge, as the brass section drops to their knees around him as if in awe of his musical prowess. The brass section then jumps back to its feet and pogos exuberantly on the spot while the rest of the musicians throw themselves into the final few bars of the tune.

While these multiple dance references are also typical of Bellowhead's postmodernist assemblage of musical and sartorial styles, the allusion both to popular performance and folk dance genres articulates important movement affiliations, distinctions and commonalities. Whereas the weighty skipping, hopping

---

(e-reference edition), at http://www.oxford-dance.com/entry?entry=t171.e1196, accessed 18 January 2012.

[32]   Although I attended the live performance, my analysis is based on the BBC television recording of the concert.

[33]   Several members of the band participate in morris dance, including Sartin and Spiers who are particular enthusiasts.

and jumping steps are recognizable from the canon of English country dance and morris dance traditions, the excessive posturing and exaggerated execution of the musical performance bring to mind the spectacle of the popular music gig.[34] Yet, although the different movement sensibilities appear to be located within discrete musical genres, they occupy common ground in that they are delivered through an everyday vernacular quality, which is relaxed and informal, and the steps do not demand high-level technical training, but are pedestrian, accessible and open to individual interpretation.

In his study of the second English folk revival, Mackinnon[35] asserts that a musical genre is not defined by musical content alone, but by values that are stated and reaffirmed through audience and performer behaviours that instruct novice audiences and iterate the norms of the genre. These codified rules include 'extra-musical behaviour' and if transgressed are immediately evident.[36] Mackinnon describes how, within the English folk club scene, audience behaviours are centred around serious contemplation. He interprets this as follows: 'a conscious demand to be taxed, to participate, to enter "into" the songs, to listen to them in an intense way, is to add a certain intellectualization, one which now pervades the folk scene'.[37] Thus the second folk revival was characterized by subdued music performances and quiet reflection, which figuratively and literally silenced the dancing body. In contrast, the live gigs of Bellowhead are typified by a spectacular musicianship and an ebullient embodied reception that are far closer to the movement aesthetics associated with the production and consumption of popular music performance.

Within the context of Bellowhead's performances, I argue that this conscious signalling of both popular music embodiments and rudimentary folk dance forms complicates the artistic, historical and political boundaries that delineate music and dance practice. First, the band's use of a popular movement aesthetic serves to underscore the popular music influences that inform its musical style and to attract popular music audiences situated outside the niche community of the folk scene. Secondly, Bellowhead employs strategic dance references as a means to acknowledge its folk heritage and to comment knowingly upon the instability of that tradition within the band's contemporary context of performance. And finally, the appropriation of multiple corporeal styles destabilizes musical contexts and categories and mobilizes complex matters of race and gender. These areas of concern form the focus of the remainder of this chapter.

---

[34] I acknowledge here that earlier bands, which also work within a 'folk rock' or 'electric folk' idiom, such as The Pogues and The Oyster Band, use a similar kind of 'rock music aesthetic' within the performance context of their live gigs.

[35] Mackinnon, *The British Folk Scene*, pp. 54-5.

[36] Mackinnon, *The British Folk Scene*, p. 55.

[37] Mackinnon, *The British Folk Scene*, p. 59.

The Appropriation of a Pop Movement Aesthetic

In a consideration of popular music performance, Shumway draws a distinction
between the 'musical text', which can either be a score or recording of the
music, and the performance itself, which constitutes a reproduction of the text.[38]
For Shumway, different musical genres approach the text and performance
relationship in quite distinct ways. In reference to pop music, he describes how
artists are expected to create an accurate production of their recorded music in live
performance; however, for some forms of popular music, such as punk and grunge,
the live performance is considered to be the musical ideal. Indeed Bellowhead
seems to share this sensibility that privileges performance over recording as the
band is repeatedly acclaimed for the dynamism of its live shows. As Denselow
comments, 'they have always sounded better live than on record'.[39] This raises the
questions then of how does Bellowhead perform this 'liveness' and how does this
impact upon audience experience?

I have already proposed that Bellowhead utilizes a popular movement aesthetic
within its live performances, and I hope to demonstrate how this articulates the
band's musical identity and invites the audience members to respond corporeally
to their listening experience. In a study of the rock band Led Zeppelin, Fast argues
that the ways in which rock musicians posture and move is critical to understanding
the music.[40] She describes how musicians produce embodied actions in response to
the presence of their fans, but more importantly their bodies articulate the music.
Indeed she describes the music as kinetic in that the performance is produced
through 'sonoric gestures'.[41] Within the live shows of Bellowhead, there are
multiple corporeal references to a range of embodiments associated with rock
music performance.

During the live performance of sea shanty *Haul Away* at Sidmouth (2010),
Spiers and Kirkpatrick face each other while pogoing on the spot both as a kinetic
articulation of the energy produced through this rousing rendition of the song and
as direct reference to the kudos of punk. The three fiddlers, Sweeney, McShane
and Sartin, shake their instruments flamboyantly like rock guitarists attempting to
produce distortion effects and pretend to machine-gun the brass section as visual
evidence of their sonic power. Later, Sweeney falls to his knees, as if to reflect the
utter exhaustion of his playing, while McShane and Sartin play aggressively over
him in their relentless desire to maintain the beat; while doing so, Sartin lewdly
waggles his tongue in heavy metal style to further illustrate the rock aesthetic.
Another example can be seen at the Shepherd's Bush Empire (2007). In the final

---

[38]   David Shumway, 'Performance', in Bruce Horner and Thomas Swiss (eds), *Key
Terms in Popular Music and Culture* (Malden, MA, and Oxford, 1999), p. 189.

[39]   Denselow, 'Bellowhead: Koko', p. 36.

[40]   Susan Fast, *In the Houses of the Holy: Led Zeppelin and the Power of Rock Music*
(Oxford, 2001), p. 114.

[41]   Fast, *In the Houses of the Holy*, p. 114.

cadence to *Prickle-Eye Bush*, in a signature rock move, drummer Pete Flood flamboyantly jumps in the air before slamming his drumsticks down to enunciate kinetically and sonically the final beat of the track.

These explicit references to a movement repertoire rooted in punk, metal and rock performance serve multiple purposes that collectively signal the musical and social identity of the band. From a musical perspective, the diversity of rock gestures demonstrate that the music is not contained within a 'pure' folk tradition but that the arrangements are informed by multiple musical reference points that are frequently drawn from the popular idiom. The movement also sets out to enunciate key musical features, such as tempo and rhythm or the point of musical closure. Furthermore, executing folk songs through forms of embodiment that are associated with a rock idiom offers folk music, which is perceived as a 'defiantly unfashionable perennial', an alliance more closely linked to a hip youth culture.[42] Yet, although these 'sonoric gestures' bring an element of cool that is attached to the intensity of rock performance, the members of Bellowhead adopt a playful stance towards these corporeal appropriations so that they can not be accused of the pomposity associated with serious rock performance.

In terms of social identity, the corporeal enactments of a rock physicality raise complex matters of racial and gendered performativity as rock music, more generally, and punk and metal specifically, identify with a white, masculine aesthetic. Given that the second-revival folk music of the post-war era sought to establish a unified English nationalism, English folk music is closely aligned with a white racial identity that is also reflected in the all-white constituency of Bellowhead. Yet the contribution of African American music styles to the canon of popular music has been well documented and problematized.[43] That Bellowhead is described as a 'big band', with influences from jazz, funk and disco,[44] clearly alludes to African American popular music traditions, which are quietly erased through the white folk idiom. A similar marginalization occurs through the gendering of the music. With the exception of Rachel McShane, Bellowhead is an entirely male outfit, and the embodied associations with the hyper-masculinized genres of punk, metal and rock serve to distance the band from the feminized image of folk music.[45]

---

[42] David Honigmann, 'Boden's Catalogue of English Folk', *The Financial Times*, 21 June 2006, p. 18.

[43] Mark Anthony Neal, *What the Music Said: Black Popular Music and Black Public Culture* (New York and London, 1998); Samuel A. Floyd, *The Power of Black Music: Interpreting Its History from Africa to the United States* (New York, 1996).

[44] Robin Denselow, 'Burlesque: Bellowhead', *The Guardian*, 29 September 2006, p. 14.

[45] A similar gender divide characterized the second folk revival in which women, such as Sandy Denny and Norma Waterson, were reputed for their singing voices, while the men were known for their fine musicianship as instrumentalists.

Waksman's study of the electric guitar offers a useful paradigm for illustrating the extent to which Bellowhead both adopts and critiques the racialized and gendered performances styles of popular music practice.[46] Waksman describes how amplification brought about a 'louder, more demonstrative style of musical performance that put the performer at the center [*sic*] of attention'.[47] Using different musical examples, Waksman demonstrates how selected male artists played the guitar to articulate racial and gender identities. For instance, he explores how guitar legend Jimi Hendrix played his guitar as a display of musical and sexual prowess that produced a racialized, sexualized and gendered performativity expressed through Hendrix's African American body, and examines how heavy metal guitar work conveys notions of male exhibitionism and homosociality, particularly in the musical power play between Led Zeppelin guitarist Robert Plant and vocalist Jimmy Page. On the one hand, I would argue that Bellowhead employs these rock clichés, such as the frequent 'play-offs' between Spiers and Kirkpatrick or the intense head-rocking of Boden consumed in playing his fiddle, to evidence the band's high level of musicianship. On the other hand, the seriousness of these gestures is frequently undermined as the band members ridicule and laugh at each other's performance antics. While the electric guitar is located in the cultural imagination as a 'technophallic' symbol,[48] that Bellowhead reproduces such flamboyant performances on traditional folk instruments, such as melodeon, fiddle and bouzouki, creates an obvious point of humour. Furthermore, that the band switches easily from folk steps to rock gestures suggests that the latter are not constructed as 'authentic' movement responses but are a playful and temporary embodiment that expresses both affinity to and distance from popular music conventions.

Another dimension of Bellowhead's performance that aligns it with a popular sensibility exists in Boden's performance as lead vocalist. I describe earlier Mackinnon's observation that, in the second folk revival, a style of performance emerged that placed the song itself at the forefront of musical expression.[49] Consequently, theatrical presentation was discouraged and 'the depression of affectations towards egotistical performance is strong'.[50] This type of expressive restraint stands in contrast to the performance persona of Boden who is described by critics as 'a natural showman'[51] and a 'wildly theatrical singer'.[52] His vocal delivery is taut, anxious and intense, while his facial expression frequently shifts from a brooding solipsism to an engaging smile. At Sidmouth (2010), during

[46]   Steve Waksman, *Instruments of Desire: The Electric Guitar and the Shaping of Musical Experience* (Cambridge, MA, 1999).
[47]   Waksman, *Instruments of Desire*, p. 7.
[48]   Waksman, *Instruments of Desire*, p. 188.
[49]   Mackinnon, *The British Folk Scene*, p. 55.
[50]   Mackinnon, *The British Folk Scene*, p. 128.
[51]   Spencer, 'Band of Hope and Glory', p. 77.
[52]   Denselow, 'Burlesque: Bellowhead', p. 14.

Whisky is the Life of Man, standing close to the microphone he holds his arms out like a rock star as if inviting the audience into his performance; in *Parson's Farewell* he sings with his knees inclined inwards, as a corporeal reference to rock 'n' roll star Elvis Presley; and in *Cold Blows the Wind* he dramatically lunges forward to the microphone, pointing to the audience in a mode of direct address.

As Fast suggests, musical utterances can not be separated from the bodies that create them and, drawing on a phenomenological perspective, she argues that 'sound touches us, physically. It connects us with the body from which it is coming.'[53] She describes how the live gig performance constitutes a tactile experience in that the volume of sound envelops the crowd and the way in which musicians move helps audiences to 'feel' the music. During the Sidmouth (2010) performance of *Haul Away*, as the band members begin to 'rock out', the audience members respond to follow this embodied lead through individually clapping, stamping, jumping and dancing to the exaggerated and heightened musical performance such that the floor begins to shake below me. This excessive physicality is typical of rock performance and, in the case of Bellowhead, it signals the band's musical identifications and instructs the audience as to the intention of this traditional 'dance music' idiom.

Embodied Reflections on the Folk Tradition

In the previous section I establish that a popular movement aesthetic is key to Bellowhead's live performance. There are other movement paradigms upon which the band draws, however, that further articulate its musical philosophy. In performance, band members frequently call attention either to notions of folk dance or movement traditions. For example, I have already described how several of the band execute a morris step during *Sloe Gin* and they frequently hop, skip or jump in a vernacular style that is akin to the pedestrian quality adopted within the context of English country dance.[54] Yet while these serve as clear corporeal acknowledgements of English folk dance, in other instances Bellowhead begins to complicate the notion of a folk tradition.

At Shepherd's Bush Empire (2007), as an introduction to *Frog's Legs and Dragon's Teeth*, Boden states, 'There is a traditional dance that goes with this one and it goes a bit like this …' He then simply jumps up and down on the spot and says, 'It takes a while to get used to, but you'll probably get there in the end.' In this very brief moment, Boden acknowledges, undermines and reaffirms the importance of tradition in the band's musical and performance identity. At first, he intimates that he will share an 'authentic' traditional dance in much the same way that the band employs traditional English tunes as its musical starting

---

[53]   Fast, *In the Houses of the Holy*, p. 131.

[54]   I have participated in English country barn dances at the Godalming Borough Hall Ceilidhs, Surrey, UK.

point. He then quickly destabilizes this image when he simply reproduces one of the most basic dance steps more readily associated with popular music reception. Yet, that the audience responds with enthusiastic jumping to the lively track that follows demonstrates that both the band and the crowd acknowledge this as a newly developed 'tradition' within the context of Bellowhead performances.[55] Another example of the band's capacity to invent tradition is evidenced when McShane states, 'We've got another little tune for you and for this one we'd love it if you'd do a silly little dance that makes us laugh'. She then asks the brass band to demonstrate the 'lasso dance', which demands swinging the arm above the head as if throwing a lasso. While the dance itself requires little movement skill and is clearly not part of an English folk tradition, shots of the audience members mimicking this move suggest a receptivity to new, albeit playful, traditions and an understanding that a danced response is central to the ethos of this music.

In a study of 'first existence' and 'second existence' folk dance, Nahachewsky suggests that what separates the two is the notion of 'reflectiveness'.[56] He describes this as a 'turning back onto oneself' as participants need to be aware of their own tradition.[57] This reflectiveness then produces changes in the meanings, context and form of the dance. In the case of Bellowhead, I would argue that it is the band's reflectiveness of the tradition upon which they draw that allows its members to celebrate, adapt and re-envision the music and its performance. As Sweers argues, 'most performers have developed highly self-aware attitudes and well-articulated beliefs about their music. The musicians I interviewed were very aware of the gaps between the tradition and their revival culture.'[58] It is precisely because Bellowhead understands that it cannot produce a pure and authentic restoration of the tradition that allows the band members to introduce other music and dance influences into its performance. This postmodernist sensibility of eclecticism, novelty and quotation supersedes the failed modernist project of a fixed folk tradition. Boden comments:

> In folk music there's this idea of the right way of approaching the material, as
> if there is such a thing as a definitive version of a song. Yet nobody owns these
> songs, or knows how they would have sounded a couple of hundred years ago,
> or has the right to say how they should be approached.[59]

---

[55]   Boden has also made reference to the 'traditional dance' of jumping up and down while introducing the same tune at the Proms (2008) and Wychwood (2009).

[56]   Nahachewsky bases this terminology on Hoeburger's (1968) notion of first and second existence folk dance. In Hoeburger's model, whereas 'first existence folk dance' is key to the entire community and is loosely improvised within a particular framework, 'second existence folk dance' is no longer central to community life and therefore needs to be taught, which produces a fixing of the form. See Andriy Nahachewsky, 'Once Again: On the Concept of Second Existence Folk Dance', *Yearbook for Traditional Music*, 33 (2001): pp. 17-28.

[57]   Nahachewsky, 'Once Again', p. 19.

[58]   Sweers, *Electric Folk*, p. 233.

[59]   Cited in Hodgkinson, 'Folk Has a New Sex Appeal', p. 13.

Indeed, the band members constantly engage in a corporeal play that clearly quotes and destabilizes the codified performance behaviours that have historically divided different music traditions. For instance, at Sidmouth (2010), during various string sections, McShane, Sartin and Sweeney play their instruments with serious, highbrow expressions as if in a classical concert, but will then suddenly strike a John Travolta disco pose or flick their fingers in a 'V' as if to snub the pomposity of high art. Thus their postmodernist call to multiple movement sources playfully reaffirms their eclectic musical identity that brings a plethora of sonic arrangements to the traditional music source material.

Mackinnon offers a useful lens through which to understand the treatment of tradition, which he conceptualizes through the distinct notions of 're-enaction' and 'revival':

> re-enaction implies a suspension of the present, allowing the past to be entered into, but in a bounded sense. Revival also requires that the past be 'entered' in some symbolic way, but once so entered artistic integrity is not so threatened by the intrusion of the present. It is entered 'once again' but allows continuity through a process of artistic evolution. Composition within a revived genre is permitted and encouraged.[60]

Thus in Mackinnon's terms, Bellowhead's incorporation of a popular sensibility and newly invented or reclaimed movement traditions allows the band to 're-enter' the body of traditional English music from the position of the present. The band's philosophy towards tradition is not one of preservation of the past, but of expressing a response towards it.

In reference to Bellowhead, I argue that this is a political reclaiming of a body that has been erased by former folk revivals specifically in the area of music performance. Given that dance is frequently read as a feminized and racially Othered practice,[61] second revival folk expressed a commitment to a position of racial privilege through the primacy of a white English and disembodied voice. That Bellowhead celebrates the dancing body clearly disrupts this imperialist position, as the band members playfully inhabit movement practices that cross popular performance, folk dance traditions and the classical idiom.

In conclusion, I argue that dance is central to understanding the performance and reception of Bellowhead's music. The band members employ dance as a pedagogic tool to instruct audiences that they are working within the framework of a dance music tradition, which demands an embodied response. The dance also serves to comment critically upon the band's musical philosophy. Their explicit use of a popular movement aesthetic offers the band members immediate connection to a hip youth market and signals Bellowhead's musical identifications

---

[60]   Mackinnon, *The British Folk Scene*, p. 63.

[61]   Jane Desmond 'Embodying Difference: Issues in Dance and Cultural Studies', in Jane Desmond (ed.), *Meaning in Motion* (London and Durham, 1997).

with a range of popular music styles. Furthermore, their frequent allusions to folk dance 'traditions', whether revived or newly invented, express the unstable and contested boundaries of Bellowhead's folk music heritage. Consequently, Bellowhead's attention to dance invites audiences to engage with the past from the embodied perspective of the present.

Chapter 3

Sound Understandings: Embodied Musical Knowledge and 'Connection' in a Ballroom Dance Community

Joanna Bosse

Every Sunday night during my fieldwork I danced at the Rose Bowl, a comfortably shabby country bar in downtown Urbana, Illinois, across from the Courier Cafe and the county courthouse. I tagged along with a group of ballroom dancers who frequented the place in order to experience a rare opportunity: to dance to a live band. Live bands are a mixed blessing for dancers, and the Western Wheels, a Rose Bowl house band playing western swing, was no exception. Their repertory of tunes did not fit any particular dance genre and their tempos were more erratic than the dancers preferred. Nevertheless, the Rose Bowl provided one more opportunity for couple dancing during the week and so a group of about twelve 'ballroomers' became regulars.

One Sunday evening, William, an accomplished dancer and owner of a small software company, caught me singing along to a George Strait ballad and there followed a conversation about slow dancing and country music. Cecil, a young engineering graduate student, listened a while and then said, 'I don't know what the big deal about the music is. I don't think my dancing would change a bit if I were to dance to a metronome.' William protested, as did the rest of the dancers once they returned to our table, but Cecil's ambivalence about music gave voice to the precarious connection between ballroom dancers and the music they dance to, an ambivalence that was expressed in myriad ways.

This ethnographic case study will engage one of the prevailing notions that I encountered regularly during my fieldwork: to 'hear' music, a concept that included a range of cognitive, performative and embodied practices that held important social meaning for ballroom performers. In particular, I suggest that, in addition to communicating a capacity for dance, the concept of 'hearing' music iconically signified an individual's potential for connection, both on the dance floor and in the broader sense of meaningful human connections. To 'hear' music encompassed a larger universe of meaning that spoke not only to the literal act of perceiving sound, but also to knowledge, embodiment and communion. As such, 'hearing' music garnered power beyond its most typical meanings and generated ambivalence from dancers who struggled with their own ability to 'hear'.

This study is based on ethnographic fieldwork in dance clubs in the American Midwest. The Regent Ballroom and Banquet Center in Savoy, Illinois served as the central hub for this work, and the examples used in this chapter stem from experiences in dance events that took place there (see Figure 3.1). The group of Sunday night Rose Bowl dancers featured above met every Friday night at the Regent and considered the Regent their 'home' dance space. Located in the heart of the Midwestern agricultural beltway, Savoy is a small bedroom community that borders Champaign-Urbana, Illinois, a twin-city region with a combined population of 100,000. Although the area hosts agribusiness, a Kraft manufacturing plant and a number of small businesses, it is primarily known as the home of the University of Illinois. It is predominantly white (78.8 per cent) with nearly 20 per cent of the population holding graduate degrees, more than double the US average.[1]

Figure 3.1   Regent Ballroom and Banquet Center, Savoy, Illinois.

I did not dance ballroom prior to undertaking my research in 1996. During the seven years of my fieldwork, I learned to dance every genre performed at the Regent, taking almost all of the courses offered, attending hundreds of social dance events, conducting formal, informal, group and individual interviews. In addition to learning how to dance, I also worked behind the scenes at the Regent, managing

---

[1]   Population data taken from the US Census Bureau, Census 2000, which documents the population statistics during the time of my fieldwork.

the front desk, helping with renovation projects, giving private lessons, tending bar and so forth, to deepen my understanding of the dance hall as a commercial space. Furthermore, I attended dance classes, lessons and events throughout the region and travelled to dances across the Midwest. Given the length of my fieldwork, and the fact that many of my informants are themselves academics or possessing graduate degrees, they were interested in my project and continue to email me from time to time with observations. I have shared some of my book chapters and article drafts with them and the work is strengthened by their input.

To be fair and respectful to those who have given me access to their personal experiences, I have used pseudonyms for every dancer mentioned in this text save David and Ellen Lin, owners and operators of the Regent Ballroom. The Lins are civic leaders in Savoy and highly visible promoters of dance in the region; they were central not only to my work, but also to the dance experiences of the individuals documented in these pages. No pseudonym could mask their unique place in this local community, and to use one would be disingenuous.[2]

Following a brief introduction to ballroom performance, this chapter will proceed in two parts. The first will address what it means to 'hear' music among ballroom dancers, the competencies required and the important issue of genre. The second part will address the social significance that 'hearing' music holds for dancers. Implied in my treatment of genre is the proposition that amateur dancers conceptualize and 'hear' music differently from scholars of music and dance. Thus to understand the relationship between music and dance in social life, scholars must recognize and account for this reality in their analysis of popular forms. Furthermore, I will argue that, for ballroom dancers, 'hearing' music is a fundamental skill because it is suggestive of the ability to connect with others in a deep and meaningful way – to be known by someone else. Thus, 'hearing' music accumulates meanings beyond the basic skills of rhythmic perception to signify one's intuition and potential for human connection.

Ballroom Dance: Style and Practice

Ballroom dance is a gloss for a variety of couple dances accompanied by twentieth-century popular music.[3] Although the style has been staged for competitions,

---

[2] I prefaced all of my interviews with the assurance that I would use pseudonyms to encourage a free exchange of thoughts without concern for privacy. Given that many of the individuals discussed in this text are likely to read it, I imagine an unintended consequence will be to stimulate curiosity and a sharing of information among my informants. In private conversations with one another, they may choose to disclose their role in the book or not as they see fit.

[3] For more on ballroom dance, see my essays 'Whiteness and the Performance of Race in American Ballroom Dance', *The Journal of American Folklore*, 120/475 (2007): pp. 19-47, and 'Salsa Dance and the Transformation of Style: An Ethnographic Study

reviews and musicals, it is most commonly performed by amateurs. The style takes its name from the social spaces, originally found in the private residences of European and Euro-American elites, in which social dancing took place. It includes over a dozen couple dance genres that enjoyed popularity in ballrooms since the turn of the century.

Table 3.1   Ballroom dance genres.

Dances in descending order of level of perceived sophistication	Competition Ballroom Dances		Social Ballroom Dances	
	Modern/ Smooth	Latin	Street/Club	Folk
	Waltz	(Paso doble)	West Coast Swing	Polka
	Viennese Waltz	Rhumba/Bolero	Hustle	Rueda?
	Tango	Cha cha	Mambo	
	Foxtrot	Samba	Salsa	
	Quickstep	Jive/East Coast Swing	Night-club two-step	
			Merengue	
Subcategories are ordered by level of perceived sophistication (left to right)				

Note: There is some degree of flexibility within this chart, especially the placement of the mid-level dances within their respective category. For example, some might argue the reverse placement of cha cha and samba. Most often, the claim for an alternative ordering is made using the discourse of prestige and valuation of sophistication. I have not met anyone who argues the lack of any hierarchical valuation at all.

One of the distinctive elements of couple dance traditions is the convention of the lead-and-follow technique.[4] For an enjoyable partnership, dancers stress

of Movement and Meaning in a Cross-Cultural Context', *Dance Research Journal*, 40/1 (2008): pp. 45-64; Julie Malnig *Dancing Till Dawn: A Century of Exhibition Ballroom Dance* (New York, 1992) and her edited collection *Ballroom, Boogie, Shimmy Sham, Shake: A Social and Popular Dance Reader* (Urbana, 2009); Juliet McMains, *Glamour Addiction: Inside the American Ballroom Dance Industry* (Middletown, CT, 2006); Edward Myers, 'A Phase-Structural Analysis of the Foxtrot, with Transformational Rules', *Journal for the Anthropological Study of Human Movement* (1979): pp. 246-68; Patricia A. Penny, 'Contemporary Competitive Ballroom Dancing: An Ethnography' (Unpublished PhD thesis, University of Surrey, 1997); and Caroline Picart, *From Ballroom to Dancesport: Aesthetics, Athletics, and Body Culture* (Albany, NY, 2006).

4   A detailed discussion of this technique, and especially its gendered dynamics, are beyond the scope of this essay. I have dealt with these issues in 'To Lead and Follow: Gender, Dominance, and Connection in Ballroom Dance', paper presented at the Annual Meeting of the Society for Ethnomusicology (Atlanta, 2005).

the importance of 'connection', the insider term connoting the non-verbal communication that takes place between the leader and follower in any given dance moment. Whether connection exists or not within a particular couple depends upon the awareness of one partner for the other. Connection is perhaps the most affective component of couple dancing and certainly the element that sets it apart from other kinds of dance. One cannot be a good dancer if s/he does not connect, regardless of one's virtuosity in other areas of dance. Connection is so powerful that many dancers liken it to a drug, and their attraction for it to an addiction, as did Matthew, a middle-aged computer programmer:

> What I look for in a partner, I guess, … I look for connection. There's the physical, the physical abilities of a person that they're able to dance. They have rhythm. There's a solid connection. There are some girls that feel like a Raggedy Ann doll. There's nothing there and you can't do anything with them.
>
> The other girls, you know it immediately when you get into dance position, you can *fffffeel* the connection. You're both in tune with each other. You feel it here and here and here [pointing to his head, his torso and his arms]. Then there's the ineffable connection that you enjoy dancing with a person and you can see they enjoy dancing with you. They know that you're enjoying them, and you know that they know that you know. You feel like you've been dancing with this woman forever.
>
> See, that's like heroin … These dances are like crack. You start looking for them. You want another and another and you keep looking for them anywhere you can find them. And you can dance with a complete stranger and it's like you've been dancing together for ten years. The music is right, everything is completely right, and it works. It's dynamite. It's like snorting crack.[5]

As Matthew suggests, the concept of connection extends beyond the technical skill to encompass a more figurative sense of connection to another individual that is authenticated by the former and corroborated by the music. As I will demonstrate below, connection is central to understanding the social value of 'hearing' music.

To 'Hear' in the Ballroom

In the strictest sense, the skill of 'hearing' music encompasses two distinct but related skills. The first is to identify the corresponding dance genre appropriate for the specific musical example in question; the second speaks to the ability to place the actual dance step in the correct place in that music. These are deeply interconnected moments of musical perception and, to some degree, the first act, identifying the genre, takes place by imagining the moment of the second, placing the steps into the musical fabric.

---

[5] Personal interview, 15 October 2005, Champaign, Illinois.

Ballroom dances are known and named by dance genre (such as waltz, foxtrot, cha cha),[6] defined in the most basic terms by the rhythm and placement of the footwork. The genres are grouped into the categories Standard (also known as Smooth or Modern) and Latin, which form the cornerstones of the repertory, and a third less-standardized category called Night-club or Street. Most of the dancers I worked with were capable of performing nearly a dozen different genres (and many of them knew upwards of 20, including variants). All genres require their own basic and elaborative steps and their own accompanying musical frameworks. All of the dances are performed several times during one social dance event. Once the music starts, the dancers have options for what dance genre to perform. The first question a dancer must answer is which dance is the correct choice.

For some dancers, the answer is an uncomplicated act of perception. They 'hear' the music, assess the rhythmic and stylistic features and within seconds are dancing in synchrony with other dancers on the floor who, likewise, came to the same conclusion. However, the continued use of the antiquated practice of a dance card in this context is but one indicator that some participants struggle with this piece of the puzzle (see Figure 3.2, below). The dance card, created by Lin for use at the Friday night dances, lists the songs that will be played by their genre alone. Among other things, the dance card indicates to the dancers what dance genre should be performed to the music being played. Having the dance card removes all doubt.

David Lin, the owner and head dance teacher at the Regent Ballroom and Banquet Center, kept abreast of music trends to keep his collection current. He also acquired recordings from distributors or 'brokers' specializing in ballroom dance music. These brokers market recordings created by record labels specializing in ballroom dance music, but also include pop music recordings and compilations of pop songs in their offerings as well. Given that he has been teaching for two decades, Lin has developed an efficient cataloguing system for his recordings. He digitizes his musical selections, catalogues them by dance genre and then burns them to mini-discs or playlists on his laptop computer. Each mini-disc contains many examples of only one genre and is then numbered sequentially as he adds more music to his library. Thus, the earliest mini-discs Lin burned were Waltz 1, Foxtrot 1, Rumba 1, and later mini-discs labelled Waltz 3, Foxtrot 3, Rumba 3, and later still Waltz 6, Foxtrot 6, and so forth.

Lin relies on the consistency of familiar music to aid his students in learning to dance, and as such the older discs are important. He maintains this core repertory while carefully incorporating new songs incrementally into the playlist. Because some dancers have difficulty 'hearing' a piece of music and knowing the proper accompanying dance, Lin uses the same music from class lessons in the evening dances. If dancers cannot discern the rhythm, they may remember the tune from

---

[6]   The cha cha chá is a Latin genre that takes its name from the rhythm and sound of the footwork (four-and-one). In social contexts, ballroomers abbreviate their style of the dance to cha cha and I have followed suit.

#1	#8	#15
Waltz Rumba	2-Step Hustle	2-Step Hustle
#2	#9	#16
Swing Foxtrot	Waltz (2) Rumba	Foxtrot Rumba
#3	#10	#17
Cha Cha Rumba	Foxtrot Samba	Quickstep (2) Triple Swing
#4	#11	#18
Swing Quickstep (2)	Swing Cha Cha	Tango Cha Cha
#5	#12	#19
Waltz (2) Cha Cha	Break Time	Swing Waltz (2)
#6	#13	
Foxtrot Triple Swing	Mixer Waltz (2)	
#7	#14	Goodnight
Rumba Tango	Swing Polka	N 11/5/99

Tango Demo
Argentine Tango demonstration will be performed next Friday by Alberto Paz and Valorie Hart from California.

Dance Competition
The Dancing Illini competition is on Saturday, November 6 from 9:00a-8:00p at the Illini Student Union-rooms A, B, and C. You can purchase tickets at the door.

New Year's Eve Reservation
Bring in the new year with all your friends at the Regent. Enjoy: Dinner Buffet, Open Bar, Party Favors, Champagne Toast and MUCH, MUCH MORE! Seating is limited. Reserve your place tonight. $75.00 per person

New Nightclub Classes
Salsa I and Westcoast Swing I will be offered in January. Both classes will be taught in a split room, space is limited. Pre-Enroll tonight!

Next Friday
Advanced Dance
Hot Chocolate at the break

If Your Birthday Or Anniversary Is Within Four Days Of Tonight,Let Us Help You Celebrate With A Bottle Of Champagne Or A Pitcher Of Soft Drink. Do Let Us Know Before The Break.

Figure 3.2   Dance card for Friday Night Dance (5 November 1999), the Regent Ballroom and Banquet Center.

class and connect it to the waltz lesson, and in this way may remember that it is a waltz, even though they cannot 'hear' the triple metre.

The practice of identifying songs by the dance genre was standard among dancers. Discrepancies exist between the dance categorization of a song and its musical identification as understood by musicians, music scholars, the music industry and other music specialists who identify songs by their musical style or marketing genre in a relatively decontextualized way. In fact, a common point of confusion between musicians and dancers lies in the criteria by which each group defines a given genre. For some genres, such as the standard waltz, there is little dispute. In this case, the music category derives its name from the dance genre, and the two styles emerged in popular culture concurrently. For other dances there is room for interpretation.

For dancers, the categorization of a particular piece of music depends upon the dance genre for which it is best suited. While the stylistic features of the piece are important, it is crucial that the rhythmic structure of the basic dance step can be comfortably superimposed over the rhythmic structure of the music. So the question 'Is this a cha cha?' would be answered with the response 'Can you dance the cha cha to it? If so, then it's a cha cha.'

For example, I once saw a televised broadcast on my local public television station of a competition couple performing a cha cha to Aretha Franklin's soul hit *RESPECT* during an exhibition performance. There is little in the history or style of this song, or its performer, which suggests Latin America, although one could draw a connection to a racialized performance that the cha cha and Aretha Franklin both share. While I did not interview the dancers or any of the audience members, it is my guess that, given the popularity of the song, the dancers and their audience understood that Aretha Franklin was not a Latina and that the song was not Latin American or of Caribbean descent. It is safe to assume that they understood that, at one level, the genre classification for this song was 'rhythm and blues' or perhaps 'soul', but as dancers they also knew that it could make for a wonderful cha cha. They were not confused as to its origins or thoughtless in their criteria for judging genres, rather they understood this song as a cha cha because the basic cha cha step (with the cha-cha-cha being articulated on beats four-and-one) fit perfectly. The song was similar to more traditional cha chas in terms of its tempo and punchy, accented rhythms that inspire fast footwork and what dancers called 'syncopations'.[7] And so, while a music scholar might categorize Aretha Franklin's performance of *RESPECT* as soul, a ballroom dancer might label it a cha cha.[8]

After identifying the dance genre to perform to a given piece of music, the second and perhaps more difficult step in the process of 'hearing' music is to coordinate the basic footwork with the rhythmic framework of the particular music in question. This action is easier for some genres than others. The waltz provides one of the least ambiguous examples, perhaps because in this instance, the waltz is such in both music and dance terms. One plays a waltz, one dances a waltz; the basic pattern of the dance step aligns strictly with the metrical structure. This alignment is not the case for most dances in which a polyrhythm is generated between the rhythm of the footwork and the metre of the music, such as in the American-style foxtrot. The foxtrot dance step is a six-beat pattern. It is performed to music that is in quadruple metre, therefore the first step of the basic does not always coincide with the first beat of the measure.

The transparency of the rhythmic component of a song is an important factor in this process, especially for less-experienced dancers, and can lend aid in 'hearing' a song. Typically, dancers find the Latin American genres the most difficult. Thus Lin uses ballroom dance arrangements for the Latin dance genres rather than performances more true to the musical genre outside the ballroom context. Most dancers report that the faster Latin dances, in particular the mambo and cha cha which require faster timing and footwork, are the most difficult to 'hear'.

The two aspects of 'hearing' music that I have outlined are interconnected at a deep level, and my separation of them here is somewhat artificial. Together they

---

[7]   When used by ballroom dancers, this term denoted a subdivision of the basic step pattern for a given dance, whether or not this resulted in the syncopation of a strong musical beat, as the term suggests when used by musicians.

[8]   On a personal note, I myself was familiar with the song before I watched this performance. I never heard the song as a cha cha prior to watching this dance performance, but ever since I cannot hear it as anything but a cha cha.

comprise what it is to 'hear' music, and those dancers who struggled with one or the other (and usually if one, then the other) were said to 'have no rhythm'. Regent dancers believed that, while one might be able to improve upon one's ability to dance 'in time', one cannot acquire it if one does not have it at the outset. In every conversation I had with ballroom dancers on the topic, they either suggested that they could or could not 'hear' music. They did not use qualifying language (no one could 'hear' just 'a little' and no one was labelled 'a beginner hearer') nor did they suggest it was a skill that they could develop, as they did with other technical aspects of dance. Of the dancers who were perceived as not being able to 'hear', some were aware of their deficit and asked for assistance. Others seemed unaware that they place their dance steps incorrectly in the music.

In my interviews, women more often claimed to possess this skill than men, and it was not uncommon to see women followers counting off or cueing with head bobs or taps on the shoulder either the pulse of the music, the first beat of the measure, or the rhythmic pattern of the footwork as it fit within the particular musical example to which they are dancing. As Joy confessed, 'If [my partner] doesn't feel the rhythm, then I will ground it, but I will not dance off-time. It's just wrong.'[9] Jane, a local dance teacher, addressed the problem in a more subtle way: 'I'll just say "Can we stop for a moment?" and then take the opportunity to signal the rhythm with my body. He may not even be aware that that's what's happening.'[10]

If one member of a partnership has studied music in a formal way, the musician was generally deferred to as the one who is best able to 'hear' music. However, in my experience, there was no necessary correlation between 'hearing' music for dance purposes and one's formal training in music. Some of the most rhythmically challenged dancers I know identify as musicians and have studied music to a high level of academic achievement.

There is another, more advanced level of 'hearing' music that dancers occasionally identified, that of 'really dancing *to* the music'. Extending beyond the mere ability to 'hear' the music, someone who 'dances to the music' can coordinate sequences of moves to the phrasing and other formal aspects of the specific musical example. For example, in swing, where the music can incorporate musical breaks, the dancer who can coordinate 'dance breaks' with music breaks – upsetting the expected footwork pattern to accommodate the musical moment – is said to be highly sensitive to musical structure and 'dances to the music' very well. This coordination works best if both partners are capable, but when it does happen it is an extremely rewarding aspect of dance.[11]

---

[9] Personal interview, 8 October 2005, Champaign, Illinois.

[10] Personal interview, 19 October 2005, Champaign, Illinois.

[11] Some people have the ability to conceptualize their dance moves as sequences that comprise a larger meaningful arc, and others do not. Some can align this dance 'phrase' in coordination with the musical phrase, though to do so in the improvisatory context of a social dance is a higher-level skill.

Very occasionally there was some debate over what dance to perform to a given song. It was not a common occurrence, but I present the issue because it sheds more light on the way genres are understood. Given that ballroom dancers are versed in any number of genres, they have options as to which dance genre they will perform to a particular musical example. While the dance card and music itself precludes a free-for-all, advanced dancers like to take liberties when possible. It was signalled by a conversation that went something like this:

'William, would you like to rumba?'

'Oh, is this a rumba? I thought it was a cha cha.'

'Oh, we can do whichever you prefer.'

'Let's try rumba, and if it's too slow we can switch to the cha cha.'

This flexibility for what I call dancing 'off-genre', because it entails challenging explicit conventions for the generic label of a particular song, is common only among the more experienced dancers and generally stemmed from a preference for a certain type of dance. Howard's election to dancing country two-step to quickstep music, for instance, or Matthew's general preference for dancing the hustle to merengue songs was one of the ways they satisfied an enthusiasm for a dance they did not get to perform often enough. For less accomplished dancers, it was a difficult task to be able to 'hear' a piece of music and ascertain what dance to perform. These less skilled dancers generally limited themselves to performing the genre as it was listed on the dance card.

Depending upon the sensitivity of the particular couple, dancing off-genre could be considered problematic because the couple was literally dancing against the flow of movement, upsetting the flow of bodies, distracting some and forcing others to alter their floor craft for fear of collision. Furthermore, even in the best of circumstances, doing so disrupted the large-scale synchrony experienced when all the dancers participate in the performance of the same genre, feeling the music in much the same way and weaving in and away from each other in time. However, performing off-genre lent a greater degree of connectedness within the partnership; as the two dancers moved as one entity in time but out of sync with the other couples, no longer able to rely on the physical cues of the others on the floor, they were forced to rely more on each other. If the rhythmic overlay was particularly complex, the dance demanded even more connectedness in order to stay on time. Generally, it was akin to participating in a playful conspiracy, and advanced dancers seemed to relish their rare opportunities to challenge the conventional wisdom or dance against the rhythmic grain.

The Social Value of 'Hearing'

Dancers repeatedly stated that the ability to 'hear' music was one of the most foundational aspects of ballroom performance, but at the same time suggested that it could not be learned. When I asked dancers about the qualities necessary for being a good dancer, they all mentioned an ability to 'hear' music and often led with this trait, coupling it with the importance of connection. As Sheri Leblanc, former competitor, states, 'What makes dancing, dancing is simple: connection. In order to truly dance you must be connected to the music, connected to your partner and connected within yourself.'[12]

'Hearing' music, however, was considered a kind of sacred or primordial gift, one rooted in the more broadly held notion that musical understanding is a complicated talent bestowed (or not) at birth. This characterization of 'hearing' was a remarkable difference from the way my informants considered dancing. They identified learning to dance as something anyone could learn to do. Even though most of them entered the dancehall for the first time not thinking of themselves as dancers, they believed that they could acquire the ability through practice. The fact that my informants were all enrolled in classes demonstrated their faith that they could learn to dance. On the other hand, 'hearing' music, they acknowledged, was not necessarily something one could learn.

This somewhat contradictory discourse about 'hearing' music, and the dire consequences for those who did not possess it, is grounded in the affective potential of connection. The synchrony and momentum created by a solid connection between the partners contributes to a feeling of getting lost in the dance, what Csikszentmihalyi has called 'optimal experience' or 'flow'.[13] These flow states are one of the driving factors for enjoyment and feelings of connection among ballroom dancers and the source of the addiction described in the above quotation from Matthew.[14]

This feeling is substantiated by the movement itself. Ballroom dance is inherently relational; it relies fundamentally on the perception of one by another. Optimal dance experiences take place when movement, momentum and ideas move fluidly, without reflection and critical awareness, between the two dancers

---

[12]   Sheri Leblanc, 'The Importance of Connection in Ballroom Dancing', *Reflections in Verse and Prose*, 2011 http://reflectionsinverse.blogspot.com/2010/03/importance-of-connection-in-ballroom.html, accessed 16 February 2012.

[13]   For more on flow, see Mihaly Csikszentmihalyi and Stith Benett, 'An Exploratory Model of Play', *American Anthropologist*, 73/1 (1971): pp. 45-58; Mihaly Csikszentmihalyi and Isabella Selega, *Optimal Experience: Psychological Studies of Flow in Consciousness* (Cambridge, 1988); Mihaly Csikszentmihalyi, *Flow: The Psychology of Optimal Experience* (New York, 1990); and Thomas Turino, *Music as Social Life: The Politics of Participation* (Chicago, 2008).

[14]   For more on ballroom as a source of addiction, see also Bosse, 'Salsa Dance and the Transformation of Style'; and McMains, *Glamour Addiction*.

causing them to form one moving entity. Being lost in this musical moment with someone else in improvised, tight synchrony iconically signifies the kind of connectedness and social acceptance dancers desire, and it is often interpreted as a 'dicent index' of that connectedness (see Figures 3.3 and 3.4, below). That is, the flow state generated from the actual *physical* connectedness of the dancers is often interpreted as proof of a *social* connection or, I think more precisely, proof of the ability to be connected.[15] As ethnomusicologist Thomas Turino states:

> Knowing and hence being able to perform appropriately in the style is itself a dicent index of belonging and social identity, because performance competence is *both a sign and simultaneously a product of* shared … knowledge and experience – shared habits. In music and dance performance a higher level of attention is placed on rhythm and synchrony; participants are acutely aware of the groove and their relation to it and through it their relation to other participants. In participatory performances, feelings of social synchrony are at a higher level of focal awareness but still involve iconic and indexical signs which typically create effects of feeling and direct experience.[16]

Married couple and college professors Chelsea and Norman put it another way:

> C: 'There is something about moving together, to the music, that is so profound, very profound.'

> N: 'Yes, for me it is all about connection. Feeling that other person to the music … [When I watch a couple dance] I want to see people looking at each other and connecting. That's what I want to feel.'[17]

Herein lies the crux of the issue: if one cannot 'hear' music, then one does not possess the potential for this kind of connection. The conviction that the ability is not obtainable through training, the discourse that naturalizes the innate ability in the body, as if it is performed by some mysterious organ that hears and feels, spells doom for ballroom dancers seeking a partner. One cannot feel another person to music if one cannot 'hear' the music. To put it in more intimate terms, if I myself cannot 'hear', then it is not only true that I cannot move in synchrony with you, but that I cannot be known in a partnership at all. If I am a bad dancer, I can learn. I can practise. I can connect with a partner who is equally bad, and we can move

---

[15]   For more on dicent indices, see James Hooper, *Peirce on Signs: Writings on Semiotic by Charles Sanders Peirce* (Chapel Hill NC, 1991); Charles Sanders Peirce, *Philosophical Writings of Peirce*, ed. Justus Buchler (New York, 1955); Thomas Turino, 'Signs of Imagination, Identity, and Experience: A Peircian Semiotic Theory for Music', *Ethnomusicology* 43/2 (1999): pp. 221-55; and Turino, *Music as Social Life*.
[16]   Turino , *Music as Social Life*, p. 43.
[17]   Personal interview, 22 October 2005; Champaign, Illinois.

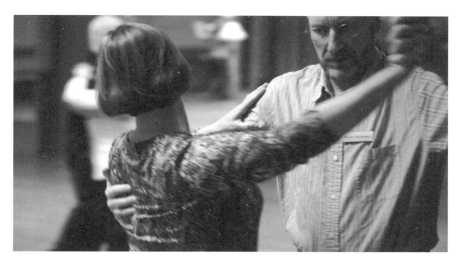

Figure 3.3   Dancers at the Regent Ballroom: flow states are generated from moments of heightened concentration, as the kind we can see on this dancer's face. The active musculature on the frame of both individuals suggests the potential for connection in this partnership.

Figure 3.4   Learning connection in class.

together at our own pace. Not being able to 'hear' music precludes my connection, literal and figurative, with other ballroom dancers.

Although music remained generally outside the focal awareness of ballroom dancers, it served a fundamental role. Music creates the context for dance and, thus, for the connections that occur within its refrains. Furthermore, it provides a kind of regulatory function, the temporal and aesthetic meeting ground, for connection. Dancing to music is embodied investment. Put most simply, music makes dancers want to move, and they do not dance without it. It creates the context in which movement was the most appropriate response. When discussing dance, the individuals I worked with often reproduced the Cartesian mind/body dichotomy when describing their own experience. 'I know what to do here (as the dancer pointed to his head) but I don't know it here (as he pointed to his torso)' was a common trope used to explain the process of learning new moves. Within this Cartesian framework, music functions as a cognitive bridge or vehicle through which the perceived components of self, the mind and body, become integrated during dance performance. This is Leblanc's aforementioned 'connection within yourself'.

Music compels movement. The deejay starts the tune, and the foot begins to tap, the knee flexes in time with the rhythm, the hip punctuates the off-beats, and the music transforms a stationary individual into a dancer. Picking up on this momentum, individuals employ their ballroom dance training, steps, figures, sequences of moves, floorcraft and the like, to create something beyond habits and reflexes, something that engages the creative intellect as well as the body. Music provides the impetus for dancers to move ideas through their bodies and to the bodies of their partners. It structures, both socially and sonically, the framework in which the body, one's own as well as another's, can be explored, celebrated and known in socially appropriate ways.

Being carried away by music stimulates the body and the imagination, and it is only in this state of being carried away from the brute facts of daily life that connection can occur. The music wafting out the front door of the Regent signals to those entering that this is a different kind of space – a space in which daily concerns do not matter, a space in which insecurities can be explored, and new kinds of relationships can be formed. In the context of ballroom dance, the process of becoming connected begins with the melodies of lush string orchestras that entice individuals not only to move, but to imagine their movement being the first step towards a meaningful human connection.

PART II
Authenticity, Revival and Reinvention

Chapter 4

Dancing Out of Time:
The Forgotten Boston of Edwardian England

Theresa Jill Buckland

In the opening years of the twentieth century, a new way of dancing to waltz music became visible in the fashionable hotel ballrooms of London's West End. Known as the Boston, this style of waltzing, as its name suggests, was believed by contemporary commentators to emanate from America and was reckoned by conservative critics to constitute a serious disjunction from the hallowed principles of Victorian dance etiquette. In vogue among British metropolitan upper-middle-class dancers, the Boston's choreomusical relations and spatial trajectories radically deviated from polite society's kinetic codes. This new style of waltzing did not become a widespread staple of the repertoire across all classes, but it was to leave indelible marks on the English manner of performing ballroom dances.

In company with many past instances of popular dancing, the Boston has escaped detailed scholarly attention. Now fallen from the collective memory of ballroom dancers, it was at the height of its popularity in England during the years immediately prior to the outbreak of the First World War. In press coverage of the time, the Boston was overshadowed by, and often confused with, the slightly later controversial importations of American ragtime and the Argentine Tango. In the wake of studies on ragtime and early twentieth-century ballroom dancing in America, and as the academic reach of dance studies widens to interrogate the significance of the popular, it is time to re-examine the phenomenon of the Boston in Edwardian England.[1]

---

[1]   See, in particular, Julie Malnig, *Dancing Till Dawn. A Century of Exhibition Ballroom Dance* (New York, 1992) and 'Apaches, Tangos, and Other Indecencies. Women, Dance, and New York Nightlife of the 1910s' in her edited collection, *Ballroom, Boogie, Shimmy Sham, Shake. A Social and Popular Dance Reader* (Urbana, 2009); Susan C. Cook, 'Passionless Dancing and Passionate Reform: Respectability, Modernism and the Social Dancing of Irene and Vernon Castle', in William Washabaugh (ed.), *The Passion of Music and Dance. Body, Gender and Sexuality* (Oxford, 1998); Danielle Robinson, 'The Ugly Duckling: The Refinement of Ragtime Dancing and the Mass Production and Marketing of Modern Social Dance', *Dance Research*, 28/2 (2010): pp. 179-99. For the British context, see Theresa Jill Buckland, *Society Dancing: Fashionable Bodies in England, 1870-1920* (Basingstoke, 2011).

Mid-twentieth-century writers on social dancing in England recognized the importance of the Boston to the later evolution of ballroom dancing. A. H. Franks, building on the work of P. J. S. Richardson, concluded that the Boston's 'style and movement were largely responsible for the early growth of what we now know as the English Style'.[2] Indeed, an evolutionist approach to dance history might classify the Boston as a 'transitional' dance or 'missing link' for its form reveals characteristics that pertain both to the nineteenth- and twentieth-century forms of waltz and couple dancing more generally. Care must be exercised, of course, in subjecting dance forms to narrow taxonomic inquiry or to interpretations based solely within a chrono-linear framework. Such perspectives often fail to engage with the variant and creative activities of human actors, ignoring earlier and co-terminous instances of similar practices and running the risk of reductionism and determinism. Nonetheless, later analysts were not alone in identifying formal differences and similarities between the old and new style modes of waltzing that the Boston appeared to herald. Similar observations were made by Edwardian participants and observers, as well as near-contemporaries who wrote with the benefit of recent hindsight.

Comparative examination of the form and relation of popular dance and music offers potential to students of dance historiography to understand shifts and continuities that move towards a closer visceral and aesthetic appreciation of transitional elements identifiable in the Boston. In addition, this analysis of structural and kinaesthetic descriptions, taken together with choreomusical and contextual developments, aims to signal modernist parallels across other dance genres of the period.

Musical Accompaniment in the Late Victorian Ballroom

At leading balls from the 1880s, it had become fashionable, especially for military bands, to accelerate the musical accompaniment. The military band conductor might well be entreated to play more slowly but, in the opinion of dance musician and dancing master C. J. Melrose, initial compliance was soon discarded: 'before the second movement is gone through they are off, and wild horses could not hold them back'.[3] The bands's *raison d'être* of course was not solely as dance musicians, for they also typically performed in musical concerts, at parades and at various civic and military events.[4] Undoubtedly, the growing popularity of listening rather than dancing to popular music contributed to increased and variable tempi: band leaders were keen both to engage the attention of their sedentary audiences and the interest of their musicians who increasingly valued their status and skills as

---

[2]   A. H. Franks, *Social Dance. A Short History* (London, 1964), p. 164.

[3]   C. J. Melrose, *Dancing up to Date* (London, 1892), p. 10.

[4]   See Gordon Turner and Alwyn Turner, *The History of British Military Bands*, 3 vols (Staplehurst, UK, 1994, 1996, 1997).

professionals.[5] Specialist dance bands similarly adopted these high speeds in order to provide 'pep' and 'go' to what had become a repetitive and monochrome dance repertoire in the late Victorian ballroom. Brisk speeds, however, rendered older dancers out of breath or inspired younger dancers to neglect dancing technique as they charged at high speed across the dance floor. By the 1890s, the standard of and enthusiasm for dancing, especially among young men, left much to be desired.[6]

Continental waltzes, as epitomized in the prolific output of composer and dance orchestra leader, Johann Strauss II (1825-99) the 'Waltz King' of *Blue Danube* fame, and the Paris-based Emile Waldteufel (1837-1915), best remembered today for his waltz *Les Patineurs*, dominated the repertoire of the Austrian and Hungarian bands that played for the balls of British high society. These fast, sparkling waltzes, constructed in several parts, complemented the rapid whirling of the waltzing couples around the dance floor. But the speed and lightness of continental waltzes appeared increasingly old-fashioned to a younger generation keen to challenge the old conventions.

Beyond the private realm of royalty and aristocracy, dancing was less a duty than an activity of choice and one in which insistence on tradition was not so stifling. The wealthier middle class, lacking their own town mansions and resources on the scale of royalty and aristocracy, increasingly began to hire the spacious and well-appointed ballrooms of the West End's newly built hotels and function rooms, which acted as magnets to attract a sophisticated clientele of rich, keen and experienced dancers.

At the very beginning of the new century, there emerged a socially exclusive subscription club for dancing known as the KDS or Keen Dancers' Society. This specifically drew together lovers of the Boston who had perhaps first encountered this style of waltzing in the fashionable summer resorts of Deauville and Trouville on the northern French Riviera. The club, which later went specifically by the name of the Boston Club, did not own its own premises but was reported to have met first at the Grosvenor Hall in Victoria and the Empress Rooms in Knightsbridge and then variously at the Portman Rooms, the Grafton Galleries and the Princes Gallery in Piccadilly. In addition to the Boston, their repertoire included the two-step, the one-step and later the Argentine tango. By the end of the first decade, enthusiasm for the new foreign dancing resulted in the founding of two similar organizations in London: the Royalist Club (1910), held variously at the Connaught Rooms in Mayfair, and the rooms of the Ramblers Club and the Empress Rooms; and the Public Schools and Universities Club (1911) at the Savoy Hotel.[7] It was in such high-class subscription clubs that the aesthetic preferences

⁵   See Cyril Ehrlich, *The Music Profession in Britain since the Eighteenth Century* (Oxford, 1985).

⁶   For fuller discussion, see Buckland, *Society Dancing*, chapters 6, 11 and 12.

⁷   'Investigator', 'Will the Boston Live?', *The Dancing Times*, October 1910, p. 9; P. J. S. Richardson, *A History of English Ballroom Dancing* (London, 1946), chapters 1-2;

and skills of their members laid the foundations for what became known as the modern English style of ballroom dancing.

The English School of Waltz Composers

The conservative British court and its followers steadfastly preferred central European melodies, composers and orchestras. The appearance of a new form of waltzing that was associated both with the middle classes and with the New World was unlikely to elicit their support. A favoured conductor, Herr Desider Gottlieb shook his head when asked his opinion of the Boston in 1911, revealing that 'though he had often heard it spoken of he had never knowingly seen it danced'.[8]

Declaring the Viennese waltz to be the 'king of dances', a *Daily Telegraph* correspondent judged that 'many men and women Boston who cannot valse'.[9] High-class dancing master Edward Scott agreed, arguing that the Boston was often nothing more than 'a mere euphemism for incapacity of performance'.[10] But for many other dancers, the Boston offered new experiences of moving to music that promised visceral pleasures that far surpassed those of the old waltz which left them hot, out of breath and disorientated after relentlessly spinning in one direction. Many high society dancers did not 'reverse', that is, change the direction of the turn when waltzing, a strategy which could obviate the effects of dizziness. The technique of waltzing, largely employed by the upper middle classes and by the better dancers (amongst whose ranks not many aristocrats might be counted) was still frowned upon at court and aristocratic events.

By 1911, the Boston had been introduced as a competitive form (together with the one-step) at the Royalist Club. As exhibition dancers and dancing teachers sought to capitalize upon its growing popularity, fresh variants were advertised: among these were the Double Boston of 1911, considered to be better suited to smaller or crowded rooms, the Long Boston, the Running Boston, and the Triple Boston. By 1912, in the capital's select public venues, P. J. S. Richardson doubted that anything other than the Boston was performed to waltz music.[11]

The music of a new generation of Viennese composers had already captured the ears of popular theatre audiences by the middle of the first decade of the twentieth century. Waltzes from the shows and operettas of musicians such as Franz Lehar (1870-1948), Oscar Straus (1870-1954), Leo Fall (1873-1925) and Karl Ziehrer (1843-1922) were commonly heard as ballroom arrangements. Indeed, *The Ball Room* observed that 'many programmes read more like a newspaper theatre

---

Walter Humphrey, *The Dancing Times*, December 1911, p. 78.

[8]   *Dancing Times*, July 1911, p. 230.

[9]   William Boosey, *Daily Telegraph*, 13 February 1913.

[10]   *Daily Telegraph*, 13 February 1913.

[11]   Victor Silvester and Philip J.S. Richardson, *The Art of the Ballroom* (London, 1936), p. 24.

announcement column than a ballroom programme'.[12] This transmission from theatre to dance floor was by no means new, but the practice accelerated in the early 1900s, in line with the passion for dancing and musical theatre among the increasingly leisured and affluent middle class. Waltzes from Straus's *A Waltz Dream* (Hicks Theatre, 1908) and *The Chocolate Soldier* (Lyric Theatre, 1910), Fall's *The Dollar Princess* (Daly's Theatre, 1909) and Lehar's *The Merry Widow* (Daly's Theatre, 1907) and *The Count of Luxembourg* (Daly's Theatre, 1911), featured prominently on ballroom programmes over several seasons.

Alongside this early twentieth-century wave of Viennese musicians arose a school of English waltz composers, several of whom, as well as writing what was later to be classed as British light concert music, were conductors of dance orchestras. Their clientele frequented West End ballrooms and the regular dances held in London middle-class enclaves such as Hampstead, St John's Wood and Blackheath. Whereas the older, the more conservative, the lower middle class and most teachers clung to the monarchy for cultural leadership, it was neither high society nor pedagogues but, as P. J. S. Richardson later reflected, the bands that 'made us get out of a rut'.[13] Foremost among these were Archibald Joyce at the Royalist Club and Grafton Galleries; Stroud Haxton, also at the Grafton Galleries, the Royalist Club, the Public Schools and Universities Club and the Four Hundred Club (later known as The Embassy); Frederick Casano at the Ritz Hotel, a venue patronized by forward-looking and fun-loving aristocrats, and out in the suburbs, Felix Godin's band at the long-running Hampstead picnic dances.

The established practice of positioning an extra dance at the end of the evening's programme provided a time and space where experiments in composition could be tested on the dancers; invariably, the 'extra', as it was known, was a waltz. Given the level of professional training and experience among these musicians, the orchestra often played fledgling compositions by sight from manuscript scores so that the composer/bandleader could make modifications in response to the dancers' reactions. If the name of the melody was requested by the dancers or if they had inquired where they might purchase the sheet music, the new composition after its trials in the ballroom was then rushed to the music publishers. According to composer and bandleader Felix Godin (alias Henry Albert Brown, c. 1864-1925), a successful waltz composition for the ballroom was most likely to be the creation of 'bandmasters who spend their lives playing for dances'.[14] 'The first, and really the most essential thing', he pronounced, 'is to know what dancers want.'[15] And with over 20 years' experience of 'high-class dance bands', Godin knew this to be a good melody with a well-marked rhythm that could suit both dance and concert tastes.

---

[12]   *The Ball Room*, January 1912, 197, p. 10.

[13]   'Are Ballroom Dancers Too Conservative?', *The Dancing Times*, September 1926, p. 530.

[14]   'A Waltz Dream', *The Dancing Times*, January 1911, p. 76. See also, 'Extra', 'Successful Waltzes of the Season', *The Dancing Times*, June 1911, p. 210.

[15]   'A Waltz Dream', p. 76.

The Dancing Times, under the editorship of P. J. S. Richardson, reflected both the importance of dance music and respect for its composers, who along with band leaders appeared on its front covers each month. Within its pages were publishers' advertisements for the latest sheet music (essential for the journal's revenue) and for the Orchestral Association, established in London in 1893, which lists string and military bands for hire. Also featured were articles on the latest melodies and their composers as well as occasional notes on musical tempi for dancing. Richardson actively championed English musicians, his efforts to promote what he perceived as a developing English school in waltz composition complementing his vision of high standards, national distinction and an infrastructure for social and theatrical dance in Britain. Adopting the quiet patriotic tone that runs throughout the early decades of his journal, Richardson emphatically pronounced in December 1910 that 'the English composer has come, and come to stay'.[16]

It was with evident pleasure that he reported Godin's observation that three of the top five waltzes voted for by readers were written by composers who not only were English but also hailed from London. First and second places were taken by Archibald Joyce with *Songe d'Automne* (1908) and *Vision of Salomé* (1909), followed by Godin's *Septembre* in third place. This latter, in contrast to most of the English school of waltz melodies, had the unusual distinction of being played at a state ball, possibly because it was closer in feeling to the Viennese style.[17]

The English waltz was typified by a simple central melody of 'ear-haunting' resonance, the triple metre written in dotted minims to produce a 'slow but fascinating swing'.[18] Archibald Joyce, marketed by his publishers as the 'English Waltz King', was a master of the style, his popular *Vision of Salomé* composed through piano improvisation at a fancy dress event and later tried out for dancing at the Grafton Galleries.[19] Even more successful, with a title indicative of the new waltz mood in the English school, was his *Dreaming* of 1911. Joyce's initial stylistic inspiration, however, came not from English melodies, but from the languorous waltz in Austrian Franz Lehar's famous operetta *The Merry Widow* (1904), which heralded a new slow pace and reflective mood in waltz composition.[20]

---

[16]   'The Rise of English Waltz Composers', '*The Dancing Times*, December 1910, p. 34.

[17]   'Which Are the Five Most Popular Waltzes', *The Dancing Times*, December 1910, pp. 50-51.

[18]   'Rise of English Waltz Composers', p. 35.

[19]   Ibid.

[20]   Jason Tomes, 'Joyce, Archibald (1873-1963)', *Oxford Dictionary of National Biography*, Oxford University Press, 2004; online edn, May 2010 [http://www.oxforddnb.com/view/article/62776, accessed 23 March 2012].

Confusing Identities

The chameleon-like nature of the Boston was recognized in 1913 by Edward Scott, who deemed it 'impossible to arrive at any really satisfactory conclusion about the origin of a dance or movement which presents such varied aspects, and admits of such conflicting interpretations'.[21] There had been a dance known as the Boston in North America during the 1870s; it reappeared in the 1880s in parts of London; the Boston was again fashionable during the 1890s in North America and in Paris, reappearing again in the French capital around the start of the new century. The Boston was, Scott concluded, like Encke's comet, disappearing and reappearing over short periods.[22]

Though the dance was practised in London's fashionable ballrooms for close to a decade, the national press discussions of 1913 reveal considerable disagreement as to its identity. Two major reasons can be attributed to this state of confusion and ignorance, one contextual, the other, choreomusical. Firstly, the Boston of Edwardian England was initially the preserve of a limited social group in an exclusive environment. To learn how to dance the Boston required leisure, money and entry through profession, family or affiliation to a wealthy class who moved easily between metropolitan and sometimes cosmopolitan ballrooms. Secondly, unlike the earlier nineteenth-century introductions of couple dances such as the polka, mazurka or schottische, the Boston was not easily recognizable as a clearly delineated set of movements performed to a distinctive musical rhythm.

In its unstable, multiple and variant forms, the Boston was typical of popular dancing before becoming adopted, commodified and cascaded across polite society and beyond, via the dancing masters of Paris. For a number of Edwardian upper-class dancers, however, long versed in strictly codified patterns of movement, the Boston posed a particular challenge in perception and aural-kinetic understanding. For those loyal to the old style of waltzing, the Boston dancer was simply a bad dancer. Even those who were more willing to accept the dance as a legitimate form considered its typical appearance on the dance floor not as an elegant alternative form of waltzing but as '[t]hat inane muddle of the two step waltz and "Merry Widow" extravagances which some people incorrectly call the "Boston"'.[23]

---

[21]   Edward Scott, *All About the Boston. A Critical & Practical Treatise on Modern Waltz Variations* (London, 1913), p. 19.

[22]   Scott, *All About the Boston*, p. 23. For descriptions of the Boston in America and France, see, for example, Allen Dodworth, *Dancing and Its Relations to Education and Social Life* (New York, 1885), p. 73; 'The Boston Dip', *The Director*, 1/1, December 1897, pp. 17-18; Alfonso Joseph Sheafe, *The Fascinating Boston* (Boston, 1913); Troy Kinney and Margaret West Kinney, *Social Dancing of Today* (New York, 1914), pp. 21-7; and, for France, G. Desrat, *Dictionnaire de la Danse Histoire, Théorique, Pratique et Bibliographique* (Paris, 1895).

[23]   *Daily Telegraph*, 13 October 1910.

The reference to *The Merry Widow* is by no means haphazard. Twice encored at its premiere in the production by George Edwardes at Daly's Theatre in 1907, *The Merry Widow* waltz, as performed by Lily Elsie and Joseph Coyne, had drawn favourable press comment for its 'dreamy, swaying qualities'.[24] It also sanctioned, in the close hold and gaze into each others's eyes, the introduction of a more emotionally expressive element to the theatrical waltz which was replicated by some social dancers in the ballroom.[25] The staging of *The Merry Widow* waltz not only appears to have added dramatic logic to the use of the waltz in musical theatre but also echoed the more combative and close body position of the Apache, a music hall 'low life' rendering of the waltz. Direct links between the choreography of *The Merry Widow* waltz and the Boston cannot be drawn but the potential for new moods in couple dancing is evident.

By the early 1900s, the Boston had spread to fashionable urban centres in America and Europe, taking on new inflections in localized dance cultures. Devotees and critics were at least in agreement that the Boston as danced in London was different from both the American and French versions, though precise comparative detail is lacking. In the national press debate of 1913, the Boston was often condemned alongside later choreographic imports as immoral and decadent,[26] though as the debate progressed, it became apparent that the real targets for censure were stage versions of ragtime dances and the Argentine tango. Old animosities between England and America often coloured the argument, the former deriding the latter for reliance upon Africanist music and dance, which were condemned as primitive and lacking in grace. Boston dancers from across the Atlantic had their English champions, of course, who, in company with American dancing teachers, condemned the English attempts. Cosmopolitan traveller and English actor and entertainer George Grossmith Jnr wrote that was there 'no resemblance' to the American version while they also missed out on the 'skating' effect of the French 'Valse Boston'.[27] Too often, in his view, the English male dancer held his partner at arm's length (as in the Victorian mode of ballroom hold) when close body contact was essential to both French and American versions. There were obviously, however, some dancers in London who attempted this new closeness of partnering.

Ever alert to dance trends, the satirical magazine *Punch* had already turned its mocking gaze on the London Boston by 1909, caricaturing the new ballroom hold in which the recommended upright posture of Victorian generations was flagrantly disregarded in favour of a lounging closeness between the sexes that challenged moral propriety (see Figure 4.1). Even allowing for exaggeration by the *Punch* cartoonist, new ways of relating to other bodies and to the space were becoming widespread.

---

[24]   *The Times*, 10 June 1907, p. 4.

[25]   Joseph Coyne in *Every Woman's Encyclopaedia* (London, 1910-12).

[26]   See, for example, 'Modern Dancing', *The Times*, 20 May 1913; 'In Defence of the "Boston"', *The Times*, 22 May 1913.

[27]   *Dancing Times*, October 1910, p. 10.

THE POETRY OF MOTION, 1909.
THE "BOSTON."

Figure 4.1   'The Poetry of Motion', *Punch*, 17 February 1909.

Dancing teachers called out for a 'modified and more graceful form' of the Boston that did not 'border on the grotesque'.[28] Moves such as the Boston dip in which dancers simultaneously executed a deep leg bend, sometimes with the man's leg in between those of his partner, caused much alarm among parents and guardians. Theatrical deviations from polite society's morally upright posture[29] that were imitated in the ballroom drew much censure. *The Ball Room* believed that it was because of these various 'extravagances' that 'the Boston has been tabooed in certain ballrooms, and it is never seen at Court'.[30] Aside from its perceived assault on moral values, the Boston posed other problems in its radical use of space and of time.

Conflicts in Space

Eschewing the crush of dances held in private drawing rooms, fashionable dancers preferred large modern public rooms where couples could travel through and

---

[28]   *The Ball Room*, 15/195, November 1911, p. 9.

[29]   On the complex of language and social action see the seminal George Lakoff and Mark Johnson, *Metaphors We Live By* (1980; Chicago, 2003); and Brenda Farnell, 'Metaphors We Move By', *Visual Anthropology*, 8 (1996), pp. 311-35.

[30]   *The Ball Room*, 15/195, November 1911, p. 9.

across space to a band playing the latest waltzes; it was 'a waste of good music when there is no room to dance'.[31] The Boston was an expansive dance in which the music of a dotted minim waltz called for a slower paced transfer of weight, sometimes with a half-turn effected by a pivot on the leading foot on the last beat of the bar. This method of waltzing, recorded in American notations of the previous century, had also appeared in London ballrooms in the late 1800s and was recognized by Edward Scott as 'our old friend the slide and a twist'. This combination was also known as the Kensington Crawl, a movement which in Scott's deprecating eyes had 'done yeoman service for tired or lazy men-waltzers ever since the waltz has been in vogue'.[32]

Sliding as a key component of waltzing, however, had been recognized as a customary practice among the younger generation of upper-middle-class dancers in Kensington during the late 1880s. Society entertainer George Grossmith Snr characterized this style as slow and lacking in exuberance, the raised arms extended stiffly to the side and the steps performed on the flat foot moving in parallel, rather than with any turn-out or rise and fall in the instep.[33] To his eyes, these dancers lacked technical competence of the kind transmitted by high-class dancing teachers, but he did at least admire the skill of the 'Kensington glider' in steering his partner around the room. Grossmith considered the geographical source of this glide and flat foot to be Boston. Other references to the Boston in Britain before 1900 designate the dance as an American method of waltzing in which emphasis is on the change in direction of the turning couple. Indeed, Edwardian singer Hayden Coffin was sure that the Boston was nothing other than the American term for reversing.[34]

By the 1880s, newly built fashionable London houses included highly polished parquet floors which provided the perfect surface upon which to slide. Another innovation in the London dancers' environment was the sprung floor. That at the new ballroom of the Savoy Hotel in 1911 was built to 'an entirely novel plan' for it rested on '150 steel springs, distributed at regular intervals over the floor area' which 'ensure[d] the desired amount of elasticity for dancing'.[35] Boston dancers sought a floor with a surface 'like smooth ice' in order to 'skim ... round the room with that delightful skating, swaying movement of the perfect Boston'.[36] The adoption of long slides rather than neat steps under the body inevitably had an impact on the dancers' footwear. In 1910, Richardson noted the increase in male

---

[31]   *The Dancing Times*, November 1910, p. 34.

[32]   Scott, *All About The Boston*, p. 22.

[33]   'The Waltz and the Ball-Room', *Pall Mall Gazette*, 7 February 1889, pp. 1-2.

[34]   C. Hayden Coffin , *The Daily Telegraph*, 13 February 1913. See also Glaswegian dancing teacher J. F. Wallace's notation which is headed 'Valse, The American or Boston', *Excelsior Manual of Dancing* (Glasgow, [1887]), p. 52; R. M. Crompton, *Theory and Practice of Modern Dancing* (London, [1892]), p. 57.

[35]   'London's New Ball-Room', *The Dancing Times*, January 1911, p. 84.

[36]   Anonymous lady quoted in *The Dancing Times*, November 1910, p. 34.

dancers wearing laced-up shoes rather than dancing pumps.[37] Recognizing them as 'Bostonians', he attributed the cause to wear and tear on the traditional light-soled dance slipper. A year later, his magazine advertised a new development, the '"Boston Court" with stout soles, light weight and flexible, recommended to all "Bostoners"'.[38]

The dance was not, however, popular with everyone in the fashionable West End ballroom, for the new rectilinear spatial trajectories literally cut across the rotary spinning couples of the Viennese-style waltz. The American hold facilitated progression in a straight line, the couple moving towards and away from the centre of the room, the turning often executed almost on the spot. This was in contrast to the perpetually turning devotees of the old waltz who travelled around the perimeter of the dance floor. The obvious complications for couples moving on a dance floor on which both styles were being performed at the same time was graphically and humorously depicted in *The Dancing Times* (see Figure 4.2, below).

Practised Boston dancers had a number of strategies at their disposal to evade potential collision on the dance floor. Not only might spatial progression be achieved through the skating style of forwards and backwards waltz in the zig-zag step, but also the dancers might quickly advance via a run on a straight trajectory. Other staples of the Boston were the crab step, a sideways movement that could be used to manoeuvre through narrow spaces between other couples on the floor, and the turn which was mostly executed on the spot, either to the right (ordinary turn) or to the left (reverse turn). Yet even when every couple was dancing the Boston, there were no guarantees of a collision-free evening. *The Ball Room* reported that in a recent Boston competition the five couples dancing in a room that 'under ordinary conditions for a waltz would accommodate about 500' struggled to avoid near misses with one another.[39]

For the popular dance historian, the gap between notations in dancing manuals and actual practice on the dance floor is notoriously difficult to fill. Dance instructors follow no ethnographic or historical imperatives, assume considerable knowledge from the contemporary reader and generally have limited expertise in describing the movement. Indeed, most pedagogic notations are prescriptive rather than descriptive, setting forth a preferred version for adoption which may seek to qualify, change or even replace existing practice with a new model. Examination of the limited number of Boston descriptions recorded reveals schisms in the once comparatively uniform dance repertoire of the British urban population: the Boston as performed by the leisured 'club dancer' and as taught by the dancing teachers in their academies. The latter looked to the spatial and temporal regulation of the past.

---

[37]   *The Dancing Times*, October 1910, p. 13.
[38]   *The Dancing Times*, October 1911, p. 9.
[39]   *The Ball Room*, 16/206, November 1912, p. 8.

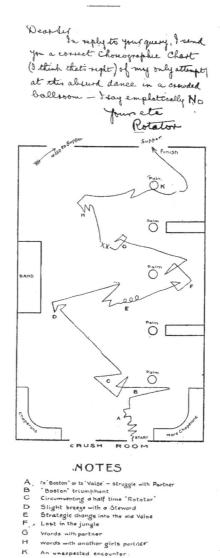

Figure 4.2   'Will the Boston Live? Another Opinion', *The Dancing Times*, October 1910, p. 20.

In 1909, R. E. A. Hildesley, a member of the Council of the recently formed Imperial Society of Dance Teachers (founded 1904), advised that dancers should use the existing waltz hold. His version of the Boston adheres closely to the balletic principles that underpinned European mainstream social dance technique, evident in his terms for the positions of the feet and movements such as *balancé à côté*, *glissade*, *dégager* and *point*. Each beat of the bar in Hildesley's Boston has a corresponding foot action just as in the classic waltz, and the implied turn-out of the feet suggests a Boston removed from the spatial and rhythmic freedoms of West End club dancers.[40]

To leading members of another pedagogic professional organization, the British Association of Teachers of Dancing (BATD), improvisation while dancing was tantamount to choreographic and social anarchy. To combat the club dancers' Boston in which there was 'no proper sequence of movement',[41] they proposed a set routine that might be performed to any moderately paced waltz constructed of an equal number of 16 bars throughout. Only then could order prevail in the social dances held at the dancing teachers' academies. This choreographic remedy was available in the form of the 'New Boston', a sequence dance adopted by the Society's conference in 1911 and profiled on the programme of their London annual ball at the King's Hall, Holborn Restaurant. The conservative nature of such creations is evident in the dance's notation which specifies the customary waltz position and 'three movements to each bar of music'.[42] The BATD was adamant that new improvisatory forms such as the Boston and the Argentine Tango were not to the taste of their clientele. The patrons of teachers' academies were to be denied the freedoms of rhythmic and spatial impulse; instead the anonymous safety and order of ready-made mass choreography was at hand to generate a sense of fashionable yet ultimately conservative community, deemed by both leaders and followers to be more suitable for – and thus likely to be welcomed by – the less temporally and spatially free members of the middling sort of society. This issue of improvisation or lack of standardization, as the debate on the 'modern' dances was to frame it, was further compounded by a widespread perception outside the dance club community that Boston dancers were committing that most heinous of crimes in Terpsichore's court: the couples were dancing out of time to the music.

Contested Rhythms

In order to investigate this claim, it is helpful to consider the preferred timing of waltzing among London's establishment. The classic Valse à Trois Temps in which the couple executed a whole turn clockwise as they progressed anticlockwise

[40] R. E. A. Hildesley, *Full Instructions for Dancing the Boston Waltz, Two-Step and Galop* [1909], pamphlet in The British Library, London.
[41] *The Ball Room*, 16/206, November 1912, p. 8.
[42] Ibid., p. 9.

around the perimeter of the ballroom required the dancers to take six steps to two
bars of 3/4 music. These were no longer evenly measured as in the early 1800s
but by the later part of the century it was advised that, to 'keep correct time in the
Waltz, it is necessary to take the first and fourth steps exactly at the beginning
of each bar, and let all the accent fall on these'.[43] This resulted in a rhythmical
stepping pattern of a dotted crotchet followed by a quaver and final crotchet in
each bar to achieve the 'tripping appearance so noticeable in good waltzing, and
which has a most pleasing effect when done gracefully, and without raising the
feet from the floor'.[44]

Not all dancers could master such precision, however, and already by the
late 1890s, dancers responded to waltz melodies by executing the Valse à Deux
Temps, in which the first step took two beats to execute at the start of each bar.
Other responses included the use of stepping patterns from the closely allied dance
forms such as the two-step and galop. Although, strictly, the latter two dances
were performed to duple metre, the fashionable speed of playing often left little
time for the less competent dancer to take three clear transfers of weight in the
first bar of the classic waltz step. Instead, the couple often did their best to shuffle
around each other in an approximation of the waltz step. Nonetheless, there was a
general understanding and effort made to make sure that the steps coincided with
the musical beat.

The Boston, however, introduced new responses to the music which critics
regarded as distinctly unmusical and as evidence of bad dancing. 'To anyone
possessed of even the faintest idea of rhythm there can be no "poetry in motion"
in the Boston', declared a correspondent to the *Daily Telegraph* in 1913, 'for the
simple reason that the movements of the body do not correspond with the beat
of the music'.[45] Indeed, pronounced another opponent, a 'Boston in which the
steps are against the rhythm of the music, is an affectation'.[46] Part of the problem
lay of course in the improvised nature of Boston dancing. 'Any step will do ...'
complained an adversary, 'visit the Connaught Rooms or the Grafton, where you
will hardly see two couples dancing the same measure.'[47] This observation is borne
out by a keen female Boston dancer who wrote:

> the time of the music is terribly puzzling, for some 'Boston' steps are quite
> unrelated to the time of the waltz to which they are danced. Some dancers do a
> walk of four steps to the music of three, some run and others crawl, yet with the
> same impulse they all move round the rhythmic scene.[48]

43   Edward Scott, *The Art of Waltzing* (London, [1885]), p. 46.
44   Ibid.
45   Reginald Tremayne, *The Daily Telegraph*, 13 February 1913.
46   William Boosey, ibid.
47   Reginald Tremayne, ibid.
48   Elizabeth Hyatt-Woolf, 'Passing of the Waltz', *The Dance Journal*, March 1910,
p. 6.

High-class Society teacher Charles D'Albert noted that, in order to dance the Boston, the 'ear must be closed to the rhythm of the waltz music, and the dance is executed to the rhythm of the dancer's personal taste and individuality'.[49] In the eyes of the dance's critics, this was viewed as technical incompetence rather than skill; good dancers, in the eyes of the BATD, '*dance to the music*' [original emphasis].[50] But herein lay another discrepancy in the perceptions of the two cohorts of dancers: for lovers and teachers of the classic waltz, dancing to the music equalled dancing to the metrical beat; for the club dancers, as Boston exponent and its respected teacher, Janet Lennard explained: '[it] is to the melody one dances in the Boston, the steps and the movements are absolutely one with it, and that being so there is an independence of the exact attention to the beat required by the old valse'. To understand how this should be done was, in Lennard's view, impossible to convey in words; only through practice might beginners 'feel it for themselves' for its interest lay not in its visual but sensory appeal in which '[m]arking time to the tune is the key to its popularity'.[51]*

High-class London dancing teachers did though try to capture the Boston's essence on paper. Walter Humphrey, at P. J. S. Richardson's request, attempted to do so in 1911 for the readers of the *Dancing Times* keen to be in the latest fashion. He set out a brief comparative table of the timing and steps of the old and new ways of waltzing. In Humphrey's notation, three steps are performed to one bar or three beats in what he calls OT or ordinary time, whereas the same moves are spread over six beats or two bars in the Boston.[52] His interpretation largely coincides with Charles D'Albert's description in his *Encyclopaedia* of the dance being 'done as though the music were written in 6-8 time'.

Humphrey's notation of the Double Boston and other variants at the start of the new dancing season later in 1911 sparked further correspondence. 'Much Perplexed' worried that, in addition to being confused by numerous teachers as to the real Boston, he was equally unable to comprehend Humphrey's description for 'the gentleman put four steps to three counts and also to six counts, and gave no idea as to how to divide the three steps into two bars'.[53] The professors of dancing no longer commanded absolute trust and it was an anonymous 'Amateur' who Richardson next published on the distinction between the old waltz and the Boston, while reserving full agreement with his contributor's views. According to 'Amateur', not only was the basic step more akin to walking in that weight was transferred from one foot to the other but also that the three steps were equal.

---

[49]   Charles D'Albert, *Dancing. Technical Encyclopaedia of the Theory and Practice of The Art of Dancing* (London, 1913).

[50]   *The Ball Room*, 16/206, November 1912, p. 8.

[51]   Janet Lennard, 'Ball-Room Dancing of To-day', *The Dancing Times*, April 1911, pp. 164-5.

[52]   'The Boston', *The Dancing Times*, March 1911, p. 144.

[53]   Walter Humphrey, 'The "Double Boston"', *The Dancing Times*, October 1911, pp. 8-9; *The Dancing Times*, November 1911, p. 48.

He was of the firm opinion that the Boston was not in fact a modified waltz but a distinctly new form.[54] This view was shared by a later correspondent 'Hametab' who remained 'convinced that the real "Boston" time is not the same as the waltz'.[55]

For Scott, the 'dancing out of time' was predominantly a matter of perception caused by the dancer retaining his or her weight over the supporting foot as the other foot slid backwards or forwards over one bar of music.[56] Scott's analysis is not entirely trustworthy, however, given his insistence upon retention of the dactylic rhythm. Other observers considered that dancers were merely moving 'half-time' in order to cope with the typically fast tempo. Lennard, however, dismissed this as nothing more than the attempts of elderly, lazy or tired dancers rather than an essential feature of the Boston's timing. If anything, she argued, the Boston in London clubs was danced 'just under the beat to the ordinary band' in 'three-quarters' time to guard against tiredness over a long evening dancing to very quick music.[57]

Attempts to rationalize and communicate the choreomusical relationship undoubtedly reflect the practice of some dancers, but for Boston devotees the essence of the aural-kinetic understanding lay in listening and responding to the melody of each waltz, not in the successful execution of any predetermined metrical patterning. For 'Amateur', the length of the steps in the Boston was 'varied at pleasure'[58] to fit the melody; and it was in pursuit of each couple's individual sensory pleasure that the Boston exercised its fascinating spell. Offering opportunity for self-expression and the quiet display of judgement on the dance floor, the dance had encouraged male undergraduates back into dance classes. Here was a fundamental aspect of modern ballroom dancing. As one female Boston devotee enthused: 'A girl must be able to move anywhere, anyhow, at a moment's notice, and always in the time of her partner. He controls the dance, and his Boston, whether it be right or wrong, must be his measure for that dance.'[59]

In spite of her misgivings about the inadequacies of written expression, Janet Lennard's article offers insightful qualitative instruction on the attraction and modernity of the Boston. In her description can be glimpsed the beginnings of contra body movement, a move now fundamental to modern ballroom technique and echoed by other Boston dancers' references to the swaying, skimming and skating sensations that the Boston evoked. The 'runs' of the Boston taken on the cross of the room, rather than turning consistently around the room's perimeter, facilitated a smoothness, grace and elegance of dancing by 'giving the body the slight turn required to enter the next position with the greatest possible ease'.

---

[54]   'The Waltz and the Boston', *The Dancing Times*, December 1911, p. 57.
[55]   *The Dancing Times*, January 1912, p. 120.
[56]   *All About the Boston*, pp. 48-9.
[57]   Lennard, 'Ball-Room Dancing of Today', p. 164.
[58]   'The Waltz and the Boston', p. 57.
[59]   Hyatt-Woolf, 'Passing of the Waltz', p. 6.

Nor were the frequent analogies with skating incidental. During the first decade of the twentieth century, at the fashionable Princes ice rink, located close to the Empress Rooms in Knightsbridge, skating had increased in popularity among the rich and leisured urban classes. On the stage, influential exhibition ballroom dancer Maurice Mouvet was famed for his skating valse performed in theatres and cabarets, and in 1913 exhibition dancers Marquis and Miss Clayton performed the tango on roller skates at the newly opened Queen's Rink in Earls Court. Here, for the same entrance fee, visitors could first try out steps in the adjacent Palais de Danse before taking to the rink.[60] Janet Lennard specifically notes the London inclusion of moves from the skating valse into the Boston 'by using a great deal more swing during the turn' and the adoption of the Drop Three Skating Valse in the reverse turn so that, instead of the three even steps of the usual Boston step, the dancers introduced a pause after the first step, reminiscent of the later hesitation of modern ballroom technique.[61]

Towards Moving in Tune with Modernity

Although A. H. Franks in 1963 had recognized the new treatment of music by dancers of the English Boston, the wider significance of his remarks with respect to transformations in social dancing during a period self-consciously observed as 'modern' has largely gone unnoticed. There can be little doubt that the Boston played a crucial role in the emergence of the English style of modern ballroom dancing, one marked by the close body hold, the basis in 'natural' walking, the improvisational potential and, especially relevant to the argument here, the choreomusical relationship which differed from the Victorian ballroom repertoire both structurally and socially.[62]

As had been the case for several centuries among the top ranking echelons, the Victorian fashionable dance floor had provided a spatio-temporal arena in which heterosexual couples were permitted to become physically, though never intimately, close. At the same time, they were under constant scrutiny by watching family, chaperones, friends and influential members of society. Social communication between the dancers was, furthermore, expected to be rehearsed via the recommended light conversation as the waltzing couple circled the dance floor.

For the new Boston dancers of the Edwardian era, such inattention to the music was anathema; they considered it 'treason to talk' when dancing to the new waltzes.[63]

---

[60]   Maurice Mouvet, *Art of Dancing* (New York, [1915]), pp. 48ff.; Gladys Beattie Crozier, *The Tango and How to Dance It* (London, 1913), pp. 140-41.

[61]   Lennard, 'Ball-Room Dancing of To-day', p. 16.

[62]   These features are, of course, shared by the one-step, Argentine tango and foxtrot, to name the more well-known dances of the period; but it was the Boston that formed the initial transformative influence on later ballroom dancing in England.

[63]   'A Waltz Dream', *The Dancing Times*, January 1911, p. 76.

In the English Boston of the Edwardian era, a new sense of interiority became socially admissible in which the dancers no longer felt compelled to be observed and judged by society when on the dance floor. Instead, the dancers eschewed Victorian patterns of social duty and self-surveillance and, as modern couples, explored new selves and relationships as they moved to the melodic flow of sound and in response to each other. As an enthusiast of this fresh style, Elizabeth Hyatt-Woolf compared the modern mode of waltzing to Post-impressionism, claiming it to be 'an expression of the emotions, the real ecstasy of the spirit of the music'.[64] Emphasizing self-expression over convention, this new practice, she asserted was the 'modern fashion of dreaming the music'. Far from dancing out of time, the Boston dancer of Edwardian London was both physically and emotionally very much in time and in tune with the sounds and spaces of modernity.

---

[64]   Hyatt-Wolf, 'Passing of the Waltz', p. 5.

Chapter 5

The English Folk Voice:
Singing and Cultural Identity in the
English Folk Revival, 1955-65

Simon Featherstone

'Hello, me dearios', said Rambling Syd Rumpo, the folk-singer in the BBC radio show *Round the Horne* (1965-69), before going on to sing a lurid song packed with extravagant neologisms and remorseless double-entendres – *Green Grow My Nadgers Oh!* or *The Pewter Wogglers Bangling Song*.[1] Syd, played by Kenneth Williams, was a regular character in a programme that worked through camp absurdity and a sharp sense of the comic potential of a range of contemporary subcultures. His popularity suggests that the audience of *Round the Horne* was both familiar with the conventions of folk performance and attuned to the comedy that could be made from an exploitation of their idiosyncrasies. For Rambling Syd was a folk-singer of his time, embodying English popular culture's ambivalent relationship with its folk traditions and the development of new kinds of folk music in the post-war period. So, whilst the tunes of Rumpo's repertoire – *Widdecombe Fair*, *Green Grow the Rushes*, *The Lincolnshire Poacher* – would be known to listeners from the canon of English folk songs that was still being taught in primary schools, his 'Rambling' epithet and a performance style that included guitar accompaniment and explanatory introductions to his songs located him firmly amongst contemporary American folk performers.[2] The cultural negotiations implicit in the voices and performance styles from which Williams's comedy was made form a neglected part of the history of post-Second World War English popular culture. This essay examines the process of manufacture of the singing voice of the English folk revival that *Round the Horne* parodied, its aesthetic and political legacies, and its relationship to the discourses, media and performance styles of popular music in the 1950s and early 1960s.

The English folk voice was (and remains) a distinctive performance style and Rambling Syd made mocking play with some of its main characteristics, deploying a nasal tone, elongating his vowels to excess and projecting an exaggerated tremolo at climactic moments. These and other vocal devices marked out a generation of

---

[1] See Kenneth Williams, *The Best of Rambling Syd Rumpo* (EMI Gold, 2005).

[2] For a scriptwriter's account of the invention of the character, see Barry Took, *Round the Horne (The Complete and Utter History)* (London, 1998), p. 79.

revivalist singers and the mannerisms could elicit harsh judgements as well as parody. Ginette Dunn records a Suffolk villager's response to changing styles of folk music in her study of local singing traditions, *The Fellowship of Song* (1980). 'I like to hear the songs sung by an old boy or somebody', Clive Woolnough stated. 'I don't like going "wah", they never used to do it years ago … I always say that the majority of young ones, they don't sing in their natural voice anyway, not folk songs. They sorta "wah", you know.'[3] Woolnough's critical sense of a generational shift in performance practice and the vivid improvisation of his description of revivalists' open vowels and tendency to decoration also suggest a more general challenge in theorizing and defining the singing voice as an instrument of cultural production. Roland Barthes, in a famous essay dedicated to the problem, makes a comparable distinction to that of Woolnough, both in terms of category and aesthetic judgement. In 'The Grain of the Voice', he contrasts performances that display competence in what he terms the 'pheno-song', a repertoire of affective devices that mimic but do not embody expression, and those that project a vocal 'grain' or 'the body in the voice as it sings'. '[T]he whole of musical pedagogy teaches not the culture of the "grain" of the voice', he concludes, 'but the emotive modes of its delivery'.[4] The distinctive 'grain' is sacrificed to conventions of emotive affect associated by Barthes with narrowed aesthetic fields of sensuous pleasure and increasingly commodified technologies of performance. In this paradigm, what Woolnough calls the 'wah' of the young revivalists is an assertion of the formal devices of the pheno-song against the old boys' informal practices, their 'materiality of the body speaking its mother tongue' in Barthes's terms.[5]

Conflicts between grain and pheno-song and embodied and disembodied voice were inscribed in the foundation narrative of the Edwardian folk-song revival, the occasion in August 1903 when Cecil Sharp collected *The Seeds of Love* from the singing of John England in Hambridge, Somerset. 'After noting it down', his biographer writes, Sharp 'went off and harmonized the song and that same evening it was sung at a choir supper by Mattie Kay, Sharp accompanying. The audience was delighted; as one said, it was the first time that the song had been put into evening dress. John was proud, but doubtful about the "evening-dress"; there had been no piano to *his* song.'[6] Sharp's removal of *The Seeds of Love* from its original singer and his rapid re-representation of it as an art song anticipated his conduct of the revival that he oversaw during the next twenty years. It was a process of collection and reproduction that systematically devalued the voice and the embodied performance of the source singer in order that the song could be transmitted efficiently into other contexts. As his collaborator Maud Karpeles

---

[3]   Ginette Dunn, *The Fellowship of Song: Popular Singing Traditions in East Suffolk* (London, 1980), p. 211.

[4]   Roland Barthes, 'The Grain of the Voice', in *Image-Music-Text*, ed. and tr. Stephen Heath (London, 1977), p. 188, p. 183.

[5]   Barthes, 'The Grain of the Voice', p. 182.

[6]   A. H. Fox Strangways with Maud Karpeles, *Cecil Sharp* (London, 1933), p. 33.

put it, 'Sharp believed that folk-music ... was capable of dissociation from the circumstances in which it was created and that, like all other musical creations, it would be upon its intrinsic merits that it would stand or fall'.[7] Such 'intrinsic merits' could be established only by the dissociation of songs from the 'grain' of their actual performance and through their dissemination within the controlled environments in which he operated, from the choir supper at which John England listened to his own song, to the Folk-Song Society that Sharp directed and the elementary schools where his editions of songs and dances found a ready market.

For Sharp and his disciples, the essential qualities of folk songs were to be found in their tunes rather than in the embodied articulation of the original performances. '[N]o melody will find a place in this series except in the precise form in which it was noted down by a competent musician from the lips of some folk-singer', Sharp writes in the preface to *Folk-Songs of England* (1908). However, the same precision was not accorded to the transcription of the songs' words or the description of their performances, those elements that most closely determined their cultural specificity. 'No vocalist would sing words that are pointless or ungrammatical', he asserts. 'Nor could he, even if he would, sing accurately in dialect ... The words, therefore, of many of the songs in this collection have been altered. Gaps have been filled up, verses omitted or softened, rhymes reconciled, redundant syllables pruned, bad grammar and dialect translated into King's English.'[8] Sharp was also notably bland in his indications for the performance of his arrangements. '[S]ing it as simply as possible', he writes in the introduction to *English Folk Songs* (1921), 'and, while playing closest attention to the clear enunciation of the words and the preservation of an even, pleasant tone ... forbear as far as may be, from actively and deliberately attempting to improve it by the introduction of frequent changes of time, crescendos, diminuendos, and other devices of a like character.'[9] The principles of 'good taste' embedded in a term such as 'pleasant tone' are those of Barthes's pheno-song, shaping performances that projected the form of 'English folk song' at a distance from its material origins in body, voice and singing style. Like John England's 'Seeds of Love', these folk songs were destined to be recast as national artefacts rather than being experienced as performances developed within the local repertoires and social contexts of individual singers.

Such deliberated erasure of traditional performance practice did not go unchallenged. An essay by the collector and composer Percy Grainger, published in the *Journal of the Folk-Song Society* in 1908, argued for a holistic sense of traditional performance that was at odds with Sharp's practice. '[T]he more I hear talented traditional singers in the flesh', Grainger writes, 'the stronger grows my

---

[7]   A. H. Fox Strangways and Maud Karpeles, *Cecil Sharp*, 2nd ed. (London, 1955), p. xv.

[8]   Cecil J. Sharp (ed.), *Folk-Songs of England, Book 1: Folk Songs from Dorset Collected by H. E. D. Hammond* (London, 1908), no page number.

[9]   Cecil J. Sharp, *English Folk Songs, Vol. 1: Songs and Ballads* (London, [1921]), p. x.

personal feeling that any noting down of an *individually* and *creatively gifted* man's songs that does not give all possible details of all the different verses of his songs, and, in certain cases, of his different renderings at different times, cannot claim to be a representative picture of such a man's complete art and artistic culture' [emphasis in the original].[10] Grainger identified an intrinsic artistry in traditional singing, in the 'flesh' rather than in the melody as Sharp would have it. The features that the latter 'corrected' in his arrangements were, for Grainger, 'radical points of enrichment, inventiveness, and individualisation'.[11] It was a judgement that determined his innovations in recording and transmitting the songs. The 1908 essay is significantly entitled 'Collecting with the Phonograph' and his appreciation of the ways in which new technologies could remove the aesthetic mediation of the collector who transcribed and amended folk-songs was put into practice in his contemporary recordings of Lincolnshire traditional singers. An audience's direct contact with such performance practices through the phonograph, he argued, allowed access to the totality of the embodied material voice. For Grainger, the purpose of collecting traditional material was to 'seize upon and preserve in *their full strangeness and otherness* just those elements that have least in common with our own music', as he put it in an essay of 1915 [emphasis in the original].[12] By celebrating, rather than eliding, the performance practice of source singers, he redefined their music from being fragile remnants of a disappearing peasant tradition to become examples of a confident, self-conscious aesthetic, one that posed radical challenges to the norms of the art music that sought to incorporate folk song within its own performance conventions.

Cecil Sharp's shrewd management of the means of production of his editions of English folk song and dance, and his skilful interpolation of them within nationalist discourses of cultural threat and revival, meant that it was his mediated version of the music that held sway. Three generations of primary school children danced to Sharp's folk dances and learned the standardized repertory of his folk song arrangements. However, as noted earlier, Rambling Syd's performances in the 1960s delineated the historical limits of Sharp's project. Part of Williams's comedy came from the parody of the earnest ruralism of the Edwardian revival's nationalist aesthetics and Rumpo's guitar accompaniment and transatlantic nomenclature flagged later versions of folk performance that began to compete with Sharp's model in the 1950s, drawing their repertoire from commercial recordings of American singers such as Ramblin' Jack Elliott and The Weavers, the songs transmitted orally in the new environments of urban folk clubs. It was a shift in the style of folk singing that was even acknowledged by the organization that Sharp founded. Douglas Kennedy, his successor as Director of the English

---

[10]   Percy Grainger, 'Collecting with the Phonograph', in Teresa Balough (ed.), *A Musical Genius from Australia: Selected Writings By and About Percy Grainger* (Nedlands, 1982), p. 22.

[11]   Grainger, 'Collecting with the Phonograph', p. 25.

[12]   Grainger, 'The Impress of Personality in Unwritten Music', in Balough, p. 79.

Folk Dance Society (later the English Folk Dance and Song Society – EFDSS), significantly made reference to Grainger rather than Sharp when he launched the periodical *Folk* in 1962 as part of his attempts to promote the Society to a new generation of revivalists. 'The First Revival brought a reverence for the music itself', he wrote, 'and transmitted itself to both classroom and concert hall. The second by means of TAPE and gramophone record has enabled the folk process of ORAL TRANSMISSION to take place, the Rough can be brought to The Smooth and vice-versa' [capitalization in the original].[13] Kennedy's celebration of the revival as a means of oral transmission was a radical revision of Sharp's dissociation of folk music from its original performative bodies. However, the reorientation of English folk music from text to orality, and from the disciplined classroom to the diverse, emergent performance spaces of folk clubs, reactivated questions about the values, meanings and practices of the long-silenced folk voice. 'How does an urban singer, not steeped in any tradition, sing a traditional song without impersonating?', asked Eric Winter in the magazine *Sing* in 1957.[14] It was to be the most pressing issue of the post-Second World War folk revival.

In the year that Winter posed his question, Douglas Kennedy was involved in two initiatives that were intended to further the possibility of answering it. The English Folk Music Festival and the commercial LP *Folk Music Today* reflected Kennedy's interest in making links between the EFDSS, urban folk singers and the traditional musicians who, it was realized after the collecting efforts of Alan Lomax, Hamish Henderson, Peter Kennedy and others in the early 1950s, were still alive and flourishing. Both suggested the Society's reconsideration of the legacy of Sharp, but both also illustrated the problems entailed upon the new significance that was attached to the folk voice. The English Folk Music Festival was held at Cecil Sharp House in October and its organizing committee was composed not only of Society officials but younger figures like Mervyn Plunkett, an independent collector and performer who had contacts both with traditional singers and the revivalists. Singers such as Bob Roberts from Suffolk, Pop Maynard from Sussex and Charlie Bates from Padstow were invited to perform and a specially designed poster advertising the event was distributed 'among various coffee bars to attract the attention of members of Skiffle Groups and other singers and players of traditional music'.[15] However, at the festival itself the innovative expansion of the constituency of traditional music came into conflict with far less accommodating aesthetics represented by the Chairman of the Festival Committee, Dr Sydney Northcote. In *Making Your Own Music* (1960), Northcote's textbook for amateur musicians, he uncompromisingly asserted that singers 'needed some definite training and this can only be done under expert guidance', a view he brought to bear in his role as a judge in the competitive section of the festival, itself a relic

---

[13]   Douglas Kennedy, 'Editorial', *Folk*, 1 (1962), p. 1.
[14]   'Made in Britain', *Sing*, 4.4&5 (1957), p. 52.
[15]   *Minutes of the Organising Committee of the English Folk Music Festival*, 19 June 1957, p. 3.

of the Society's past.[16] In *Sing*, Fred and Betty Dallas reported the 'angry scenes that followed most of the adjudications [and] the various rude things said by … Northcote to some of Britain's finest traditional singers, venerable old gentlemen who should have been treated with more respect'.[17] Kennedy himself later recalled a singer 'brought up in the conversational mode of ballad singing [being] told that he must open his mouth and make his tongue tell against his teeth'.[18] In his contribution to the *Sing* report on the festival, the singer and scholar A. L. Lloyd, demonstrating his customary tact, concluded that 'when listening to folk song performers, genuine or revival, adjudicators have to be looking for a different set of artistic virtues from those immediately recognized by the singing teacher'.[19] What those different artistic virtues actually were, though, proved just as hard to negotiate when contrasting the revival singer with the traditional singer as when comparing the latter with Northcote's trained amateur. The Society's second venture that year, the LP *Folk Song Today*, released by HMV using the EFDSS's recordings, only served to sharpen the question.

Commercially recorded folk music had previously been limited to such items as 'Peter Pears singing "The Foggy Foggy Dew" and Owen Brannigan "The One-Eyed Reilly"', as a contributor to the magazine *Ethnic* put it in 1959.[20] *Folk Song Today*, by contrast, used the capacity of the long-playing format to display contrasting styles of singing, with seven field performances collected by Peter Kennedy in the early 1950s alongside three recordings by young revival singers. Rory and Alex McEwen appeared prominently on the sleeve with guitars, open-necked shirts and matching cravats, emphasizing the youthful target market of the record.[21] This fusion of generations and singing styles provoked mixed responses. Lloyd, in a review in *Recorded Folk Music*, noted '[t]hree are in city-billy style, the rest are the real thing' – an uncharacteristic use by him of one of the disparaging neologisms of the post-war revival.[22] A comparable distinction was made by *Ethnic*'s reviewer who described Fred Lawson's performance of *Dance to th' Daddie* as representing more the 'tradition … of the drawing-room than the Folk' and criticized Shirley Collins for displaying 'a fatal echo from across the Atlantic'. 'From the first notes of the melodeon in "High Barbaree" [sung by Bob Roberts] you're in a different world from that suggested by Miss Collins and Mr Lawson', he asserted.[23] Significantly, these reviews identified the singing style associated with Cecil Sharp ('drawing-room' arrangements) and more recent transatlantic

[16] Sydney Northcote, *Making Your Own Music* (London, 1960), p. 33.
[17] 'Made in Britain', p. 52.
[18] Douglas Kennedy, 'A Fourth Folk Festival', *Sing*, 6.10 (1962), p. 107.
[19] 'Made in Britain', p. 52.
[20] Peter Grant, 'The Pure Spring', *Ethnic*, 1.1 (1959), p. 10.
[21] *Folk Song Today: Songs and Ballads of England and Scotland* (HMV, 1957).
[22] A. L. Lloyd, 'So You Are Interested in Folk Music?', *Recorded Folk Music*, 1 (1958), p. 6.
[23] Peter Grant, 'A Package Deal', *Ethnic*, 1.4 (1959), p. 12.

popular styles ('city-billy') as constituting equally 'inauthentic' approaches to folk-singing in opposition to the newly audible performances of the 'real thing' by source singers such as Roberts, Jeannie Robertson and the McPeake Family.

Folk Song Today advertised the 'different worlds' of a revival that placed performance at its centre and held embodied authenticity to be a central value. *Ethnic*, the folk magazine that examined the issue of singing styles most restlessly, encouraged 'all would-be traditional singers to learn their songs directly from live sources'.[24] 'While we wish to give every assistance to those who want to sing in the traditional way', a later editorial declared, 'we have no desire to provide material for those who want to sing like Lonnie Donegan, Engel Lund or Ewan MacColl' – a list of performers that covered Anglo-American skiffle, conservatoire folk song and the most influential figure of the post-war revival.[25] But 'singing in the traditional way' posed practical and theoretical problems. The most basic of these concerned access to British, and more particularly English, voices. As the record reviews in *Sing* confirm, the recorded folk music that was commercially available in the 1950s was predominantly American, with Topic, the only British record company that specialized in folk music in the period, concentrating on Scottish and Irish rather than English singers. Even when an English traditional voice could be heard, though, the question of how a revivalist singer was to engage with its style and technique remained pressing. Harry Cox, the only English unaccompanied singer on *Folk Song Today*, vividly illustrates the difficulty of moving from the pheno-song of Sharp's arrangements back to the grain of English folk voices. For if any singer embodied grain in his or her performances, it was the farm-worker from Catfield, Norfolk.

Cox's singing of *The Foggy Dew* was celebrated rapturously in the *Ethnic* review of the record. 'Here is the authentic ethnic voice', Peter Grant writes, deploying the journal's always ill-defined eponymous term, 'with its noble simplicity and inimitable inflections, as natural as cold water and bird-song'.[26] Such romanticism misrepresented the singer, however. The nearest thing that the post-war revival had to a Gramscian organic intellectual, Cox was the inheritor of his family's songs, an assiduous collector of the songs of others and a careful, self-conscious stylist in his singing. Francis Collinson, who recorded Cox for the BBC in the early 1950s, noted his 'command of melodic decoration, his power of varying the melody from verse to verse [and] the characteristic *tenutos*, the folk singer's uninhibited tonal modification of the scalic intervals according the context and direction of the melody'.[27] Such techniques did not make him an easy model for other singers, even if his readily available recordings had not been limited to a single track on *Folk Song Today*. Although he proved willing to perform occasionally in the emergent

24   'Policy Statement', *Ethnic*, 1.1 (1959), p. 2.
25   'Policy', *Ethnic*, 1.2 (1959), p. 2.
26   Grant, 'A Package Deal', p. 12.
27   Francis Collinson, 'A Reminiscence', *Journal of the English Folk Dance and Song Society*, 8.3 (1958), p. 146.

cultural spaces of metropolitan folk clubs and on the newly welcoming stage of Cecil Sharp House, he was also fierce in his determination to maintain an intensely localized aesthetic of performance and a repertory that had been established in the pubs of East Norfolk and latterly in his 'singing house' in Catfield. Peter Kennedy noted the '"dry" impersonality and monotony of his style' and the 'dry cynicism' of his songs, qualities that amply demonstrated the function of folk song that Percy Grainger had defined as presenting in their '*full strangeness and otherness* just those elements that have least in common with our own music'.[28] What 'our own music' meant for young English folk singers in the period, though, was harder to define than the art music tradition that was Grainger's point of reference. Those who had grown up with the idioms of transatlantic popular and 'traditional' music, whether skiffle or The Weavers, were more accustomed to the performance style of Louisiana-born Leadbelly – albeit mediated by Lonnie Donegan – than to that of Harry Cox.

The scarcity of available recordings of English traditional singers and the plural attractions of American models of folk music led to anxious discussions in the little magazines of the time about what an English revivalist should sound like. *Sing*, an imitator of *Sing Out!*, its American 'big brother',[29] had always published an eclectic selection of songs from Britain, America and Eastern Europe since its first appearance in 1954 and it made no aesthetic discrimination between unaccompanied singing, guitar arrangements and choral styles. Nevertheless, in 1957 it published an appeal addressed to 'SINGers, Skifflers [and] Choir members'. 'We are always hearing that too many performers rely on American material', it noted, posing the question 'How can we develope [*sic*] a British urban folk song without imitating anybody's style?'[30] That question – with varying degrees of precision in its differentiation between 'British' and 'English' as a term of cultural description – was reframed persistently in subsequent years without a clear conclusion being reached. *Ethnic* identified 'a three-cornered fight between the neo-Victorians, the city-billies and the traditionalists', but, whilst firmly allying itself to the third party in the battle, could not provide a clear strategy for combating the 'non-traditional antics'[31] of the revival beyond its impractical project of supplying readers with home-produced tapes of field recordings.[32] The two leading theorist-performers of the period, A. L. Lloyd and Ewan MacColl, articulated divergent responses to the issue. Lloyd, always the more conciliatory of the pair, advocated moderation. 'By all means try new ways of performing', he advised in an article in *Spin*, 'but familiarise yourself too with what's best in the old ways.' He turned to watchwords that he associated with

---

[28]   Peter Kennedy, 'Harry Cox: English Folk Singer', *Journal of the English Folk Dance and Song Society*, 8.3 (1958), p. 142.
[29]   'A Singer's Notebook', *Sing*, 1.1 (1954), p. 11.
[30]   'An Invitation: SINGers, Skifflers, Choir members', *Sing*, 4.1 (1957), p. 9.
[31]   'Editorial', *Ethnic*, 1.4 (1959), p. 3.
[32]   'Policy Statement', p. 2.

Cecil Sharp (itself a sign of Lloyd's inclusivity) in recommending revivalists to: 'Respect *continuity*; be judicious in *variation*; be generous in *selection*' [emphasis in the original].[33] Quite what that meant in practice remained vague. MacColl's approach was confrontational. In an essay entitled 'Going American?', ostensibly co-written with Sydney Carter and (the American) Peggy Seeger and published in *English Dance and Song* in 1961, he issued dire warnings about the dangers of American voices and performance techniques subsuming native traditions. 'If we subject ourselves consciously or unconsciously to too much acculturation', the authors argued, 'we'll finish with no folk culture at all. We'll finish with a kind of cosmopolitan, half-baked music which doesn't satisfy the emotions of anybody.'[34]

Fears of cultural dilution led MacColl to establish a new kind of performance space in June 1961, a folk club with an intensively policed ideology. He declared darkly in *Sing* that it was 'necessary to rescue a large number of young people, all of whom have the right instincts, from those influences that have appeared on the folk scene during the past two or three years – influences that are doing their best to debase the meaning of folk song'.[35] Salvation was to be found in the Singers' Club, the policy of which was that performers should 'limit themselves to songs which were in a language the singer spoke or understood'. 'We felt it was necessary to explore our own music first,' MacColl explained in his discussion of the project in his autobiography, 'to distance ourselves from skiffle with its legions of quasi-Americans.'[36] This first attempt to theorize and organize the practice of the post-war revival only served to complicate the question of voice, however, dependent as it was upon fractious definitions of ethnic identity, kinship and vocal legitimacy. The criteria for the 'ownership' of songs and singing styles, beyond the obvious transatlantic divide that was the main cultural and political bugbear of the enterprise, were inevitably slippery – MacColl, born and brought up in Salford, nevertheless continued to sing Scots ballads by virtue of a Scots 'inheritance', for example.

Issues of performance practice and cultural value were also apparent in the activities of the Critics' Group, MacColl's development of the principles of the Singers' Club into a training scheme for revival singers that aimed to establish professional standards grounded in historical understanding and aesthetic rigour. It began its meetings in 1964 and was described by MacColl as a 'mutual-aid group where everyone gave a hand in solving each other's problems'.[37] '[S]o many people go into folk singing these days without a knowledge of anything really', he lamented at a meeting in April 1964, 'without any scientific tools, any scientific aids ... Some of the most difficult songs to sing are not sung, have not

---

[33]   A. L. Lloyd, 'Guest Spot', *Spin*, 1.6 (1962), p. 6.
[34]   Sydney Carter, Ewan MacColl and Peggy Seeger, 'Going American?', *English Dance and Song*, New Year 1961, p. 20.
[35]   Ewan MacColl, 'Why I Am Opening a New Club', *Sing*, 5.4 (1961), p. 65.
[36]   Ewan MacColl, *Journeyman: An Autobiography* (London, 1990), p. 288.
[37]   MacColl, *Journeyman*, p. 305.

been sung over the last hundred years or so, because they *are* difficult and because singers have lost some of the expertise.'[38] The tapes and transcripts of the early sessions, now held in the Charles Parker Archive in Birmingham Public Library, indicate a far less collective process in the development of the 'scientific tools' and 'expertise' than its founder suggested. MacColl, who dominated proceedings, introduced vocal techniques established by Nelson Ellingworth, ('an Australian, who taught at the Scala, Milan', as he informed the group), 'exercises based on Laban's effort-scales', Stanislawskian performance training and Workers' Educational Association-style historical lectures delivered by himself.[39] Such directive experiments in communal art were, of course, at odds with the informal organization that characterized the post-war revival and, ironically, had much more in common with Sharp's well-marshalled Edwardian original, at least in its emphasis upon aesthetic discipline and its suspicion of an unregulated diversity of folk culture. One early attendee of the Critics' Group, Luke Kelly, was asked by a suspicious MacColl at a session in 1964, '[H]ave you done any work since last week or have you been singing around in the clubs all the time?'[40] Kelly left for The Dubliners shortly afterwards.

The Critics' Group's attempts to train singers and establish performative criteria for the revival had only limited influence on a movement that had always drawn its energies from eclectic sources and improvised practices.[41] Indeed, the most influential aspects of the work of MacColl and Lloyd were not mediated by such organizations (and Lloyd, by temperament as much as by politics, was distanced from the Critics' Group enterprise). Instead, it was the two singers' highly idiosyncratic voices and performance styles, developed outside any explicit theory of revivalist aesthetics, that came to shape the distinctive vocal resources of the revival. Neither could claim to be a traditional singer in the way of Harry Cox, and consequently both were forced to develop performative responses to the challenge of singing folk songs in the early days of the revival, responses that in their very distinctiveness made them unsuitable as models for the kind of instruction envisaged in the Critics' Group. Both MacColl's and Lloyd's singing developed through a need to both engage with and resist a range of vocal styles that were active forces in the post-war revival, from Sharp's conservatoire approach maintained by the likes of Sydney Northcote, to Harry Cox's idiosyncratic, localized performances, to the imported American singing of Jack Elliott and Pete

---

[38] *The Critics' Group, Transcription of Tape 5, Recording of Meeting April 1964* (Charles Parker Archive, Birmingham Public Library), p. 45.

[39] *The Critics' Group, Transcription of Tape 1, Recording of Meeting March 10 1964*, p. 9.

[40] *The Critics' Group, Transcription of Tape 7, Recording of Meeting June 23 1964*, p. 9.

[41] For a discussion of the influence of MacColl's Singers' Club policy, see Niall MacKinnon, *The British Folk Scene: Musical Performance and Social Identity* (Buckingham and Philadelphia, 1993), p. 28.

Seeger. The English folk voice that MacColl, Lloyd and their imitators established was consequently an invented traditional voice, a necessarily synthetic response to demands for authenticity. Two brief examples from the very different repertoires and approaches of the singers can serve to suggest the ways in which each created a distinctive performative means to negotiate the cultural questions that vexed the nascent theorists of the revival – including MacColl and Lloyd themselves.

MacColl's version of *Sixteen Tons*, released in 1956, was one of Topic's first recordings of a British singer and represents a surprising choice of material for someone who was later to be so determined in his opposition to the importation of American repertoire.[42] However, his approach to Merle Travis's song of hardship in the Kentucky coalfields, which had been a recent British hit for Tennessee Ernie Ford, suggests the way in which MacColl as a singer was far more flexible in his approach to such songs than the later uncompromising doctrines would seem to allow, deploying a strategy that claimed the song for the British folk-song revival through vocal adaptations and an emphasis upon the implicitly radical politics of the original. Small elements of MacColl's performance acknowledge its transatlantic origins – the 'wadda' for 'what do you' in the chorus, for example, and a swelling of volume on the word 'soul' that might be a nod to Paul Robeson, one of the revival's favourite American radicals (Robeson had contributed a message of support to *Sing* the previous year[43]). However, there is no sustained attempt to mimic either country, popular or African American styles. Instead, the majority of the performance decisions serve to distance the song from its cultural origins, foregrounding a roughened grain of the voice and a strain in the singing in implicit contrast to Tennessee Ernie's mellifluous baritone and easy-going delivery. MacColl's version, reflecting the politics of the record label, serves to emphasize common international experience of labour and the capacity of song to respond to its injustices. It was a strategy that was developed in a British context in the following year when he recorded *Shuttle and Cage* for Topic, a collection of folk songs from mining and industrial areas that reiterated the politics of *Sixteen Tons* and which again displayed vocal codes that were not located in any specific accent or dialect. Neither conservatoire nor transatlantic nor regional English, MacColl's singing worked to establish a performative grain that signified authenticity without being in any sense authentic.

Bert Lloyd's singing, very different in character to that of MacColl, nevertheless shared its cultural strategy. Lloyd's repertoire included more English traditional songs than that of MacColl, but, as with the latter's performance of *Sixteen Tons*, he approached them by simultaneously acknowledging and distancing himself from their original performance practices and cultural contexts. His version of Harry Cox's *The Long Pegging Awl*, for example, reproduces only the slow pace

[42] Ewan MacColl, *Sixteen Tons* (Topic, 1956). The recording is included on *Three Score & Ten – A Voice to the People* (Topic, 2009).
[43] 'Greetings', *Sing*, 2.2 (1955), no page number.

and deliberation of Cox's singing.[44] The source singer's distinctive articulation is referenced (but not imitated) through open diphthongs and swallowed word-endings ('verra' for 'very', for example) and a studied wavering of pitch, just the suspicion of a 'wah' and a characteristic vocal 'catch' at the end of some lines establish a distance from art-song techniques (his singing would certainly have been corrected by Sydney Northcote). But, like MacColl, Lloyd makes reference to the cultural frame of the original only through specific details of the performance whilst avoiding wholesale mimicry. His amelioration of the peculiar demands of Cox's performance style into an engaging conversational delivery was well suited to the new environments of the folk clubs in which audiences could experience intimate performances that projected a version of 'tradition' in the imaginary folk embodiments that the revival singers created. Lloyd and MacColl established a repertoire of aural and performance practices – from the hand cupped over the ear during performance to references to the styles of source singers to the idiosyncracies of tone and decoration – that were all responses to the central question of the revival: how to sing traditionally outside of the social and aesthetic contexts of a tradition. Their answer was to create a synthetic grain, defined by no one local place and referential to no one tradition, but in active tension with the pheno-song of both Cecil Sharp's legacies and the post-war American folk revival.

The English folk revival of the 1950s and 1960s was defined by its interest in performance and by its consequent re-examination of the ways in which vernacular English cultures could be maintained in new circumstances. One of its singular achievements, and one that has attracted little academic notice, was its establishment of spaces, physical and imaginary, in which regional English voices and repertoires could be re-appraised, revived and developed. At the same time, though, it had also to confront questions concerning the politics of its performances: the relationship of revival singing with source singing, the persistence of the strategies and aesthetics of Sharp's Edwardian revival, and the means of incorporating (or resisting) the influence of American styles of folk performance. In response, revival singers invented a new kind of voice that in its tone, style and sound negotiated with these issues of authenticity, mimicry and the competing demands of local and international influences. The singularity of the folk voices invented by Lloyd, MacColl and their contemporaries and successors led to the parodies of *Round the Horne*, of course, but the strange vowels and 'wah' that formed the basis of Rambling Syd Rumpo's comedy were not just eccentricities of English popular music. Rather, they expressed a complex performative response to a legacy of the dissociation of folk song from material performance and to the problems and possibilities of remaking living traditional singing cultures.

---

[44]   Lloyd's recording is on A. L. Lloyd et al., *The Bird in the Bush: Traditional Erotic Songs* (Topic, 1966). For Cox's version, recorded in 1953, see Various Artists, *Songs of Seduction* (Rounder, 2000).

Chapter 6
Halling as a Tool for Nationalist Strategies

Anne Margrete Fiskvik

The finale of the 2009 Eurovision Song Contest: three male dancers move vigorously across the stage, their agile bouncing movements following the energetic duple meter of a melodious tune composed and performed by pop singer Alexander Rybak. 'I'm in love with a fairy tale' sings Rybak, alternating between singing and playing what sounds like an eight-stringed *hardingfele* [hardanger fiddle] to accompany the male dancers. Two women sing along with Rybak and the Eurovision Song Contest orchestra keeps a steady beat under Rybak's ornamentation. The dancers, through acrobatic *Halling* moves, demonstrate what dance can look like when you are young and in love … backflips are followed by somersaults and deep knee-bends or *kruking*.[1] The dancers jump around on all fours, chase and vault over each other with ease. The audience enthusiastically cheers the combination of folkdance and pop music.

In the passage above, I describe the successful finale of the 2009 Eurovision Song Contest held in Moscow.[2] Alexander Rybak, joined by backing singers Jorunn Hauge and Karianne Kjærnes and accompanied by a mid-sized orchestra provided by the competition organizers, performed with dancers Hallgrim Hansegaard, Torkjell Børsheim and Sigbjøn Rua from the professional folk dance company Frikar. When Rybak and the Frikar dancers won the contest, it brought to light an innovative fusion between a melodious pop tune and a vigorous restaging of the Norwegian folk dance *Halling*.

Halling is a dance practice with a long and diverse history. Traditionally it was performed in social settings accompanied by the *hardingfele*, a fiddle with double sets of strings whose resonating overtones produce a rich and piercing sound. *Halling* music is in duple metre, usually notated in 6/8 time and further divided into two groups of triplets. Danced at parties, particularly in the mountains and the inner fjord valleys of central southern Norway, the best-known form of *Halling* is a solo for a group of men who simultaneously compete against each other, although it can also be danced individually by men and sometimes by women.

Because of the virtuoso and acrobatic aspects of *Halling*, it has been appropriated for the concert stage at various times in Norwegian dance history, including the long period during which Norway was ruled by Denmark and

---

[1]   *Kruking* consists of knee-bends with continuous extensions of one foot alternating with the other, not like the Russian Cossack dances. See Figure 6.1, below.

[2]   http://www.youtube.com/watch?v=y4D_hguWPQE.

Sweden.[3] *Halling* has been performed throughout Norway in a variety of contexts, with roots identified at least as far back as the fifteenth century and likely to the Middle Ages.[4] Traditional descriptions emphasize it as a male solo dance, both competitive and improvisational, where dancers execute difficult leaps, *kruking*, somersaults, backflips, kicks and other acrobatic stunts to demonstrate masculine vigour and virility.

Figure 6.1   Hallgrim Hansegaard performs *kruking* in *Kruk* (2006).

In this chapter, I examine three theatrical performances of *Halling* and explore the strategies and agendas that shaped the choice of music and movement within these re-stagings. The examples range over a period of more than 200 years: the Danish ballet *Amor og Ballettmesterens Luner* [*The Whims of Cupid and the Ballet Master*] choreographed by Vincenzo Galeotti in 1786; the 1948 Norwegian ballet *Veslefrikk* by choreographer Gerd Kjølaas; and the 2009 Frikar performance of *Fairytale* from the Eurovision Song Contest. While the aims of the three choreographers demonstrate a shared desire to create an accessible dance event, the aesthetic agendas of the choreographers and how these relate to cultural politics and the creation of national images emerge as my focus. I aim to show how the image of the agile male *Halling* dancer served as a nationalist strategy that produced an idealized representation of 'Norwegian-ness'.

---

[3]   Political and intellectual power, as well as the royal court, were located in Copenhagen until 1814, and then briefly in Stockholm until 1905.
[4]   Egil Bakka, *Norske dansetradisjonar* (Oslo, 1978), pp. 25–7.

Halling is well-documented in visual and written sources from the seventeenth and eighteenth centuries.[5] Written descriptions are available only from the nineteenth century, and film and video sources have been collected in the twentieth century.[6] More recent research shows that many women have been active *Halling* dancers throughout its history, sometimes dancing parallel to the men, but without receiving the same attention.[7] While this new research complicates traditional gender roles in folk dance, the male *Halling* dancer remains the trope through which to express Norwegian national identity.

Vincenzo Galeotti and his Wish to 'Recommend Himself'

The earliest known example of *Halling* material recontextualized for the theatre stage comes from 1786 when a 'Norsk Springdands' became part of the ballet *Amor og Ballettmesterens Luner*.[8] *Amor* was staged by the Royal Danish Operaballet in Copenhagen by the Italian Vincenzo Galeotti (1733-1816), ballet master of the Royal Danish Theatre and consists of short divertissements portraying dances of 'the folk' from various parts of Europe, as well as from Africa. Jens Lolle, a member of the theatre orchestra and first répétiteur during the absence of Galeotti's preferred composer, Claus Schall, supplied the music.[9] The ballet is famous for its continuous performance history under many different Danish ballet masters. The original musical score survives and provides valuable information including information about changes and additions to the music.[10] Like the movement, which likely was altered to the different dancers' techniques, the score has also undergone changes. The one used today was revised during the early part of the 1880s by the professional orchestrator Fredrik Rung.[11]

---

[5] Jørgen Moe's famous painting from 1869, 'A Visit to a Peasant Wedding', depicts *Halling*. For a written source see Christopher Hammer, 'Sogne-Beskrivelse over Hadeland udi Aggershuus Stift i Norge, tilligemed et geographisk Kort og Tegning over de tvende Grans Hoved-Kirker paa en Kirkegaard', *Årbok for Hadeland*, 33 (2000): p. 157.

[6] Egil Bakka, of The Norwegian Centre for Traditional Dance and Music in Trondheim, has collected thousands of video recordings of *Halling*.

[7] Halldis Folkedal, 'Den kvinnelige hallingdansaren. Om kropp, kjønn og seksualitet i norsk folkedans', (MA dissertation, Trondheim, 2009).

[8] Part of this material has been developed with Egil Bakka in 'Vicenzo Galeotti's Springdance', in Uwe Schlottermüller (ed.), *Vom Schäferidyll zur Revolution* (Freiburg, 2008), pp. 53-70.

[9] Sven Lund, 'Jens Lolle. Komponisten til Amors og Ballettmesterens Luner', *Fund og Forskning I det kongelige biblioteks samlinger*, XIII (1966), pp. 83-8.

[10] The Royal Library, Copenhagen, Sign, MA MS 2951-52. The score consists of a handwritten violin and other instrumental parts. Later modifications include the addition of a Greek dance and a French gigue shortly after the 1786 premiere.

[11] Lund, 'Jens Lolle', p. 84.

    The ballet begins with a prologue followed by couples who dance before
Cupid using movement vocabulary 'typical' of their cultures: we see dances from
Denmark and France followed by the Norwegian *Springdands*. Each dance follows
the same three-part structure in which the opening and ending parts are the same.
The *Halling* appears as the middle part of the dance, framed by the *Springdands*.
In the excerpt from the opening provided in Figure 6.2, the 'Norsk Springdands'
follows a 3/4 metre, which due to the triplets, could feel like a 9/8 metre, and
the dancing consists of *Springdands* steps, a common type of running step in 3/4
time. In the middle section, the rhythm changes to a 2/4 (or 6/8) metre typical
of *Halling*. The change from triple to duple metre is also emphasized through
movement: in the *Springdands* section, the couple dances together, mirroring each
other's movements with quick running steps and deep knee bends, whereas in
the *Halling* part they dance individually. Notably, the woman occupies a more
passive role, watching the acrobatic stunts of the male dancer. Galeotti's *Halling*
for the female solo bears no resemblance to the *Halling* or any other Norwegian
folk dance; instead she performs typical ballet movements like arabesques and
penchées, after which she stands and watches the male dancer's *Halling* moves.
While adhering to the choreographic tradition of creating 'equal duets' in time and
attention, Galeotti placed the national identity markers on the male dancer.

Figure 6.2   Dance 6, 'Norsk Springdands', by Jens Lolle, arranged by Frederik
              Rung for 1884 publication.

    In both the *Springdands* and *Halling*, the frequent repetition of short phrases
and the rhythmic stresses in Lolle's music are typical of those used in Norwegian
folk dance. The music creates a distinct and continuous rhythmic drive and, in
choreomusical terms, Lolle provides *musique dansant*, music that adds rhythmic
and melodic structure to the ballet without being overly literal or mimetic. In

the *Halling* section, the male dancer moves with ease and agility through typical *Halling* movements such as *kruking* and back flips, all in accordance with the musical rhythm. Lolle's attempt to create Norwegian *Halling* music is successful in its reproduction of a certain dancelike quality, and most likely he drew from available Norwegian *Halling* folk music, even though a specific example cannot be identified.

The programme notes state that Galeotti wished 'to present a cheerful ballet and to recommend myself',[12] suggesting that with *Amor* he sought to expand the contemporary conventions of ballet and theatre in order to gain popularity. Since he was of Italian ballet heritage Galeotti integrated pantomime into *Amor* as well, in his desire to 'thrill' the audience.[13]

Almost all programmes from other works by Galeotti reveal the inclusion of roles for people of the 'lower classes', either from Denmark or other countries where the given ballet takes place. And he often portrayed these 'lower classes' through the use of folk dance material. This appropriation of folk movement may have been one of his trademarks, but was probably also related to the taste of his contemporary public as both the exotic and the peasant life interested the upper-class audiences of Copenhagen at this time. In the wake of the French Revolution, audiences began to influence theatre and dance productions across Europe. The influential Danish ballet master August Bournonville reflects upon this influence in his memoirs *Mit Teaterliv* (1848), claiming that the late eighteenth-century audience no longer appreciated the grand dramatic spectacles of the *ballet d'action* from the 1750s, which drew on themes from Greek Mythology. Instead, Bournonville observes that Galeotti's audiences wanted small *divertissementi* that humoured them.[14] Consequently, lighter and shorter ballets, combined with operas or theatre productions, became the standard in Copenhagen, as well as in Sweden and the rest of Europe.[15]

Galeotti's 'agreeable ballets' integrated folk material in the music, movements and costume and restaged traditional Norwegian folk dances. Yet this usage raises the question of how much of the material in the 1786 version would have had roots in original folk material. While it was common for the eighteenth century to be *inspired* by folkloristic traits, it would have been considered crude to copy folk models too closely. Several contemporary dance scholars argue that the use of folk material on stage during the eighteenth century was emblematic rather

---

[12]   'At frembringe en munter Ballet var min Hensigt og mig anbefalet.' Galeotti, *Amors,* 1786, translation by author.

[13]   Galeotti, *Amors*.

[14]   According to Bournonville, Galeotti's works that humoured the audience include *The Gypsy Camp*, *The Whims of Cupid*, *The Weavers* and *The Washing Maids and the Tinkers*, August Bournonville, *Mit teaterliv: erindringer og tidsbilleder* (1848; Copenhagen, 1979), p. 28.

[15]   Lena Hammergren, Karin Helander, Tiina Rosenberg and Willmar Sauter, *Teater i Sverige* (Hedemora, 2004), p. 34.

than realistic. Dance scholar Lena Hammergren, in a study of Swedish dance and opera history, claims that, even though the idea that dance could express national and ethnic character was accepted, the dances on stage were not 'authentic' during the eighteenth century. Instead, distinctive conventions developed for how certain steps or movements could show the intended identity.[16] This 'emblematic trend' had already arisen in the late baroque period according to Joellen A. Meglin. When analysing the French opera ballet *Les Indes Galantes* (1735), Meglin identifies the folk elements as 'imagined entities or cultural constructs' inspired by ideas of Native American culture without being accurate reproductions of these.[17] The choreographer Louis Dupré did not use actual Indian dance movements, but created new ones inspired by images of the 'gallant' Indian people.

Evidence for Hammergren and Meglin's view can be found in the writings of important dancing masters of the eighteenth century. Several of Galeotti's contemporary colleagues felt that elements of the folk needed to be tailored to fit the 'high art' tastes of their audiences. The advocate for the *ballet d'action*, Jean-Georges Noverre stated in his *Lettres*, published in 1760, that folk dance material had to be changed to suit the theatrical purpose:

> If one were too scrupulous in depicting the characters, manners and customs of certain nations, the pictures would often be poor and monotonous in composition … I think, Sir, that neither a Turkish nor a Chinese festival would appeal to our countryman, if we had not the art to embellish it, I am persuaded that the style of dancing common to those people would never be captivating.[18]

Thus Noverre claimed that the stage portrayals of the lower classes or 'exotic nations' should not be too realistic, because 'This kind of exactitude in costume and imitation will only present a very insipid spectacle, unworthy of a public which only applauds in proportion as artists possess the art of bringing delicacy and taste to the different productions which they offer to it'.[19] Similarly, Giovanni-Andrea Gallini, an Italian dance master working in England, claimed that 'even in the lowest classes of life, the composer must seize only what is the fittest to give satisfaction; and omit whatever can excite disagreeable ideas … He must cull the flowers of life, not present the roots with the soil and dirt sticking to them.'[20] These sentiments reconstruct the high-low binary, where exotic nations are primitive,

---

[16]   Hammergren et al., *Teater*, p. 36.

[17]   Joellen A. Meglin, 'Galanterie and Glory: Women's Will and the Eighteenth-Century Worldview in *Les Indes Galantes*', in Lynn Matluck Brooks (ed.), *Women's Work: Making Dance in Europe Before 1800* (Madison, WI, 2007), p. 228.

[18]   Jean Georges Noverre, *Letters on Dancing and Ballets* (1803), trans. Cyril W. Beaumont (Brooklyn, NY, 1966), pp. 153-4.

[19]   Ibid.

[20]   Giovanni-Andrea Gallini, *A Treatise on the Art of Dancing* (1762; London, 1967), pp. 80-81.

simple and 'dirty'. Motivated by an evolutionist agenda, choreographers refined and 'cleansed' movement before 're-presenting' it on the concert stage. The 'crude' art of the lower classes needed to be rearticulated by 'fine artists' to make the result suitable for the higher-class audiences.

Galeotti likely followed the tastes of his time by responding to his audiences in their desire for exotic folklore, but keeping the folk elements refined enough to fit theatrical values. At the same time, Galeotti could not just invent a new kind of folk dance. Upper-class Copenhagen audiences probably had some conception of what the vernacular Norwegian *Halling* looked like given the close contact between the two countries, and many Norwegians living in Copenhagen performed the *Halling* on occasion.[21] Galeotti therefore would have had to take into consideration the 'perceived reality' when choreographing his dances.

In summary, in order to satisfy his audience's expectations, Galeotti selected ideas from rural dancing and modified the choreography, while retaining those elements believed appropriate for the purpose. He transformed the improvised *Halling* into set motifs, which he structured into a fixed order with symmetrical repetitions that were in accordance with the musical structure. Furthermore, Galeotti transmitted constructions of the Norwegian peasant through the male dancer, but not through the female.

Veslefrikk as a Nation-Building Strategy

In 1948, the ballet company *Ny Norsk Ballett* [New Norwegian Ballet] staged the ballet *Veslefrikk med Fela* [*The Magic Fiddle*], a work typical of Norwegian post-war cultural politics. Based on a popular Norwegian fairy tale about the poor, simpleminded and kind-hearted Veslefrikk who is rewarded with a magic fiddle by a supernatural being (the devil) because he good-heartedly gave away his money to the poor, the ballet utilized folk-derived movements, music and costumes. Choreographer Gerd Kjølaas, then the leading figure in Norwegian contemporary dance, shared an agenda similar to Galeotti; she aimed to create an agreeable ballet for post-war bourgeois and upper-class Norwegian audiences. This audience was both fascinated by and supportive of Norwegian elements, and Kjølaas created her ballet by blending Norwegian folk dance elements with the German 'free-dance' style and ballet technique of Laban, Wigman and others. A variety of folk dance and folk music-style material can be found throughout the 30-minute ballet. At the beginning of the ballet, the protagonist Veslefrikk performs typical *Halling* movements including *kruking*, somersaults, back flips and running steps on his

---

[21]   Norway had no noticeable aristocracy in the eighteenth century. A number of Norwegians went to Copenhagen and several nineteenth-century sources note that sons of civil servants in rural areas knew these dances. See Nicolai R. Østgaard, *En Fjeldbygd: Billeder fra Østerdalen* (Christiania,1852).

way through the forest. He appears carefree, even when challenged by the devil himself.

The musical score, an arrangement of different folk tunes for a small ensemble of instruments, was compiled by the company's pianist Sverre Bergh, better known today for his work in musical theatre. He used several well-known folk tunes, such as 'Vesle guten oppi bakken', but his arrangement for a small conventional orchestra is more akin to light salon-music than genuine folk music and noticeably does not utilize the *hardingfele*. There are no references in the score regarding the sources that Bergh drew upon, even though folk music was much debated at the time. The powerful *Leikaringen i Bul*, an organization in charge of teaching folk dance and music in Oslo, dictated many practices, and it favoured music for the *Turdanser* [contradances], similar to English country dances, and *Songdanser* [song dances], performed to sung accompaniment. There was less interest in the older types of folk music that would have accompanied the *Halling*.

By today's standards, the music in *Veslefrikk* can best be described as 'folk music light', inspired by the *Turdanser* and *Songdanser* of the day. The music is melodious with steady rhythmic patterns, but lacks the play with rhythmical stresses or melodic patterns found in contemporary folk music practices. In choreomusical terms, it represents *musique parlant*; music that underlines the story line or dance action. The character Veslefrikk dances *Halling* steps to the same musical phrase throughout the ballet creating an aural and visual leitmotif. In contrast to the *musique dansante* found in *Amor*, the music in *Veslefrikk* visualizes the movement. For instance, when the protagonist Veslefrikk dances *Halling*, his jumps and *kruking* are timed and supported by a rhythmic upbeat that underscores the movement.[22]

Kjølaas and Bergh's use of accessible folkloric material had roots in contemporary cultural politics. When *Ny Norsk Ballett* began in 1948 as the first professional dance company in Norway, the leaders purposely chose the outdoor stage at the Bygdøy Museum for Folklore as their performance site, creating an appropriate frame for their 'Norwegian heritage' repertoire (see Figure 6.3).[23] Interest in folk culture grew in the period after the Second World War, and Kjølaas used such material in several of her choreographies, such as *Ballade* and *Tyrihans*. In her autobiography, she proudly claimed that 'Ny Norsk ballet established a special style of story ballets based on our Norwegian fairy tales and stories'.[24]

---

[22] For a discussion of 'musique dansante', see Marian Smith, *Ballet and Music in the Age of 'Giselle'* (Princeton, 2000); and Anne Fiskvik, *Koreomusialsk Idealisering og Praksis. En komparativ koreomusialaks analyse av balletten Ildfuglen* (Trondheim, 2006).

[23] During its first season, *Ny Norsk Ballett* gave more than 50 performances.

[24] Gerd Kjølaas, *Dans, ropte livet* (Skillingsfors, 1998), p. 103, translation by author.

Figure 6.3   *Veslefrikk* performed at the outdoor stage at the Bygdøy Museum
for Folklore in 1948.

Veslefrikk became one of the company's best known works.[25] The use of
folklore-related material mixed with a balletic style became popular with
audiences and contributed to the company's national and international success.
The church and culture minister at this time, Knut Moen, is reported to have
been especially fond of *Veslefrikk* because he recognized its fairy-tale story and
understood the movement and plot. He appreciated that Kjølaas could make high
art ballet understandable for the middle- and upper-class audiences of the day
without descending to crudity. Moen was thus instrumental in securing important
funding for *Ny Norsk Ballett* in its first year of existence.[26] The nationalist image
of the company was further reinforced when it toured England where reviews
acknowledged its unique style: 'This young company, directed by Gerd Kjølaas, is
founding a ballet tradition based mainly on its national folk-lore and literature, and
some characteristic movements can be noticed recurring in the different themes.'[27]

---

[25] The Norwegian government considered it worthy of being filmed: Statens
Filmsentral produced a prize-winning film version of *Veslefrikk* in 1953.

[26] Kjølaas, *Dans*, p. 94.

[27] *The West London Observer*, 15 September 1951.

Kjølaas understood what would 'sell' in the post-war period. When the war and Nazi occupation ended in 1945, the nation needed to unite, and thus the desire to revive a cultural heritage became increasingly important. Folk dancing became a medium for connecting to a Norwegian folk spirit. Already in the autumn of 1944, the *Hjemmefronten* [Homefront] brought the largest political parties in Norway together in order to develop a common programme for rebuilding the country, which included an emphasis on the 'national aspects' of cultural politics.[28] One such programme, *Arbeid for Alle* [Work for Everybody], aimed to use cultural activities to encourage a new national identity, thereby hoping to secure a unity between the country and its inhabitants.[29] Thus, the cultural political climate between 1945 and 1955 embraced the need to strengthen cultural life as 'a weight against the strange and foreign commercialized mass culture that flooded the country' and 'to resist the culture pressure coming from outside'.[30] *Ny Norsk Ballet* demonstrated this ideology. Although it worked with a foreign *Freier-Tanz* and a balletic style, its performances remained accessible through the integration of nationalist folk dance material (see Figure 6.4, below).

While the democratization of culture dominated Norwegian cultural policies between 1945 and the early 1970s, ideas of cultural democracy ascended between the 1970s and 1990s. In her 2003 article, sociologist Marit Bakke identifies distinctions between the post-war democratization of culture, a top-down policy, and the later bottom-up policy of cultural democracy from the 1970s onwards.[31] Kjølaas's *Veslefrikk* contributed to this top-down nationalist policy. Kjølaas daringly used the *Freier-Tanz* as a starting point, but to counterbalance this new and foreign style, she integrated her own acceptable cultural heritage. Streamlined music and folk dance elements provide a kind of 'folk dance light' where the *Halling* movements are disciplined and stylized, danced with an upright body and with none of the bouncing in the knees that is so typical of the vernacular *Halling* dancer. Furthermore, Kjølaas chose to underline the *Halling* as a purely male solo dance, leaving the women in the ballet to dance other forms reminiscent of the waltz and gallops. While her use of Norwegian folk dance material made her work accessible to a large number of Norwegians, theatre dance largely remained an entertainment for the middle- and upper-class audiences.

---

[28]   Helge Sivertsen, 'Norsk kulturpolitikk 1945-1965', in Edvard Beyer (ed.), *Norsk kultur og Kulturpolitikk* (Oslo, 1985), p. 22, translation by author.

[29]   Ibid.

[30]   Ibid.

[31]   Marit Bakke, 'Cultural Policy in Norway', in Peter Dueland (ed.), The Nordic Cultural Model (Copenhagen, 2003), p. 155. I am grateful to Lena Hammergren, whose article 'Dance and Democracy in Norden', in Karen Vedel (ed.), Dance and the Formation of Norden (Trondheim, 2011), pp. 175-96, identified Bakke's theories on Norwegian cultural policy.

Figure 6.4   Veslefrikk throws his leg back in a typical *Halling* movement from a 1949 performance.

Fairytale: *Halling* as Commercial Enterprise

As the third case study, *Fairytale* differs from the previous two because it features traditionally trained folk dancers who moved into the ranks of professional dance. Founded by highly skilled folk dancer Hallgrim Hansegaard in 2006, Frikar was the first professional folk dance company in Norway. The company advertises its style as 'unique', as it employs *Halling* fused with breakdance, capoeira and acrobatics.[32] Frikar has achieved both artistic and commercial success, performing nationally and internationally to sold-out houses. As further testament to its status, in 2008 Frikar became the first folk dance company to receive funding from the Norwegian government.

Winning the Eurovision Song Contest in 2009 owed little to chance, but was the result of careful strategic planning. A team from Norwegian Broadcasting carried out a detailed analysis of the outcome of the 2008 Eurovision Song Contest and saw that the top four numbers all employed male dancers. They chose Rybak, a relatively unknown songwriter and fiddler, as the vocal artist and hired the three male dancers from Frikar to perform to the music and lyrics composed by Rybak and the producers. The result, *Fairytale*, became an energetic and compelling number with a strong rhythmic drive and accessible melody.

The theme of the song is lost love: 'I'm in love with a fairytale ... I am already cursed ...' sings Rybak, while the male dancers flip backwards and forwards, jump up and down, and kick their legs in the air. The singers and dancers playfully interact with each other on stage, creating a humorous and attractive atmosphere. The energetic performance earned *Fairytale* a score of 387 points, the highest ever received. The music itself has little to do with Norwegian folk music other than the opening rhythmic phrase that is repeated over and over again. In 4/4 metre, it does not have the 6/8 metric subdivisions common to traditional *Halling* music, although Rybak attempts to recreate the sound of the *hardingfele* on a standard violin. However, the movements compensate for the lack of 'Norwegian-ness' in the music as they demonstrate the most technically demanding and aesthetically pleasing aspects of the *Halling*. The movements fit the 'oom-pah oom-pah' rhythm of the music, with stresses on *one* and *three* of the measure. The overall impression is almost that of 'Mickey Mousing' whereby the dance and music fit together quite literally through simple choreomusical devices, in which the movement mimics the musical drive and energy as closely as possible. Most of the energetic dancing takes place when Rybak stops singing and accompanies the dancers on stage with his fiddle-playing. The movements look improvised at first glance, but a closer analysis reveals that there is nothing accidental about the dancing; Hansegaard received the prize for best choreography among the 43 competing countries.

One of the strategies used by the producers of *Fairytale* was to capitalize on the image of *Halling* as a nationalist male dance of virility, strength and friendly competition. Following the competition, Frikar and Rybak created an evening-length show that further exploited these stereotypical images. *Halling* was the backbone of the show, performed more than 100 times in 20 different countries, and Frikar purposely did not integrate other non-Norwegian dance styles such as breakdance and capoeira that they have used elsewhere. The show created a renewed interest in *Halling* both nationally and internationally. According to Frikar, 'fanclubs poped [*sic*] up in several countries and people started guessing

---

[32] http://www.2011.frikar.com/, accessed 29 September 2011.

Halling dance will take over from the Irish folk dance'.[33] Thus, in the wake of the Eurovision Song Contest, the choreographer carefully tailored his material to please audience expectations, much in the same fashion that Galeotti did more than 200 years earlier. But instead of 'refining' the *Halling* to suit audience tastes, Hansegaard chose to emphasize the folklore aspect both visually and, to a lesser extent, sonically. Strong, good-looking, athletic males performed energetic and acrobatic steps traditional to the *Halling*. Significantly, Frikar left women out of the show, choosing instead to focus on the gendered stereotype of an attractive and virile Norwegian farmer refined through the cultural activity of dancing.

Hansegaard and Frikar have become 'super agents' for transporting traditional *Halling* into a theatrical setting. The company's dancers have transgressed boundaries and popularized the *Halling* both within and outside Norway through integrating modern dance styles and acrobatics into their work, as well as by using female performers in performances such as *Kruk* (2006), *TidarÅ* (2009) and their latest production, *Jamsíis* (2011). As one critic notes, 'it's very exciting to see folk dance in dialogue with contemporary dance. Hansegard is branching out and opening up new territory here.'[34]

Frikar has earned the respect of the Norwegian Folkdance Society, no small achievement given its sensitivity to the representation of Norwegian heritage. Contemporary Norwegian folk dance has its own agenda and the theatricalization of folk dance material can be seen as part of a plan for securing the existence and continuation of traditional dance and with it national identity. The 1995 *Action Plan for the Furthering of Norwegian Traditional Folk Music and Folk Dancing* published by prominent folk dance researchers Egil Bakka and Ingar Ranheim, while acknowledging a growing awareness of Norway as a multicultural nation, also expressed the wish to 'take care of' or preserve the old traditions.[35]

As already mentioned, a distinct Norwegian cultural policy developed after 1945, but national aspects of cultural policy became increasingly important from the 1970s onwards. The preservation of a national heritage as well as the cultivation of a unique national identity became priorities, and in the early 1990s, folk music and folk dance organizations focused on the issue of authenticity: retaining a common point of origin, while at the time allowing for the uniqueness of local variants. One of the goals of the 'Action Plan' was to know how 'your own' Norwegian dance and musical heritage had helped the creation of a more solid identity.[36] Whereas in the mid-1940s culture was thought to have the potential for enhancing people's social conditions, this line of thought was replaced in the 1980s by 'notions of

---

[33]   http://www.2011.Frikar.com/, accessed 29 September 2011.

[34]   Karen Frøsland Nystøyls, review of *Jamsíis*, in *Bergens Tidende*, 24 May 2011.

[35]   The Action Plan was the result of a 1990s gathering of representatives from different organizations. Together, they wrote a strategic plan for how Norwegian folk dance and folk music should play a more prominent role in Norwegian cultural policy. See Egil Bakka and Ingar Ranheim (eds), *Handlingsplan for Folkemusikk og Folkedans* (Trondheim, 1995).

[36]   Bakka and Ranheim, *Handlingsplan*, p. 24.

culture as a means for promoting national prestige abroad',[37] and Frikar puts both
of these ideas into practice. Its work emphasizes the company's unique heritage
and at the same time acknowledges a need to transgress traditional boundaries
and use other types of movements to create performances that are theatrically
and artistically satisfying. Frikar seems aware of the commercialized aspect of
the Eurovision Song Contest 2009 and the resulting show. On its webpage the
company draws attention to the site-specific work *TidarÅ*, premiered in August
2009 and regarded by the company as a more original and artistic example of
choreography than *Fairytale*.

Hansegaard himself points out that *Fairytale* was a 'sidetrack' for the
company, and that they engaged in other projects that have high artistic standards
and humanistic goals. Hansegaard claims 'A lot of time it is the showbiz's part
that is emphasized and I would hope that researchers would appreciate our more
serious work to larger extent'.[38] Hansegaard's statement suggests that he wants
to emphasize the artistic qualities of Frikar as, through *Halling*, they perform
Norwegian national identity for an increasingly international audience.

The idea of the nation and what constitutes the nation-building process has been
a much debated issue, and the post-colonial theorist Homi K. Bhabha offers two
different modes, the pedagogic and the performative, as central to this process.[39]
As noted by Lena Hammergren, these two modes can be helpful in explaining
political strategies implemented in Norway's cultural policies.[40] The pedagogic
assumes a fixed origin for a nation's cultural heritage and would view Norwegian
dance traditions as part of a steady, linear progression of time from past to present
to future.[41] Thus, the origins of dancing can never change; they can only be added
to by new developments in later times. The performative mode views cultural
practices as continuous, and since they are performed repeatedly in various ways,
traditional dance can have no essential origin. The performative representation of
the nation enables new versions of a dance culture to be developed and practised.
The pedagogic and the performative usually exist side by side, as a 'double
narrative movement'.[42] The 'Action Plan' represents the pedagogic view that folk
dance and music have fixed origins in the historical past. At the same time, the
'Action Plan' also has a performative strategy since it identifies folk dance as a

[37]   Bakke, 'Cultural Policy', p. 163.
[38]   Hansegaard writes: 'Som eg håpar du har fått med deg var Fairytale ei sideprosjekt
for "Frikar" dance company. Sidan "FRIKAR" dance company faktisk driv med viktig
scenekunst på eit humanistisk plan (som er ein mykje større del av arbeidet vårt) ville eg
håpa at forskarar ville vore like seriøse og framheva dette. Likvel ser eg i lærebøker at det
er showbuissen som blir framheva.' Email correspondence with author, 30 September 2011.
[39]   Bhabha, quoted in John McLeod (ed.), *Beginning Postcoloniaslism* (Manchester,
2000), p. 118.
[40]   See Hammergren, 'Dance and Democracy in Norden', pp. 185-7.
[41]   Bhabha in McLeod, *Beginning Postcoloniaslism*, p. 118.
[42]   Homi K. Bhabha, *The Location of Culture* (London, 2004), p. 208.

corporeal and contemporary practice – a lived practice continuously changing and developing.

Both the pedagogic and performative modes are at play in Frikar's work and evident within its stated performance policies. Hansegaard presents the pedagogic narrative of the authenticity and uniqueness of Norwegian traditional dancing and has repeatedly argued for the need to go back to the roots of *Halling* and recapture the variety of movements that existed before it became standardized through national folk dance competitions (see Figure 6.5).

Figure 6.5   Frikar dancers in a friendly *Halling* battle in Hansegaard's *Kruk* (2006).

Hansegaard certainly bases his own dancing on traditional practices; he has interviewed many of the old dancers and examined written sources for movements from the past that enhance his acrobatic and virtuosic dance style. While Frikar emphasizes its Norwegian roots and close connection to the *Halling*, Hansegaard also aims to create something unique through integrating contemporary and globalized dance forms. There is another dimension to this performative mode as well. Through *Halling*, he makes contemporary dance more accessible to Norwegian audiences: 'At the same time that he [Hansegaard] approaches contemporary dance, he opens doors. If he succeeds in making contemporary dance accessible to a wider audience than today's, the genre of contemporary dance should learn to endure a "halling-roundkick" or two.'[43]

Halling as a Tool for Nationalist Strategies

This chapter has examined strategies used when transferring *Halling* into theatrical performances. The agendas of the three choreographers discussed here have been informed by the societies in which they lived, even as they share common elements in their search for accessibility and commercial success. Galeotti entertained his mostly upper-class, royal Copenhagen audience with carefully tailored elements of 'the folk'. Following the end of the Second World War, Kjølaas made her ballet *Veslefrikk* accessible to Norwegian audiences through the use of folk dance material. Her strategy was part of a larger, post-war, nationalist cultural agenda that aimed at rebuilding the country through focusing on a shared Norwegian heritage. Additionally, Kjølaas wanted to educate her audience in contemporary dance and, by combining *Halling* and other folk dance material, the ballet *Veslefrikk* became accessible to audiences of all classes. Today, Frikar aims at preserving its Norwegian heritage while simultaneously creating new and unique choreography. Rybak, Hansegaard and the Frikar ensemble were part of a huge enterprise when they won the Eurovision Song Contest. Financial interests as well as national prestige were at play in the creation of *Fairytale* and the show that followed it. Frikar won acclaim for its potent and energetic performances, and Hansegaard achieved his personal goal to popularize *Halling* both inside and outside Norway.

In contrast to the codified structures of ballet and modern dance, the aesthetic ideal in the vernacular *Halling* is complex, free-flowing, improvised and unregulated. Both Galeotti and Kjølaas re-envisioned the tightly knit, complex material of the traditional dance as a display of isolated, repeated elements for the male dancer alone. Hansegaard, deeply rooted in a folk dance tradition, likewise choreographed his material when taking it to the stage and maintained the national focus on the male dancer. His work, too, becomes presentational rather than improvisational in nature. Regardless of the strategies used, these three choreographers utilized their own folk culture to enhance nationalistic strategies in Norwegian cultural life.

---

[43]   Nystøyls, review of *Jamsiis*.

PART III
(Re)Framing Value

Chapter 7

Rocking the Rhythm: Dancing Identities in Drum 'n' Bass Club Culture

Joanna Hall

A wall of noise and shuddering strobe lights make me blink, catch a breath and my heart race. Deep underground bass sounds rumble through the floor and shudder up into my body. Fast, skipping drum patterns sizzle right through me, seizing my body and commanding me to dance. Moody, hooded clubbers stare down at the floor with intense concentration as they trace shifting patterns with their shoulders and hands; others look excitedly across the space to the DJ and salute with a thrusting arm and jabbing hand. The emcee shouts out to the crowd, 'rocking the rhythm and never forget, check, check down with the lyrical set'. Dancers bounce and slam into one another as the DJ sends a rewind shuddering across the club.[1] Wide eyed clubbers stand arms aloft, waiting, swaying … until finally, the beat kicks in and the whole room moves as one. Pure kinetic energy celebrates the beat of the drum and bass.[2]

The extract above describes the experience of dancing to drum 'n' bass music at a London electronic dance music (EDM) nightclub in 2006. The popular dances of such clubs in the United Kingdom (UK) are key social activities through which the personal and collective identities of British youth are actively produced and performed.[3] The specific musical sub-genre within EDM is often the focal point that distinguishes each club event from others and attracts a particular dancing crowd. For example, at drum 'n' bass, hip hop and dubstep events an emcee is regularly employed to rap over records played by the DJ, whereas at techno or house events the DJ is the sole provider of the soundscape. House music has been popular with gay clubbing crowds since the initial development of the style in Chicago and New York in the early 1980s, whilst drum 'n' bass, hip hop and techno events identify more with a heterosexual community. The popular dances performed at EDM events vary but there are clear differences between

---

[1]   A 'rewind' is a DJ-ing technique where the record is stopped manually and spun backwards with the needle in contact with the vinyl. The record is then released to play the section again.

[2]   Joanna Hall, Unpublished personal field notes from Switch at The Ministry of Sound, London, 31 March 2006.

[3]   I use the term 'popular dance' to refer to dance practices that take place in vernacular settings, such as night clubs, and are often accompanied by forms of popular music.

those associated with each specific musical sub-genre. Techno, for example, encourages an introspective style of movement, whereas dancing to house music is celebratory and interactive.[4] Despite such clear differences between EDM club cultural crowds and their particular dance styles, previous scholars have failed to differentiate between events by musical genre and have neglected these distinct movement practices.

The specific combination of music and dance is integral to club-goers' construction of subjectivity. In this chapter I show how UK drum 'n' bass clubbers' performances of identity can be characterized, like the music, by hybridity, ambiguity and contradiction. I use empirical data gathered from participation and observation at club events, as well as semi-structured interviews with regular clubbers, to reveal how drum 'n' bass club-goers' performances of identity are achieved through their inscription of value on the dancing bodies of 'Others', both within and outside the club cultural scene.[5] Clubbers' subjectivities are constructed through conflicting moves of affiliation (with specific identities) and distinction (from Others). I examine how these movements result from complex and dynamic systems of value associated with popular representations of collective identities, and I reveal how the multiple images of identity with which club-goers engage are both supported and contested in the popular dancing body associated with a distinctive musical sound. Thus, I demonstrate as well how drum 'n' bass club cultural identities are closely connected to perceptions of the clubbers' dedication to, knowledge of and passion for the music, as one clubber describes: 'it's just really, really happy because everyone so loves their music … it's the first thing in the morning I think about … when I go to bed at night I think about it, you know, all through the day'.[6]

Drum 'n' bass is a sub-genre of electronic dance music that first developed in the UK in the early 1990s and is characterized by a combination of a slow, heavy bassline, such as those used in dub reggae records, with fast, frenetic breakbeat drum rhythms that move at double speed in relation to the bass. The presence of these contrasting stylistic influences has led scholars to describe drum 'n' bass as 'double-voiced', a genre where seemingly contradictory or conflicting elements work in simultaneity. For example, Gilbert and Pearson describe how the combination of these characteristics allows the genre to occupy a 'double space' as the music appeals to audiences both as a 'black' musical form and as part of the

---

    [4]   Joanna Hall, 'House Queens and Techno Drones: the Social Construction of Gender in the House and Techno Club through Dance Movement and Other Embodied Practices' (Unpublished MA thesis, 2002).

    [5]   The use of the term 'Other' makes reference to Edward Said's groundbreaking text *Orientalism* (New York, 1978). In the context of my chapter, it is used to establish a relationship between drum 'n' bass club-goers and the different groups from which they distance themselves.

    [6]   Reuben, Unpublished interview, Hemel Hempstead, Hertfordshire, 29 April 2006.

(typically 'white') intellectualized avant-garde.[7] It is these 'oppositional' values identified within the musical style that I will argue are present concurrently in the dancing bodies of drum 'n' bass fans.

Drum 'n' bass has a dichotomous history as well as style. The musical genre was first known as 'jungle', with the term 'drum 'n' bass' only used to describe a new direction from 1993. Jungle initially evolved within the UK breakbeat hardcore scene but was heavily influenced by North American hip hop, and Jamaican reggae and ragga. Many of the scene's early producers were involved in the London reggae and hip hop sound system culture and incorporated reggae and ragga sounds and traditions into their music. The inclusion of these elements encouraged African and Caribbean British youth to attend early jungle raves and club events, and led to the racial branding of the music as 'black'.[8] Yet several music scholars, journalists and production artists describe the genre as located at the intersection of a range of musical and cultural influences, proclaiming the style as a product of 1990s urban, *multicultural* Britain.[9] Although early descriptions of club audiences support this notion by depicting them as racially mixed,[10] scholars Gilbert and Pearson identify a later splitting of the genre into 'black' and 'white' audiences.[11] This tension is still apparent in contemporary British drum 'n' bass club culture: whilst young, white, male clubbers now dominate the scene, their movement practices are arguably 'appropriated' from popular representations of a racialized 'Other'.

My Identity through Yours: The Role of the Other in Constructing Self

Stuart Hall describes identity as a process of identification with, and from, others, through which a split occurs that marks 'one that is and one that is Other'.[12] The 'Other' is a necessity in determining our own identity, whether that is in terms of gender, sexuality, race, ethnicity or class. Identity, therefore, can be characterized as a relational concept. Skeggs extends Hall's concept of identity through difference to include the notion that subjectivity is actively produced through a process of marking value on the bodies of others.[13] Referring to Deleuze and Guattari's notion

---

[7]   Jeremy Gilbert and Ewan Pearson, *Discographies: Dance Music and the Politics of Sound* (London, 1999), p. 79.

[8]   Rupa Huq, *Beyond Subculture: Pop, Youth and Identity in a Post-colonial World* (London, 2006).

[9]   Jumping Jack Frost in Matthew Collin, *Altered State: The Story of Ecstasy Culture and Acid House* (London, 1987).

[10]   Sheryl Garratt, *Adventures in Wonderland: A Decade of Club Culture* (London, 1998).

[11]   Gilbert and Pearson, *Discographies*.

[12]   Stuart Hall, 'Old and New Identities, Old and New Ethnicities', in Les Back and John Solomos (eds), *Theories of Race and Racism: A Reader* (London, 2000), p. 147.

[13]   Beverley Skeggs, *Class, Self, Culture* (London, 2004).

of 'inscription',[14] Skeggs describes how a body is labelled or 'marked' in a process that produces subjectivity: 'inscription is about making through marking'.[15] The products of inscription are identity classifications (such as race, gender, sexuality and class), and this process occurs through the marking of value on bodies.

Skeggs highlights the shifting nature of inscriptions of value by identifying how it can be transferred to bodies and read off them, 'how value may be retained, accumulated, lost or appropriated'.[16] In addition, this process is not contingent as it is the *history* of inscription that produces the conditions of marking and allows privileged groups the ability to challenge the dominant symbolic order. Skeggs identifies how the process of inscription attributes different values to specific identity-markers. These values accord different positions of power and privilege to an individual: for example, being marked as black, working-class and male produces a different value to that ascribed to a white, female and middle-class identity. These systems of value are dynamic as they shift according to the context with the ability for re-evaluation and contestation.

Drum 'n' bass clubbers use dance movement to construct and perform personal and collective identities, which are signified through the use of movements and gestures that suggest an affiliation with particular identities and their associated values. Their verbal descriptions of the club 'culture' (by which I mean the practices and behaviours associated with drum 'n' bass clubs events) and of clubbing crowds are often in juxtaposition to their embodied performances. Clubbers use these descriptions to ascribe themselves particular identities through a disassociation from 'Othered' groups. These ways of marking or inscribing value on their own and Others's dancing bodies reveal complex and shifting hierarchies operating within this club culture.

Boys, Bass and Bother: Dancing against the Mainstream

There is a predominance of young, male club-goers, producers, promoters, DJs and emcees at drum 'n' bass events, and clubbers commented on the unequal gender balance: 'I think it's kind of accepted that it is male dominated'.[17] Tasha, a final year psychology university student at the time of our interview, is one of a small number of female clubbers who have become interested in DJ-ing through their involvement in drum 'n' bass club culture. Ben A, a 19-year-old administrator for a haulage firm, told me that the majority of women at drum 'n' bass clubs are there because they are the girlfriends of male club-goers, and suggested that women

[14]   Gilles Deleuze and Felix Guattari, *Anti-Oedipus: Capitalism and Schizophrenia* (New York, 1977).
[15]   Skeggs, *Class*, p. 12.
[16]   Skeggs, *Class*, p. 13.
[17]   Tasha, Unpublished interview, Farncombe, Surrey, 2 June 2006.

would not be as interested in the music as their male partners.[18] Ben's comments highlight the importance of music in the clubbing experience, but also reveal a marginalization of the role that women are expected to play and a privileging of masculinity in this club culture.

The majority of male interviewees were not able to explain why there were not more female clubbers at drum 'n' bass events, although Chris, a 23-year-old technical engineer from Bristol, identified the particular style of the music and club atmosphere: 'there are usually far more males … but I can only put this down to the style of music and atmosphere … being slightly more agreeable to guys, than girls. Why? I have no idea.'[19] The men in the scene position going out to drum 'n' bass in opposition to other forms of 'mainstream', 'chart music' club events by emphasizing the importance of the music above socializing. Ben B, a 20-year-old music technology student from Brighton, contrasted drum 'n' bass club culture with 'mainstream' clubbing, which he associates with the feminine:

> People who go to drum 'n' bass nights, the majority of them will go because of the music, but a lot of people who go clubbing in general to get pissed, have a good time, and then try and pull you know? Erm, and so, *women* get all in their nice clothes and their makeup and stuff, spend hours and then go out and shake their booty [my emphasis]! You know? Whereas drum 'n' bass is more about the music … I'm not really sure what it is but not a lot of women tend to get into it as much.[20]

Ben's association of 'clubbing in general' with 'pulling', and his description of drum 'n' bass as focused on the music rather than socializing, dancing or sexual interaction is a common theme within accounts of EDM club culture.[21] The characterization of 'mainstream' male clubbers as less dedicated to the music and more interested in meeting women is further supported by a comment posted on the forum of the popular website *Drum & Bass Arena*: 'girls like cheese, girls go to cheese clubs. Boys like girls, boys go to cheese clubs.'[22] In addition, the following post associates 'mainstream' clubbing with women, drinking and *violence*: 'Cheese clubs = fights / pulling / getting smashed'.[23] These are particularly interesting

---

[18]   Ben A, Unpublished interview, Dartford, Kent, 18 May 2006.
[19]   Chris, Unpublished email interview, received 26 January 2006.
[20]   Ben B, Unpublished interview, Brighton, Sussex, 24 August 2006.
[21]   For example, see Ben Malbon, *Clubbing: Dancing, Ecstasy and Vitality* (London, 1999); and Maria Pini, *Club Cultures and Female Subjectivity: The Move from Home to House* (Basingstoke, 2001).
[22]   Corpsey, 'Dancing to music you love / enjoy v music you don't', *Drum & Bass Arena*, 17 June 2008. AEI Media Ltd. 25 November 2008, at http://forum.breakbeat.co.uk/ tm.aspx?m=1970609211&mpage=1&key= dancing&#1970610756 .
[23]   Adzh, 'Dancing to music you love / enjoy v music you don't', *Drum & Bass Arena*, 17 June 2008. AEI Media Ltd. 25 November 2008, at http://forum.breakbeat.co.uk/tm.aspx ?m=1970609211&mpage=1&key=dancing&#1970610756.

characterizations of 'Other' club scenes as drum 'n' bass club cultural practices are often violent and aggressive as discussed later in this chapter.

Whilst there are difficulties inherent in categorizing genre,[24] at the time of this research it was possible to identify three recognized sub-genres in the UK drum 'n' bass scene. 'Dark' drum 'n' bass is beat driven and often includes synthetic and sparse industrial sounds with a dystopic theme. 'Jump up' drum 'n' bass artists use deep synthesized ragga basslines alongside high impact, energetic, fast-paced drum loops, which are less dark in tone than 'dark' drum 'n' bass tracks. Lastly, 'liquid' drum 'n' bass artists use vocals reminiscent of house and disco tracks alongside broken beats and jazz- and funk-influenced rhythms. These stylistic musical differences have led to some variation in the composition of their respective clubbing communities.

A greater number of women attend liquid drum 'n' bass as opposed to jump up or dark drum 'n' bass club nights. Tasha explained how she particularly liked attending liquid club events, as there was a better balance of men and women. Reuben commented on how the vocals and 'lightness' of liquid alongside the absence of a 'blearing' emcee would be more attractive to women. By describing elements that female drum 'n' bass club-goers would value in music (melody, lightness, calmness), he ascribes oppositional shorthand 'masculine' values that privilege 'hardness' and 'noise' for his own identity.[25] This distinction is particularly interesting as Reuben's valuing of 'hardness' is in contrast to previous interviewees' comments that distance drum 'n' bass clubbers from the *violent* 'Othered' mainstream.

These clubbers' comments reveal the existence of complex hierarchies of value in drum 'n' bass club culture that privilege masculinity and the associated notions of intellectualism, complexity, seriousness and 'hardness'. These qualities are ascribed to (male and female) drum 'n' bass club-goers through their dedication to, and knowledge and connoisseurship of, the music, as well as an active distancing from the supposed feminized, simplified and violent mainstream. Yet club-goers' disassociation from violence sits in juxtaposition to the physical embodiment of these qualities in their dancing.

The dance movement and dynamic qualities performed by male, and some female, clubbers at drum 'n' bass events suggest strength, power and aggression. The dancers' body postures vary between two main positions that contrast by a difference in direction of focus and upper back alignment. In the first, the clubbers hunch their shoulders forward over a curved upper back, often raising them up

---

[24]   See Joanna Hall, 'Mapping the Multifarious: the Genrification of Dance Music Club Cultures', in Janet Lansdale (ed.), *Decentring Dancing Texts: The Challenge of Interpreting Dances* (Basingstoke, 2008).

[25]   By 'shorthand' I refer to simplified, popular stereotypes of gender that circulate in popular discourse and associate the female with body, emotion and nature and the male with culture, language and technology (Barbara Bradley, 'Sampling Sexuality: gender, technology and the body in dance music', *Popular Music*, 12/2 (1993): pp. 155-76).

towards the ears as if protecting their torso. They hold their arms close to the body with their elbows bent and forearms forward. Their bodies appear grounded, with a strong and powerful centre, as if preparing to fight. Keeping the upper back curved, the shoulders twist and thrust from front to back (causing a movement in the whole spine). One shoulder leads the movement, accentuating the forward thrust in syncopation with the dominant 4/4 duple metre drum beat. The feet are planted apart and the knees bend and straighten in a strong, energetic bouncing movement.

This body position is also used with a stepping movement from side to side, which is either performed with a loose kicking motion to the front or a floor tap next to the active foot. In addition, some dancers use a different static stance where one foot is diagonally in front of the other with weight shifting forward and back. The dancer's focus is often down to the floor or looking around the space with the chin dipped. The dynamic of this movement is dictated by the music, becoming forceful, thrusting and tense when the music becomes more driven and industrial, or with a rolling quality when tracks are more fluid. Dancers often use a variety of these feet positions during their time on the dance floor and change from moving their feet to being static when more dancers join the area and restrict the space around them.

The second main body posture is more vertical than the first and often includes the dancer's torso 'lounging' back with one or both shoulders dropping past the line of the lower spine and hips. Focus is projected outward towards the DJ or staring confidently and knowingly around the dance space. The arms are heavy and appear long by the dancer's sides as they swing languidly in opposition (often with a cigarette or drink held in one or both hands) and the knees bounce softly. Some dancers rest one hand in the crotch area, whilst the other gestures confidently to the DJ across the dancing crowd. The dynamic of this movement is often one of suppressed or contained energy; however, when the music builds in intensity the arm gestures and bouncing knees become more powerful, jabbing and aggressive. These gestures appear confrontational and evoke images of anti-social youth, 'lager louts' and the 'vulgar' corporeality that scholar Robson describes as embodied by working-class, football fans.[26]

'Classy' Moves / Moving Classes?

Earlier I argued that drum 'n' bass clubbers actively construct subjectivity by positioning their club culture in opposition to the mainstream. However, club-goers also differentiate between groups within the club culture. Such strategies for internal differentiation draw on other aspects of identity and demonstrate the close relationship between gender and class. Female interviewees actively distanced

---

[26]   Garry Robson, 'Millwall Football Club: Masculinity, Race and Belonging' in Sally Munt (ed.), *Cultural Studies and the Working Class: Subject to Change* (London, 2000).

themselves from other female drum 'n' bass clubbers by ascribing particular class-based identities to both self and 'Other'. These clubbers align themselves with middle-class values through their active distancing from other female fans that they ascribe as working class.

Anthias notes how the generation of social class and the production of gender and sexuality are closely linked.[27] The connection between these aspects of identity can be seen in drum 'n' bass clubbers' comments when they discuss female performance troupes, such as the Narni Shakers, TNT Dancers and the Vixens, who became popular entertainment at jump up club events in the early 2000s.[28] These dance groups perform on raised stages often next to the DJ and wear revealing clothing such as bra tops and hot pants. The movement content of their routines is heavily influenced by contemporary popular music videos by hip hop and R&B artists, such as The Pussycat Dolls and Rihanna, as the dancers use sexualized movements such as body ripples that emphasize the breasts and buttocks, 'strutting' walks and 'booty' shaking, combined with acrobatic movements such as cartwheels.

Club-goer Tasha voiced concern that the female dancers detract from a focus, again, on the music and suggested that they were only used because of the unequal audience gender balance: 'coz I'm really into the music ... why do you need to have girls with next to nothing on just dancing because there's no girls at an event, you know, is that what it's all about?'[29] Tasha and Rai, a 24-year-old fashion student, described how performance groups would usually be found at jump up drum 'n' bass events. Rai noted how she has 'seen them quite a few times but it tends to be at like proper raves ... grimey raves ... you wouldn't see them in Fabric, which is quite a middle class club'.[30] These comments clearly indicate that club-goers employ class-based affiliations and distinctions to distinguish between kinds of drum 'n' bass club culture and their attendant communities. Jump up drum 'n' bass events, which feature sexualized performances of female dance groups, are seen as 'working class', whereas events (or venues) that would not host such groups are positioned as 'middle class'.

Rai's association of sexuality with a working-class identity can be clarified by referring once more to the writings of Skeggs, who suggests that morality lies behind all ascriptions of value.[31] Skeggs describes the working classes as traditionally represented by excess, including explicit sexuality, whilst the

---

[27]   Floya Anthias, 'Social Stratification and Social Inequality: Models of Intersectionality and Identity', in Fiona Devine, Mike Savage, John Scott and Rosemary Crompton (eds), *Rethinking Class: Culture, Identities and Lifestyle* (Basingstoke, 2005).

[28]   The Narni Shakers have now significantly expanded their activities to include performances at other types of EDM club nights, corporate events and erotica festivals.

[29]   Tasha, Interview.

[30]   Rai, Unpublished interview, Hemel Hempstead, Hertfordshire, 29 April 2006. Rai is referring to the nightclub Fabric in Farringdon, London.

[31]   Skeggs, *Class*.

middle classes are represented by their distance from this quality and are thus characterized by restraint, repression, reasonableness, modesty and denial.[32] In addition, the value of modesty is used as a marker of middle class femininity and can be contrasted to working-class representations of the feminine that were coded by conduct; to pay too much attention to how one looked was a sign of sexual deviance or excessive sexual desire.

Rai told me that she 'goes out to dance and have a good time ... not to be looked at',[33] and both female interviewees described 'other' female drum 'n' bass clubbers as displaying unwarranted sexuality through wearing 'next to nothing'[34] or 'short denim skirts and tight tops'.[35] Tasha also thinks that the female performance groups bring a 'tacky' or 'porno' image to drum 'n' bass. In denouncing female fans' and performers' clothing and movement as excessively sexual, Rai and Tasha distance themselves from a working-class identity and in doing so ascribe to themselves middle-class values of restraint, respectability and seriousness. This act of ascription situates them as worthy inhabitants of a masculinized and 'authentic' drum 'n' bass club culture. Both women justify their place in this culture by heavily stressing their dedicated interest in the music: Tasha describes herself as 'really into the music'[36] and Rai states 'I just love the music. Love it.'[37]

Clubbers describe jump up drum 'n' bass events as having the potential to attract a 'rogue element', with a 'rude attitude'.[38] Groups of young men engage in aggressive behaviour and fights, alongside more serious criminal acts such as stabbings and muggings (referred to as 'jackings'). During fieldwork visits to jump up events I regularly observed aggressive behaviour and fighting between clubbers. Clubbers Amie,[39] Chris and Deefa explained how they have witnessed 'jackings' for mobile phones, money or drugs: 'I've known quite a lot of people who have been threatened or robbed at DnB events'.[40] These depictions of jump up drum 'n' bass club-goers are similar to Munt's descriptions of historical representations of the working classes as associated with excessive vulgarity.[41] Whilst Munt discusses the portrayal of a female working-class identity, similar values can also be seen in representations of their male counterpart: the working-

---

[32] Skeggs draws on particular cultural associations related to European historical traditions dominated by Protestant and Catholic religions.

[33] Rai, Interview.

[34] Tasha, Interview.

[35] Rai, Interview.

[36] Tasha, Interview.

[37] Rai, Interview.

[38] Reuben, Interview.

[39] Amie, Unpublished email interview, received 6 March 2006.

[40] Deefa, Unpublished interview, Brixton, London, 6 April 2006.

[41] Sally Munt (ed.), *Cultural Studies and the Working Class: Subject to Change* (London, 2000).

class 'scally' or 'lager-lout', which I earlier noted as evoked in the dance language of drum 'n' bass fans.

Most clubbers describe popular representations of working-class identities as displayed by 'Others' in the scene who are perceived to occupy the more simplistic, mainstream-orientated, excessively sexual, aggressive and feminized jump up drum 'n' bass events. In doing so, these clubbers actively distance themselves from characteristics of vulgarity, tastelessness and potential loss of control in relation to the 'rogue element's' rowdy or violent behaviour. However, the dance practices observed in dark, liquid and jump up drum 'n' bass events display the same movement lexicon. Therefore, whilst the majority of clubbers distance themselves from working-class identities, the dance movement they embody reinstates these representations in the corporeal.

Clubbers' use of violent and aggressive body slamming and barging into others on the dance floor, thrusting body and shoulder rocks, jabbing hand gestures or the violent punching of the air or parts of the club environment is in direct conflict with their verbal distancing from these 'Othered' identities. Club-goers simultaneously denounce and embody popular representations of working class identities. The music and dance work together to create this experience as it is the clubbers' need to valorize the music that prompts them to distinguish between those who are dedicated to the scene and those who are not, and it is the dance that allows the club-goers to experience 'working-class' values of loss of control, hardness, vulgarity, aggression and rage from the relative safety of a 'middle-class' sensibility. Here, I do not suggest that all drum 'n' bass clubbers are 'middle class', but that drum 'n' bass clubbers' subjectivity is constructed through 'middle-class' values.

A Case of Cultural Looting? Evoking the Racialized 'Other'

Drum 'n' bass clubbers distance themselves from 'Othered' identities that are articulated in terms of gender and class, but how are racial identities or ethnicities evoked or employed in the embodied performances or verbal articulations of drum 'n' bass clubbing fans? In this final section I examine how clubbers affiliate themselves with the values associated with popular representations of the racialized 'Other' by using socially and historically constructed representations of 'black' expressive culture, sexualities and style.[42]

Drum 'n' bass club cultural practices are similar to those found in hip hop culture, which scholar Rose describes as 'propelled by Afrodiasporic traditions'.[43] Drum 'n' bass events often feature an emcee whose role is to rhyme or 'toast'

---

[42]   I use the term 'black' to emphasize the way in which popular representations of African diasporic identities homogenize these diverse cultural groups.

[43]   Tricia Rose, *Black Noise: Rap Music and Black Culture in Contemporary America* (Hanover, 1994), p. 25.

over the recorded tracks to create additional layers of sound and rhythm, as well as to excite the dancing crowd.[44] Drum 'n' bass DJs use techniques that were originally created by African American hip hop artists, such as the 'rewind', and clubbers, especially at jump up events, often wear hooded sweatshirts, tracksuits and baseball caps, such as that worn by hip hop and gangsta rap artists and fans.[45]

Dancers, emcees and DJs also perform movement similar to that seen in hip hop music videos. For example, in the video for *Race Card* (Ice Cube, 2006, Lench Mob Records), rapper Ice Cube uses a hand gesture extending the thumb and first finger (whilst the other three are bent inward) in a pointing motion towards the camera. This movement is also performed by a crowd of fans in the music video for *Lose Yourself* (2002, Shady Records) by hip hop artist Eminem. Drum 'n' bass clubbers use this and similar hand gestures whilst repeatedly pointing their arms above their heads towards the DJ and emcee. They are also used with a sharp flicking movement of the arm, held above the head and forward of the body, to mirror a drop in the music at the end of a climatic build-up.

Some female clubbers at jump up drum 'n' bass events use provocative movement that sexualizes the dancing body by emphasizing the hips and buttocks through shaking and rippling. This movement is similar to that used by the female drum 'n' bass performance groups and is reminiscent of that described by Hope as present in Jamaican dancehall culture.[46] However, this movement style is more readily accessible to British youth in contemporary American hip hop and R&B music videos, such as *Drop It Like It's Hot* by hip hop artist Snoop Dogg (2004, Geffen Records), *Buttons* by The Pussycat Dolls (2006, A&M Records; with Snoop Dogg), and *Rude Boy* by Rihanna (2010, Def Jam Recordings), all of which feature confident and highly sexualized images of women. The dance movement of these female drum 'n' bass clubbers shows a clear similarity with the portrayal of women in these styles of music.

Dance movement that borrows heavily from popular representations of 'black' male and female identities in North American hip hop and R&B music videos replicates popular representations of 'black' bodies that play on 'orientalist' constructions of the 'black' woman as sexually promiscuous, and 'black' men as associated with criminality and violence. Drum 'n' bass clubbers' 'appropriation' of African American hip hop movement, expression and style can therefore be seen as a 'participatory Orientalism', a phrase used by Bannerjea to describe 'white'

---

[44] 'Toast' is a term used in Jamaican sound system musical culture to refer to the emcee's dialogue that is heard over the top of recorded tracks. African American rap music incorporated this practice in the late 1970s.

[45] Michael Quinn, '"Never Shoulda Been Let out the Penitentiary": Gangsta Rap and the Struggle over Racial Identity', *Cultural Critique*, 34 (1996): pp. 65-89.

[46] Donna Hope, 'The Lyrical Don: Embodying Violent Masculinity in Jamaican Dancehall Culture', *Discourses in Dance*, 2/2 (2004): pp. 27-43.

participation in 'black' cultures as a form of 'carefully constructed exotica'.[47] Whilst here I engage momentarily with narratives of 'orientalist appropriation', I do so to highlight the ways in which clubbers associate themselves with and disassociate themselves from different representations of 'Othered' identities. Elsewhere I argue that whilst it is vital to recognize marginalized groups who have been written out of history, the notion of cultural appropriation is limiting as it infers the 'ownership' of cultural forms and perpetuates the internally homogenizing and essentialist categories of 'black' and 'white'.[48]

Drum 'n' bass clubbers associate themselves with popular representations of a racialized 'Other' in order to ascribe particular qualities that are valued within the musical scene to their own identity. Verbal descriptions of fans' attraction to drum 'n' bass club culture demonstrate their mobilization and revaluation of negative, historically determined constructions of the racialized 'Other' as marginal, 'dirty … and almost animal-like'[49] to positive, desired qualities. Drum 'n' bass fans describe being attracted to the music and club scene because of its underground and marginal status. For example, Jack, an 18-year-old student from London, explained how 'drum 'n' bass people are quite proud of how kind of underground it is and how grimy and dirty and un-mainstream it is'.[50]

Clubbers construct drum 'n' bass club cultural identity as a marginalized 'Other' that they seek to embody through characterizations of the music and club scene as 'dirty' and 'grimy'. The associations with dirt and darkness appear to be particularly attractive for some female and younger male interviewees. Rai describes how she 'love[s] really dirty, dark basslines', Ben A voices his passion for 'dirty bass, dirty tune[s]' and Tasha told me 'I do enjoy mixing … a really dark, sort of, heavy set'. Amie, a 21-year-old student living in Sheffield, claimed that she was attracted to the subversive location of the Mass club in Brixton, London and particularly to the atmosphere: 'especially like this club as it's dark and gloomy and in a church … a more dirty atmosphere in the venue'.[51]

The attraction to the risky or subversive elements of drum 'n' bass club culture is in contrast to clubbers' descriptions of their backgrounds and everyday lives, and appears to offer them the opportunity to embody a risky 'Other' whilst maintaining 'safe' (white, middle-class) identities outside the club space. All those interviewed described how their parents had encouraged them to conform to hegemonic

---

[47]   Koushik Bannerjea, 'Sounds of Whose Underground? The Fine Tuning of Diaspora in an Age of Mechanical Reproduction', *Theory, Culture & Society*, 17/3 (2000): pp. 64-79, after Said, *Orientalism*.

[48]   See Joanna Hall, 'Heterocorporealities: Popular Dance and Cultural Hybridity in UK Drum 'n' bass club culture' (Unpublished PhD thesis, 2009).

[49]   Michelle Fine, Lois Weis, Judi Addelston and Julia Marusza, '(IN)SECURE TIMES: Constructing White Working-Class Masculinities in the Late 20th Century', *Gender and Society*, 11/1 (1997): p. 58.

[50]   Jack, Unpublished interview, Wandsworth, London, 22 December 2005.

[51]   Amie, Interview.

societal values through emphasizing the importance of gaining a good education and secure employment. Most had been educated to degree level and were in full-time employment, or in full-time further or higher education. By engaging in these subversive activities, drum 'n' bass fans appear to be satisfying an 'orientalist' desire to engage, temporarily, in a fetishized alterity, whilst maintaining a safe distance between self and 'Other'.

Dancing around Someone Else's Handbag: Some Conclusions

A drum 'n' bass clubber's subjectivity is constructed through an assertion of difference from the dancing bodies of 'Others', which is articulated through their relationship to the music. Whilst the concept of subjectivity through difference has been long established,[52] drum 'n' bass club cultural identity is actively produced through the inscription of value in the popular *dancing* body of both self and 'Other'. These qualities and values are ascribed to (male and female) drum 'n' bass club-goers through an evaluation of their dedication to, reverence for and connoisseurship of, the music. The relationship between the clubber, the dance and drum 'n' bass music is central to the club experience.

Drum 'n' bass clubbers ascribe positive value to notions of intellectualism and complexity that they associate with the music and distance themselves from 'mainstream' nightclub events that are typified by the presence of *dancing women* who place excessive emphasis on their appearance, as well as male violent and aggressive behaviour. In addition, the role of women within drum 'n' bass club culture is marginalized as interviewees describe female club-goers as the 'girlfriends' of 'authentic' fans. Drum 'n' bass music and club culture is constructed by these accounts as complex, intellectualized and masculinized in its polarized distance from the mainstream 'Other'.

Some drum 'n' bass clubbers distance themselves from jump up fans (and the performance groups seen at these events) who, because of their explicit sexuality, 'rude' and aggressive attitudes or clothing choices are ascribed a working-class identity. In the act of ascription of 'Others', female club-goers position themselves as deserving inhabitants of an 'authentic' (middle-class) drum 'n' bass club culture. Whilst these individuals move away from traditional expectations of the feminine to authenticate their position in the club culture, women who engage in more sexual movement content on the dance floor or in organized performance groups, are forging their own space in drum 'n' bass club culture through their promotion of explicit sexuality.

Despite moves of distinction away from working-class identities, an analysis of the dance reveals that clubbers engage in movement practices that demonstrate qualities of aggression, hardness, vulgarity, disorder and rage. The verbal

---

[52] For example, see Frantz Fanon, *Black Skin, White Masks* (London, 1986); and Stuart Hall, 'Old and New Identities, Old and New Ethnicities'.

distinction from and physical embodiment of values normally associated with a working-class masculinity suggests a simultaneous refusal and *revaluing* of these qualities; 'class is made as a cultural property, a resource that can be used (or not) depending on the value attached to it and the markets in which it can realize value'.[53] Similarly, in the use of movement and gestures from R&B and hip hop culture, clubbers ascribe themselves *revalued* qualities normally associated with historically and socially constructed popular representations of 'black' identities.

Negative qualities associated with popular representations of the racialized 'Other' are positively revalued by drum 'n' bass clubbers who are attracted to the dark and subversive elements of the club culture. Clubbers evoke a marginalized 'Other' that they seek to embody through characterizations of the music and club scene as 'underground', 'dirty' and 'grimy'. The ambivalent and contradictory attitude displayed by clubbers towards criminality in drum 'n' bass club culture is shown in descriptions of the dance floor as both a site of pleasure and excitement and yet as potentially dangerous and violent. These comments demonstrate an association with popular representations of 'black' identities that are associated with criminality, violence and, at times, sexuality. Whilst some clubbers are clearly disturbed by incidents such as muggings and stabbings, violence and aggression is permitted and embodied through the dance movement.

Thus, drum 'n' bass is replete with hybridity, contradiction and ambiguity, demonstrated in the complex hierarchies of shifting values that draw on popular representations of the middle and working classes, male and female identities and 'black' culture, expression and style in conflicting moves of affiliation and distinction. In contemporary UK drum 'n' bass club culture, gender, class and race are mobile resources, used to ascribe negative values to 'Othered' groups (the mainstream or jump up drum 'n' bass clubbers); yet these same qualities are positively revalued when embodied as part of the dance and movement practices.

---

[53]   Skeggs, *Class*, p. 99.

Chapter 8

Authenticity, Uplift, and Cultural Value in Bahian Samba *Junino*[1]

Danielle Robinson and Jeff Packman

'Samba is from Rio, not Bahia.' This statement made by a Brazilian taxi driver is emblematic of a common assumption: that samba as practised in Rio de Janeiro is the benchmark of authenticity for Brazil's national music and dance. Both scholarly and popular accounts of samba's development and nationalization likewise minimize the role and contributions of practitioners elsewhere despite sometimes acknowledging Bahian samba as foundational to the nationalized practice.[2] Typical histories suggest that Bahians brought a crude music and dance practice to Rio which was slowly urbanized and refined, eventually coming to represent the nation as Brazilian music and dance par excellence. Overlooked until recently is that this pre-national samba lives on in Bahia, where it is known as *samba de roda* (circle samba). Even in Bahia, *samba de roda* has not been accorded as much respect as its Rio-born progeny as it is associated with poor, often black, residents of rural areas. Yet the status of the practice and its practitioners changed dramatically in 2005 when UNESCO, as part of its programme to preserve cultural diversity and protect endangered heritage, recognized *samba de roda* of the Bahian Recôncavo (the farmland to the west of Salvador, Bahia's capital) as a Masterpiece of the Oral and Intangible Heritage of Humanity.[3]

The international acclaim accorded to the once marginalized practice of *samba de roda*,[4] has allowed it to be re-imagined as a valued 'tradition' by many of Brazil's

[1]   The authors would like to acknowledge and thank Canada's Social Sciences and Humanities Research Council and Britain's Leverhulme Trust for their support of this research.

[2]   Examples include: Hermano Vianna, *The Mystery of Samba: Popular Music and National Identity in Brazil*, ed. and trans. John Charles Chasteen (Chapel Hill, 1999); José Ramos Tinhorão, *História Social da Música Popular Brasileira* (São Paulo, 1998); Jairo Severiano, *Uma História da Música Popular Brasileira: Das Origens à Modernidade* (São Paulo, 2008); Alma Guillermoprieto, *Samba* (New York, 1990); Chris McGowan and Ricardo Pessanha, *The Brazilian Sound: Samba, Bossa Nova, and the Popular Music of Brazil* (Philadelphia, 1998).

[3]   http://www.unesco.org/culture/ich/index.php?lg=en&pg=00103, accessed 15 October 2011.

[4]   Ralph Waddey, 'Viola de Samba and Samba de Viola in the Recôncavo of Bahia (Brazil)', *Latin American Music Review*, 1/2 (1980): pp. 196-212.

elite through a discourse rich in what, following Brazilian ethnomusicologist Martha de Ulhôa Carvalho, we gloss as 'folk authenticity', a notion rooted in the practice's perceived purity and pre-modern-ness.[5] This remapping from quaint, marginal, neglected practice to authentic folk 'masterpiece' through UNESCO recognition has, in turn, had important implications for Bahia's samba participants, especially those from the 'popular' classes.[6] Within a diverse and changing range of samba sounds and movements, newly bound by competing notions of legitimacy and cultural ownership, self-identified working-class black Bahians now harness *samba de roda's* elevated status in ways that assert new models for community empowerment and uplift often through reconfigured notions of samba authenticity.

To illustrate the newly complicated context and political potential for Bahian *samba de roda* following UNESCO's recognition, we will consider an urban samba variant in Bahia's capital city, Salvador. Specifically, we discuss a dance contest held in the working-class neighbourhood of Tororó during the *festas juninas* (June Festivals), which commemorate three Catholic saints and the fall harvest. Of interest are the ways in which participants in a community-based performance group, known as Samba Tororó, actively align themselves with a 'traditional' *samba de roda*, both through speech acts and through sonic and movement practices. In particular, various means of valorizing *samba de roda* infuse Samba Tororó's events and especially its dance contest's evaluation criteria. The result, we argue, is a particular expression of samba, one that is distinct from the nationalized versions associated with Rio, other local urban samba variants from Salvador, and even the rural UNESCO 'masterpiece'. Such performative positioning, we contend, intersects with, and at times challenges, cultural and political discourses that are strongly tied to Brazil's colonial legacies and deeply rooted in Bahia's history as a centre for slave importation and labour. Our engagement, then, queries the normalization of particular attitudes and values in expressive culture – in this case 'proper' dancing and 'good' music, as they are articulated in relation to constructed and problematic notions of 'tradition' and 'authenticity'.[7]

To situate this particular dance contest, an annual event at which Samba Tororó selects its queen, we first introduce the forms of samba commonly practised in

---

[5]   Martha de Ulhôa Carvalho, 'Tupi or not Tupi MPB: Popular Music and Identity in Brazil', in David J. Hess and Roberto DaMatta (eds), *The Brazilian Puzzle: Culture on the Borderlands of the Western World* (New York, 1995), pp. 159-79.

[6]   In Brazil, 'popular' commonly refers to places and practices that are not regarded as elite. In this context, the term has an even more restricted meaning that implies 'of the people', and refers specifically to the working classes and poorer members of society who comprise the majority of the population of Salvador and the focus of our study.

[7]   Eric Hobsbawm, 'Introduction: Inventing Traditions,' in Eric Hobsbawm and Terrence Ranger (eds), *The Invention of Tradition* (Cambridge, 1983), pp. 1-14; Carvalho, 'Tupi or not Tupi MPB'; Benjamin Filene, *Romancing the Folk: Public Memory and American Roots Music* (Chapel Hill, 2000).

Bahia and the debates surrounding these specific music and movement practices. We then engage in a close analysis of the dancing and judging practices of Samba Tororó's Queen contest and locate a tactical racial intervention by its members. Drawing on Michel de Certeau's theorizing of 'tactics', the ways people improvise in the everyday to avoid the dominating discourses of the more powerful, we note how June samba participants reassert and redefine notions of 'blackness' during a season of celebrations that shifts focus away from Bahia's Afro-Brazilian culture.[8] Our emphasis is on Samba Tororó's delicate negotiation between contradictory, intertwined and, for most participants, subjugating discourses of race and class. Ultimately, we argue that Samba Tororó's practices and their embedded values tactically steer the neighbourhood towards greater safety, uplift, and social inclusion.

Bahia and its Sambas

Scholarly writing, popular discourse and tourist literature typically emphasize African influence in Bahia and especially Salvador. Characterizations such as 'the most African city in Brazil' derive not only from the region's past as a plantation centre and slave port, but also its present, which is infused with Afro-Diasporic expressive cultural practices.[9] Salvador was Brazil's first capital, but its replacement by Rio de Janeiro in the mid-eighteenth century exacerbated the economic stagnation of the entire northeast that is still evident today. Perhaps unsurprisingly, poverty in Bahia is concentrated among its darker skinned residents. Such conditions persist despite a national discourse that, since Gilberto Freyre's writings in the early twentieth century, has asserted Brazil's absence of racism, the centrality of racial and cultural mixing in notions of national identity and the nation-state's 'racial democracy'.[10]

Samba de roda emerged out of Bahia's slave past and continues to be informed by its racial legacies. A cousin of the North American ring shout, it has roots on Bahian sugar plantations that dotted the Recôncavo at least until abolition in 1888. The practice can also be traced to the many maroon communities, or *quilombos*, established in the area by escaped slaves as early as the sixteenth century. Owing to this geographic atomization and its primarily oral transmission, numerous variants of *samba de roda* exist throughout Bahia. Despite this variety, several

[8] Michel de Certeau, *The Practice of Everyday Life*, trans. Steven Rendell (Berkeley, 1984).

[9] José Jorge de Carvalho, 'The Multiplicity of Black Identities in Brazilian Popular Music', in Larry Crook and Randall Johnson (eds), *Black Brazil: Culture, Identity and Social Mobilization* (Los Angeles, 1999), pp. 261-95.

[10] Gilberto Freyre, *The Masters and the Slaves: A Study in the Development of Brazilian Civilization*, trans. Samuel Putnam (1933; New York, 1964); Thomas E. Skidmore, *Black into White: Race and Nationality in Brazilian Thought* (Durham, NC, 1998).

features unify the practices, including continued association with the rural poor, especially the descendants of African slaves.

Also uniting what is otherwise a highly varied music and dance complex (a generalized structure within which participants improvise) are a number of sonic and movement conventions. As the name *samba de roda* suggests, music-making and dancing typically take place in a circle formation.[11] Call and response singing and dancing, accompanied by hand percussion and often plucked string instruments, are the norm. In addition, all participants forming the circle clap a particular timeline (Example 8.1) and/or one of several common variations, the most typical of which is shown in Example 8.2. Certain instruments appear in *rodas* with some regularity, including *atabaques* (a Brazilian cousin of the Cuban conga) and *pandeiros* (Brazilian tambourines), as well as various string instruments such as guitars, *cavaquinos* (a small four-stringed lute similar to a ukulele) and, in some instances, an instrument called a *viola*. Regardless of what instruments accompany *samba de roda*, any harmony tends to be unelaborated and repetitive, in many cases limited to alternation between the tonic and dominant chords. Percussion, on the other hand, typically features dense polyrhythms and highly varied, elaborated syncopations.

Example 8.1   Basic *samba de roda* timeline.

Example 8.2   Typical *samba de roda* timeline variation.

A particular movement vocabulary overarches all *samba de roda* variants. Despite tremendous variety and frequent personalization, nearly all *samba de roda* participants practise a basic foot movement known as *miudinho*, which translates loosely as 'mincing' or 'niggling', and refers to very small, tight steps. It begins with an accented forward step (often with a heel smacking the ground), followed by two quieter backward ones on the balls of the feet. Accordingly, many of our collaborators referred to their manner of dancing as *samba no pé* (foot samba), emphasizing the importance of footwork and distinguishing it from the extravagant full-body movements of common urban samba variants in Salvador and, implicitly, those from Rio de Janeiro.[12]

---

[11]   Post UNESCO, *samba de roda* is increasingly presented commercially on proscenium stages; participants replace the closed ring with an open semi-circle facilitating the audience's view.

[12]   We use 'collaborator' to express respect for those who assisted us with our research and to acknowledge the active role these men and women have had in shaping our understandings.

Women are the primary dancers of *samba de roda*, with men typically providing the musical accompaniment. Men do dance on occasion, though, and their movement style is also based in the *miudinho*. However, they deviate from this basic step more frequently than women, often dramatically shifting their balance through lunging and crossing steps to create playful accents with the whole body. Although men seem to enjoy greater liberty in their choreography and the women's vital foot motion is usually all but hidden underneath the voluminous skirts they customarily wear, the *miudinho* remains crucial to *samba de roda* in terms of how the practice is discussed and experienced by dancers and informed observers, both male and female.

When performed correctly, *samba de roda* dancing echoes, but does not match exactly, the musical timeline. In a manner reminiscent of Charles Keil's 'participatory discrepancies', a slippage between rhythms creates a pleasurable feeling of pushing, sliding and pulling within the dancer's body.[13] Above the patter of their feet, the dancers's arms and hips are subdued but active. In comparison to other samba variants, such as that seen at Rio's carnival (especially as performed by women), the torso actions of *samba de roda* are understated and subtle, and help construct what many Bahians refer to as *samba de roda*'s sensuality (as opposed to overt sexuality).

The women*'s miudinho* footwork makes their hips sway quickly, but gently, providing visual accents that complement sonic ones. As each foot is thrust forward, the opposite hip is pushed out horizontally, diagonally, or backwards, all within a tight range of motion. These movements are usually greeted by a soft shoulder dip and/or elbow arc to the side. Other times, gently undulating arms sway and flow above the hips and feet, usually below shoulder level – mimicking ocean waves. Accompanied by a humble down-turned face, the women's movements express and interact with *samba de roda*'s musical rhythms and render them visible.

In addition to being distinct from Rio-style samba in terms of sound, movement and gender conventions, *samba de roda* also stands apart from another Bahian samba variant known as *pagode*. This practice, distinct from one with the same name from Rio de Janeiro, gained popularity in the 1990s with the flourishing of Bahia's carnival music industries.[14] Bahian *pagode* is an urban and now thoroughly commercialized genre that developed in Salvador as a hybrid of existing local music practices (including *samba de roda*) and other music from Brazil and international

---

[13]   Charles Keil, 'Participatory Discrepancies and the Power of Music', in Charles Keil and Steven Feld (eds), *Music Grooves: Essays and Dialogues* (1987; Chicago, 1995), pp. 96-108.

[14]   Philip Galinsky, 'Co-option, Cultural Resistance, and Afro-Brazilian Identity: A History of the *Pagode* Samba Movement in Rio de Janeiro', *Latin American Music Review,* 17/2 (1996): pp. 120-49; Bill Hinchberger, 'Bahia music story', in Robert M. Levine and John J. Crocitti (eds), *The Brazil Reader: History, Culture, Politics* (Durham, NC, 1999), pp. 483-6; Mônica Neves Leme, *Que Tchan é Esse? Indústria e Produção Musical no Brasil dos Anos 90* (São Paulo, 2003).

locations. While there are many Bahians who resist associations drawn between *pagode* and samba (given the national status of samba and *pagode*'s purported lewdness and banality), the influence of samba, both Rio-style and *samba de roda*, is clear in its musical and movement vocabulary. In fact, in the only full-length study of *pagode*, Monica Leme confirms that Bahian *pagode* developed out of *samba de roda* and shares a considerable history with June samba.[15]

Even when links between *pagode* and other respected forms of samba (both Rio-style and now *samba de roda*) are publicly acknowledged, this music-dance practice is still commonly condemned, especially by members of the middle and upper classes, as an impoverishment of samba. Bahian *pagode* features a great deal of harmonic and textual repetition. Relatively simple chord progressions (that is, I vi ii V I) are ubiquitous, as are playful lyrics describing easy movements and gestures to be performed by the audience. In many cases, the dance that accompanies Bahian *pagode* includes arm and hip movements drawn from Rio samba that are typically performed by women and many men in an even more exaggerated manner.

While *pagodeiros* (*pagode* musicians, dancers and fans) value the easily grasped expressive and participatory elements of *pagode*, those not part of the scene view them disapprovingly. Critics regularly attack the exuberance and overt sexuality in the movements and the banality of the coordinated choreography. Even more frequently, they criticize *pagode* lyrics as trite, nonsensical, misogynistic and even obscene. Despite its efficacy for animating crowds during Carnival and its commercial success, *pagode* is constantly decried by a cross-section of Bahians for not being good music and for using movements that are perceived as insipid, offensive, or both.

Thus, a broad-reaching samba complex (including *samba de roda*, Rio-style/ national samba, and Bahian *pagode*) creates an historical and discursive frame for June samba that is crucial to its musical and movement values. Indeed, June samba exists within the perceived refinement of Rio-style (non-local) samba; the devalued putative crudeness and commercial popularity of local urban *pagode*; and the newly valorized folk authenticity of rural Bahian *samba de roda*. Consequently, dance contestants in Samba Tororó's queen-selection event must navigate these entrenched understandings to win the crown. With each step, gesture and facial expression, competing performers position themselves, and Samba Tororó, in relation to the complex significations and histories of these related samba practices.

Samba's Places in Bahia and Samba Tororó

Inaccurate as claims for the lack of samba in Bahia may be, they are understandable given that the state's biggest, most visible and most lucrative celebrations feature

---

[15]   Leme notes the links between *pagode*, *samba de roda* and what she calls 'street sambas' in Salvador. Leme, *Que Tchan é Esse?*, p. 25.

other music and dance practices. *Pagode* is prominent during carnival, but it is secondary to another genre, *axé*, that is distinct in both sound and movement conventions. Similarly, samba is only a minor feature of Bahia's second largest seasonal festival, the *festas juninas*. Known popularly as São João, one of the Catholic saints honoured during the events, this series of celebrations highlights all things rural with harvest-themed food, drinks, attire, music and dance. The most prominent music and dance practice of São João is a Brazilian kind of country music known as *forró*. This accordion-based genre is danced in a closed couple formation, with footwork reminiscent of polka but featuring hips that punch, curve, arc and circle in a bouncy way. Performers of various styles of *forró* are the central attraction of the large-scale parties held in rural Bahian cities that have, in recent years, become the June holiday season destinations favoured by those Bahians who have the financial means for travel. Notable in all of the most prominent manifestations of São João is a conspicuous absence of overt reference to Bahia's Afro-Brazilian culture, people and slave past. Instead, nostalgia for an idealized bucolic bygone era dominates, as does an emphasis on north-eastern regional *caboclo* (European/Indigenous mixed) culture and identity. Glaringly absent in both representation and discourse are references to the people of African descent who carried out the Recôncavo's harvest, both in the past and today.

The agricultural theme of São João is a likely catalyst for what has become a holiday mass exodus primarily by middle- and upper-class Bahians to *forró* parties held in Bahia's rural interior. In the last five years, however, we have also noted an increase in samba events within Salvador's city limits. These celebrations take place away from the most visible parts of the city in working-class neighbourhoods populated mainly by Bahians of visible African descent. Despite being largely unknown to people who do not live in such places, June samba in Salvador dates back well over 30 years. According to our collaborators, participation decreased and almost ceased for a time, in some instances because of increasing violence between neighbourhood samba groups. However, since 2007 and UNESCO's recognition of *samba de roda*, June samba groups have become more active and visible, with Samba Tororó emerging as one of the organizations most central to this shift.

Notably, and we contend not coincidentally, Samba Tororó's discourse – along with that of many of the other groups – involves assertions of belonging to the *samba de roda* complex. By tactically situating themselves as part of *samba de roda*, participants in urban June Samba effectively appropriate the prestige and cultural value that is now associated with the rural practice by virtue of its UNESCO recognition. Once marginalized, *samba de roda*'s international acclaim has reframed it, and it is now viewed by a cross-section of Bahians, and indeed Brazilians, as treasured heritage. We argue that June samba, as a similarly neglected practice also associated with a marginalized population, is gaining its own legitimacy as a valued tradition through the actions of participants, in part through their discursive connections with *samba de roda*.

Certainly, attendance and interest in June samba has increased in the last five years following UNESCO recognition. This greater visibility, though, means that the June *sambadores'* alignments with *samba de roda* are also risky and raise the stakes for their tactics.[16] On the one hand, participants risk being derided as quaint (*samba de roda* is deeply rooted in Bahia's past) and outside mainstream June Festival customs that embrace *forró*. On the other hand, they stand to draw ire for corrupting a (now) valued tradition, as has been the case with *pagode*. Yet, our experience suggests that groups such as Samba Tororó ably negotiate a space for their participants within the context of Bahia's *forró*-focused June celebrations and the newly complicated politics of *samba de roda* stewardship and related concerns over authenticity. Samba Tororó, in particular, has accomplished such an intervention through its unique take on samba, which asserts a specific and, we would argue, tactical subjectivity with respect to music, movement and social values.[17]

Negotiating Cultural Values and Choosing a Samba Queen

Samba Tororó's take on samba politics, São João tradition, and local music and movement values is especially visible during the annual selection of their queen. In keeping with the customs of choosing queens for various carnival organizations as well as the *Rei Momo* (Carnival King) in the weeks leading up to the pre-Lenten celebration, Samba Tororó dedicates one night in the weeks prior to São João to the selection of the young woman who will represent the group. The selected queen leads the group's parades through the city and dances in a prominent location during the weekend *ensaios* (literally rehearsals, but actually public parties) that are held in Tororó through the month of June. Similar to the annual beauty contest held by the famous Afro-centric carnival group Ilê Aiyê, which challenged the exclusion of dark-skinned Bahians from prominent carnival *blocos* in Salvador beginning in the 1970s, selection of the Samba Tororó queen is based primarily on the dancing ability of the candidates. Indeed, movement skill is central to how beauty is expressed and appreciated. Whereas Ilê Aiyê's beauty criteria emphasizes a movement vocabulary that they gloss as 'Afro', Samba Tororó's queen competitors are evaluated instead on their ability to dance Bahian samba. In particular, judges look for a very specific movement approach that emphasizes footwork skill and understated sensuality (much like *samba de roda*), and that avoids the perceived self-indulgence of Rio samba and especially the asserted lewdness of Bahian *pagode*.

---

[16] Bahian practitioners, primarily from rural areas, use the terms *sambador* and the feminine *sambadeira* in distinction to the Rio-based nationalized term *sambista*.

[17] Jeff Packman, 'The *Carnavalização* of São João: Forrós, Sambas, and Festive Interventions during Bahia, Brazil's June Party Season', *Ethnomusicology Forum*, 21/3 (2012): pp. 327-53.

We have attended numerous Samba Tororó rehearsals and parades dating back to 2005 and have seen several different queens in action. Moreover, we have attended two competitions to select those queens, one in 2007 and another in 2011, where, at the invitation of long-time participants and members of the directorate of Samba Tororó, Danielle served as a judge. This involvement offered an especially effective means of gaining insight into what values were central in the selection of the contest winner though direct discussions with judges as they chose the queen.[18]

While there are differences in the yearly implementation of Samba Tororó's June festivities and queen competitions, there are also numerous aspects that are maintained. The selection of the queen takes place in late May or early June, several weeks before the official São João celebration on 24 June. Since the commemoration of São João is the peak of the entire June party season (and an official holiday, hence the travel en masse out of Salvador), the night of 23 June sees the most activity in the city and throughout the state.

In preparation, Samba Tororó begins to hold Saturday *ensaios* in March or April after carnival season. The selection of the queen takes place once the gatherings are in full swing, attracting large crowds of regulars from the neighbourhood, and increasingly beyond, all of whom become familiar with the music and each other. Such familiarity maximizes audience participation through singing and dancing along with performances. The timing of the contest also allows the new queen to settle into her role as the group's centre of attention a few weeks in advance of its parade excursions outside of Tororó, the majority of which take place on and around the end of June and São João itself.

The *ensaios* all take place in the heart of Tororó, a well-established neighbourhood in the centre of Salvador. Tororó is generally regarded by Bahians as a 'popular' neighbourhood and its residents are primarily working class. Nevertheless, it does have an area that is considered lower-middle or even middle class toward the top of the hill upon which it sits. Further down the hill, dwellings are more humble, with open windows and exposed brick that approaches the familiar owner-made look of Brazil's infamous *favelas*. Our collaborators view Tororó as very much a working-class space, whose residents are by and large of visible African descent. This self-mapping further informs Samba Tororó's agenda in terms of its samba practices and politics.

The typical gathering place for the *ensaios* and the dance contest is towards the end of the principal street that loops through Tororó, passing above the poorer

---

[18]   Being selected as a judge has been awkward and exciting for Danielle. While she was likely invited given her dance expertise and friendly relations in the neighbourhood, she also provides Samba Tororó with a degree of prestige through her presence as a North American academic. However, as an outsider, she also experienced moments of tension. Danielle has been careful not to assert any authority and instead asked many questions and invited feedback throughout the evaluation process. Thus she aimed to defuse the possible awkwardness of a *gringa* (white, foreign, female) judge, however familiar in the neighbourhood, helping select Samba Tororó's most visible representative.

area nestled on the hillside below and underlying the middle-class homes that sit at the crest of the hill. At these parties, the focus of attention is on a small stage with a thatched roof that juts out into the street against the backdrop of the crumbling, stained walls of an apartment building. The stage faces and is flanked by several small markets and neighbourhood bars. Many small *barracas*, or huts, also dot the street, temporarily erected by neighbourhood residents to sell beer and other drinks as well as food typical of the São João season. The stage upon which the musicians and dance contestants perform has grown over time. During the first queen selection we attended in 2007, dancers performed in the street, between the judges' table on one side and a small thatch-roofed, street-level stage for the musicians on the other. In 2011, by contrast, the stage was an elevated platform with lights and a public address system.

Figure 8.1   Samba Tororó Judging Table 2011. Author Danielle Robinson is
                seated at the table between several community members. In front of
                the table stand Raimunda Boa Morte, a key contest organizer, and a
                cluster of queen contestants preparing to go on stage. With the help
                of another contestant, the dancer in the pastel dress is about to pin
                closed her skirt.

The sequence of events for the queen's selection is relatively straightforward. After the musicians have played for several hours to energize the crowd, the invited judges take their seats in front of the stage. They are served roasted corn, boiled peanuts and endless refills of ice-cold beer. Contestants gather in an area alongside the stage and are introduced in turn by Marcos 'Porco Olho' Boa Morte, a founder of Samba Tororó, one of the group's singers and the principal lyricist for its original sambas. During a typical *ensaio* or parade, the group performs a wide range of music, including its own compositions and favourite songs from the repertories of classic *sambas de roda*, contemporary Brazilian Popular Music (MPB – *música popular brasileira*), Afro-centric Bahian carnival music, and *forró*, all performed in Samba Tororó's particular samba style. For the dance contest, however, the song list consists primarily of original compositions by members of the group. After being introduced and briefly sharing with the crowd her unique vision for being queen, each dancer removes her shoes and then demonstrates her samba to the crowd with the voice and percussion accompaniment of Samba Tororó's musicians. Much like in a rural *samba de roda*, all of this activity is supported by the enthusiastic rhythmic clapping and singing of onlookers. But unlike typical *samba de roda* events – at least, those in rural, non-commercial settings – there is no circle. Rather, the musicians form an arc behind the dancers, leaving the audience's view unobstructed. Each contestant dances to one samba. A medium initial tempo allows the contestant to settle into a groove and demonstrate her footwork and musicality. After a few minutes, however, the drummers step up the pace dramatically, testing the abilities of the competitor and allowing the most skilled movers to demonstrate their virtuosity. Upon building to a frenetic climax, the group cadences and the dancer's turn ends, usually to wild applause.

Although most of the dancers are greeted enthusiastically by the audience, they are being evaluated simultaneously by both the crowd and the judges, in ways that may not correspond. That is, some of the behaviours that elicit the most enthusiastic response from audience members are frowned upon by the judges. The most vocal faction of the audience, typically young, heterosexual males, respond enthusiastically to somewhat overt sexuality (clearly reminiscent of Bahian *pagode*) and nearly all of the audience reacts to the grand arm gestures, virtuosic footwork and lightening-fast hip gyrations that recall the Rio samba schools (see Figure 8.2, below). Yet the judges, along with many of the long time participants in Samba Tororó, tend to evaluate the dancers based on a movement aesthetic rooted in rural *samba de roda*, exemplified by subtly undulating arms, mincing feet (*miudinho*) and comparatively quieter hips. This aesthetic framework speaks to efforts by the older participants in Samba Tororó to not only hold on to what has recently become a valued tradition, but also to instil a sense of cultural pride and dignity that avoids the negative imagery associated with newer trends in Afro-Bahian music and dance, while still remaining distinctly Bahian.

Six to ten invited judges from inside and outside the community rate candidates on a ten-point scale in four categories: *desenvoltura, carisma, criatividade* and *samba no pé/suwing* [sic]. The first category translates literally as unfolding, development and amplification, but the judges described this term as 'the body' and 'everything together'; in practice, we have come to understand *desenvoltura* as meaning bodywork or whole body integration. *Carisma* literally translates as charisma, but according to the judges means charm: in this context, whether the person is likeable and attractive. *Criatividade* refers to creativity and imagination, and in action addresses invention: how does the dancer generate new movement ideas within the range of acceptable movements? *Suwing* [*sic*], a Portuguese adaptation of 'swing', refers to groove and the rhythmic play in the feet that creates pleasurable energy shifts in the body.

Figure 8.2   Samba Tororó Queen Contestant 2011. This young woman earned cheers from the crowd, but not the crown. She performed *pagode*-like movements, such as planting her feet wide apart and circling her bottom progressively towards the ground.

Samba no pé (foot samba) is the key aspect of this final category and it is a highly political one. It addresses footwork as well as rhythmic engagement and complexity, and thus discursively links June samba to rural *samba de roda*. The dancers' kinaesthetic expression of an idealized notion of *samba no pé* makes these links material and visible at the same time that the clapping of the *samba de roda* timeline renders them audible. Perhaps unsurprisingly, evaluation in this category ultimately figures most prominently in the queen selection process. In addition to resonating with the discourse and valorization of *miudinho* in *samba de roda*, the stakes for *samba no pé* are all the higher because *pagode*, with its exaggerated hip movements, is commonly criticized by locals (especially those adept at *samba de roda*) for its lack of footwork. On the other hand, despite acknowledging the virtuosic footwork of Rio samba, many *samba de roda* dancers regard its foot movements as 'backwards'.[19] It is this category, then, that most strongly ensures

---

[19]   Rio samba's whirling feet that press forward, arch to the side and then step back one at a time, carry a dancer backwards; *samba de roda*'s *miudinho* gently pushes a dancer forward.

that the queen's dancing will be *samba de roda* and not another samba. Footwork, along with the presence of the *samba de roda* timeline, therefore, also becomes central to the assertion of any claims of belonging to the *samba de roda* tradition since, like both *pagode* and Rio samba, June samba is urban and performed without a circle.

In addition to tactical alignments with *samba de roda*, we have also noted that a performance that distances a contestant from other forms of samba, especially *pagode*, is crucial for a candidate to be considered seriously for queen honours. Contestants are told to remove their shoes upon entering the stage, which signifies that the dancers are different from *pagode* or Rio ones, who typically wear heels. Past winners have not worn short skirts, reserve uncommon in the other urban samba types. Moreover, the dramatic hip gyrations of *pagode* and grand showmanship of Rio samba, often expressed through active and outward-reaching arm gestures, were not marked highly by judges who instead embraced the more demure upper-body movements seen among long-time, female practitioners of *samba de roda*. Through the overt valuing of such notions of propriety and conventional gender roles (as in women dancing and men comprising the musical ensemble), more explicit sexuality like that associated with Bahian *pagode*, along with the extravagance linked to Rio *samba*, is deliberately muted at the Tororó dance contest.

The judges's prioritization of *samba de roda* values, especially subtle sensuality over sexuality, is not necessarily in alignment with the crowd's preferences. Dancers who performed exaggerated hip movements and pelvic thrusts incited wild cheering every year we attended. However, those contestants who relied primarily on such movements were consistently scored lower by the judges, who told us that they viewed these choices to be disrespectful and inappropriate in this context. Despite some dissonance between crowd reaction and contest results, the eventual winner each time was accepted enthusiastically by onlookers, while family and friends comforted the unsuccessful candidates quietly off to the side.

By validating a more conservative view of femininity, Samba Tororó's judges reward those who do not transgress their notions of appropriate female sexuality and who forgo the immediate gratification (in the form of enthusiastic audience response) such transgressive acts might provide. In a sense, then, the criteria of the contest and the judges's selection of winners act as a form of disciplining that, to borrow from Katherine Bergeron, orders bodies.[20] On one hand, the discourse and performances of Samba Tororó suggest a tactical evasion of the disciplining legacies of colonialism and slavery by asserting an Afro-centric politics and claiming inclusion during the June festivals, which have historically excluded them. On the other hand, by enforcing their own notion of movement propriety, one that is in some ways, but not entirely, complicit with dominant, Eurocentric

---

[20]   Katherine Bergeron, 'Prologue: Disciplining music', in Katherine Bergeron and Philip V. Bohlman (eds), *Disciplining Music: Musicology and its Canons* (Chicago, 1992), pp. 1-9.

notions, certain group members also engage in a form of disciplining. Here, their own notion of proper movement, acceptable female sensuality and samba tradition is modelled and subtly enforced in the face of pressures to act otherwise. Notably, where Foucault's 'panopticism' hinged on surveillance in which the subjects were always aware of the potential risks of acting improperly, here the knowledge of surveillance brings with it both the very real risk of punitive action (not winning the contest) and reward (being chosen queen) (see Figure 8.3).[21]

Figure 8.3   Samba Tororó Queen Contestant 2011. This young woman almost won the crown with her subtle, playful and sensual movements, but the judges felt she did not exhibit the *carisma* necessary. She looked down while dancing most of the time.

On our most recent visit to Bahia, we noted that efforts to distance Samba Tororó's practices from other forms of samba were often more evident in action than in words: for example, Rio-style samba was almost always embraced in conversation. As mentioned above, however, *pagode*'s movement conventions, musical tendencies and lyrical customs continued to be harshly criticized, especially among members of the middle and upper classes. And while we heard condemnations of the practice among residents of popular neighbourhoods, it was striking that, at the 2011 contest, judges were more reluctant than in the past to say anything directly negative about it. Rather, they emphasized that, while

---

[21]   Michel Foucault, *Discipline and Punish: The Birth of the Prison*, trans. Alan Sheridan (New York, 1977).

pagode is fine for other types of parties, their event was simply not the place for it. Discussions of *pagode* in Tororó and with other self-identified Afro-Bahians now often included the statement '*nada contra*' (nothing against it), even if the interlocutor was explaining why it was not suitable for the context at hand.

While *pagode* is still not embraced across a wide cross-section of Bahians in the same way that Rio samba is, its local discourse has changed in recent years. In a manner similar to the reclaiming of *samba de roda* from primitive relic to valued tradition, the new perspectives voiced by our working-class, Afro-Bahian collaborators about *pagode* signal a rethinking, and perhaps gentle resistance to a dominant discourse in Bahia that has normalized this music-dance practice's overt condemnation. Since *pagode*, like *samba de roda*, is typically associated with black Bahians, we view this shift as not only a matter of loyalty to local practices, but also as a rejection of the all too common race- and class-based hierarchies of expressive culture in Bahia that have become hegemonic. Indeed, in years prior, we frequently heard condemnations of *pagode* even by residents of popular neighbourhoods.

Certainly it could be argued that the words and actions of Samba Tororó's judges are contradictory and suggest a capitulation to the views of the elite and even colonial legacies. However, we interpret the events of the most recent queen contest as part of an on-going negotiation, through samba(s), of emerging issues in Tororó and beyond. In many ways *samba de roda* represents Bahia and the history of its African descendants. By claiming affiliation with it, Samba Tororó by extension moves to demarginalize its own history as a collective of Afro-Bahians. Similarly, by distinguishing their music and dance practices from Rio Samba, which stands in for the more Europeanized, economically and culturally dominant south of Brazil, participants symbolically elevate Bahia within their imagining of the nation-state, reversing more typical hierarchies that give primacy to the South. Finally, through the markedly less passionate dismissals of *pagode*, Tororó residents stand up for black-mapped cultural practices within Bahia and, by extension, themselves.

Thus we argue that the overt valuing in this context of *samba de roda* over other sambas, both from Bahia and Rio, emerges out of the desire to help and control Tororó as a discursive and social space. After a century-long effort toward establishing the area as a popular neighbourhood rather than a *favela*, and after several decades of trying to reclaim their streets from drug-related crime, the community leaders who are the driving forces of Samba Tororó have a clear vision for their home: one of greater respectability and peacefulness. *Samba de roda*, with its newfound status as a cultural masterpiece and its musical, movement and discursive linkages with traditional, rural values, offers an appealing alternative to *pagode* and its widespread associations with hyper-sexuality, urban poverty, drug use and lack of artistry (see Figure 8.4). Creating such alternatives is key; in our interviews, Samba Tororó's leaders expressed their desire to improve both the circumstances and representation of working-class black communities within Salvador. In the process, though, they must win the attention of many young residents who are drawn to *pagode* and its adult sexuality, commercial glamour, and prominence during carnival. At the same time, Samba Tororó's leadership now clearly aims to make such interventions without diminishing appreciation for local, and especially black-mapped, expressive culture. Such denigration is a longstanding concern that, according to collaborators, has contributed to further erosion of such practices and apathy toward investment in local community building. The embrace of a local music and movement practice, then, deliberately shifts the focus back home, and away from Rio – a place that for years has served as the centre for Brazilian cultural production and remains in many ways the benchmark for national cultural values.

Figure 8.4   Samba Tororó's Queen 2008. This photo was taken on São João eve, just before the neighbourhood paraded from Tororó to Pelourinho, the historic city centre. The queen wears a colourful and feminine costume that matches the all-male musicians' shirts.

This complex agenda dovetails with efforts to make the streets safer by providing an environment where various demographics (younger, older, wealthier, poorer, black(er), whit(er)) can enjoy São João in Salvador in a distinctly Bahian way. This includes celebrating with less *forró* from the vast plains of the Brazilian northeast and more local samba. It also means less emphasis on nostalgia for an idealized agrarian past that ignores slave legacies and plantation violence, greater inclusion for non-elite black-identified residents of Salvador during June celebrations, and broader recognition of Afro-Bahian contributions to valued Brazilian culture. In this way, aesthetic and cultural values become entwined at Samba Tororó's Annual Queen Contest, when a neighbourhood comes together and particular local ideals are tactically enforced, taught, and subsequently performed in the public spaces of citywide São João celebrations.

Chapter 9

Hierarchical Reversals: the Interplay of Dance and Music in *West Side Story*

Rachel Duerden and Bonnie Rowell

Integration of the Vernacular and Classical

The iconic Broadway musical *West Side Story* (1957) was the result of a four-way collaboration between composer Leonard Bernstein, choreographer Jerome Robbins, playwright Arthur Laurents and lyricist Stephen Sondheim. Although its initial critical reception was mixed, it soon established itself as a significant work, and the award-winning 1961 film consolidated its place in the Western art canon.[1] While the film departs from the original theatre version in a number of respects, such as the order of scenes and the length of some dances, the central relationship of dance and music remains and forms the basis of the following analysis.

West Side Story is based on Shakespeare's *Romeo and Juliet*, transposed to New York's West Side in the mid-twentieth century, where the feuding families are rival gangs of youth trying to carve out their place in the culturally diverse city. The Sharks are the relative newcomers from Puerto Rico; and the Jets consider themselves to be the legitimate street 'rulers', although they too are of immigrant stock (European – or 'Polack') albeit less recent arrivals than the Sharks. Young, desperate to 'belong' and to feel in control of their lives, these gangs share more than they realize, which contributes to the tragic irony of the scenario.

In this chapter we explore ways in which the choreography and music embody this irony, individually and in relationship to each other, through a subtle referencing and integration of different cultural influences. The focus of our discussion is 'Dance at the Gym', the scene which immediately precedes the meeting of the star-crossed lovers, Maria (sister of the Sharks' leader) and Tony (formerly a Jet and friend of the Jets' leader, Riff). In it, the rival gangs are brought together in what is ostensibly a social event, designed to encourage friendship and integration among the different groups. What we see, however, is a display of insistent gang identity that reveals surprising cultural mixes and prompts us to

---

[1] Directors Robert Wise and Jerome Robbins; producer Robert Wise; screenplay Ernest Lehman, based on the book by Arthur Laurents; music Leonard Bernstein; lyrics Stephen Sondheim; choreography Jerome Robbins.

look again at the complexity of identity and of what is important to these young people and their sense of belonging.[2]

We analyse the movement vocabulary and music, engaging in a close reading of characteristic demeanour, centre of weight, articulation of the body and stylistic influences, alongside consideration of comparative musical factors such as tonality, orchestration and stylistic reference. Our analysis is informed by the work of Joseph Swain, Elizabeth Anne Wells and Deborah Jowitt, among others, whose illuminating studies of music and choreography in *West Side Story*, respectively, underpin and guide our detailed interpretation of 'Dance at the Gym'.

Before focusing on 'Dance at the Gym', however, we examine the classical and vernacular sources and attendant values, that Robbins and Bernstein drew upon. These sources are germane to understanding the ways in which the creators characterized the gangs, and in the 'Prologue' Robbins and Bernstein set up these characterizations and the dance and music ideas that then pervade and animate the narrative throughout. The centrality of contemporary popular dance forms to 'Dance at the Gym' in particular becomes the focus, as we consider the range and significance of Robbins's research into movement styles for this key scene.

We then turn our attention to the content of 'Dance at the Gym': the way the scene is set; the sharp distinctions drawn between Jets and Sharks in terms of both movement style and relationships between the sexes; the mambo and its embodiment of jazz and Latin influences; and the 'dance off' between the leaders of each gang and their respective girlfriends. All of these signifiers speak of the gangs' desire to assert their cultural identity and difference from their rivals; yet they also reveal much that is common between them, underlining the message of the story's dénouement. We conclude with a consideration of the importance of popular forms and the presence of hierarchical inversions, both central to the construction of gang and individual identity in *West Side Story*.

Bernstein and Robbins suggest the gangs' contrasting cultural identities initially by referencing Cuban mambo-style hip swings and layered rhythms for the Puerto Rican Sharks' signature moves, and jitterbug athletic swings and turns for the Jets. Both styles were highly popular dances of the era. But Robbins also refers to the Puerto Rican Sharks' Spanish heritage with certain characteristic flamenco moves, such as bull's horn arms, and he gives jitterbug dance qualities, such as the relaxed carriage of the body and low centre of gravity with their roots in Afro-Caribbean culture, primarily to the European Jets, resulting in their characteristic 'laid back' attitude. Furthermore, for both gangs these styles are mixed with classical and jazz

---

[2]   Our analysis has led us to challenge many of the objections concerning the representation of race and cultural difference that have been raised by earlier authors. See, for example, Rachel Rubin and Jeffrey Melnick 'Broadway, 1957: *West Side Story* and the Nuyorican Blues', in *Immigration and American Popular Culture* (New York, 2007), p. 89; and Frances Negrón-Montaner, 'Feeling Pretty: West Side Story and Puerto Rican Identity Discourses', *Social Text*, 63, 18/2, Summer (2000), p. 84.

influences – the main genres in which composer and choreographer were trained – but they intermingle and comment on each other, we argue, in surprising ways.

West Side Story has achieved both its critical and its cultural status on the strengths of its narrative, its musical and choreographic sophistication,[3] and its use of the Broadway stage as an unlikely forum through which to discuss fundamental social issues of the day. Robbins and Bernstein advance the plot through their manipulation of the interchange between musical and dance references. They achieve this by characterizing individual and group identity and, further, by telling a nuanced version of the narrative, thereby offering a perspective that is both sympathetic to the passions of the liminal post-war generation and able to recognize and draw attention to the tragic irony of a situation in which the protagonists share so much more than divides them.

Classical and Vernacular Sources and Values

Throughout *West Side Story*, Bernstein and Robbins draw on popular dance and music styles, such as mambo and jitterbug, broadly to identify social and racial identity. There are additional ways, however, in which the Puerto Rican Sharks also embody classical ballet values, whereas the European immigrant Jets' movement vocabulary derives significantly from Afro-Caribbean forms, and these embodiments contradict a superficial reading. Similarly, Bernstein's interweaving of vernacular forms – in particular jazz and Latin-influenced dances – within a classical symphonic structure avoids simplistic equivalences between music and character or group. Instead, the musical choices, like their choreographic counterparts, both affirm and interrogate their historical and cultural significance by revealing the aesthetic values associated with each style. Consequently, the choreography and music lead us to question our assumptions about social hierarchical structures and reveal the problematic nature of gang 'identity' and the intractable depth of conflict in *West Side Story*. The fact that all the collaborators were themselves from immigrant stock provides a context for their sympathetic treatment of the gang members. Moreover, we are reminded by Wells[4] that they were all Jewish and either gay or bisexual and these factors are similarly relevant when we come to consider the collaborators' interest in representing an inclusive rather than divisive American identity.

In his insightful study of the Broadway musical, Joseph Swain illuminates important characteristics of Bernstein's score, drawing attention not only to musical features in themselves, but also to the range of cultural influences at work

---

[3]   Deborah Jowitt, *Jerome Robbins: His Life, His Theater, His Dance* (New York, 2004); Joseph, P Swain, 'Tragedy as Musical', in *The Broadway Musical. A Critical and Musical Survey* (Oxford, 1990), pp. 205-46.

[4]   Elizabeth Anne Wells, *West Side Story: Cultural Perspectives on an American Musical* (Lanham, MD, 2010), p. 14.

and Bernstein's manipulation of them. Elizabeth A. Wells also throws light on key factors relating to the music, with particular focus on the ubiquity of 'Hispanic' connections.[5] Wells argues that the influence of the 'Hispanic' had, since the previous century, become widely pervasive in Western music, as evidenced in the works of European composers such as Ravel and Debussy, and also through jazz. This Hispanic presence thus contributes significantly to the way in which Bernstein's score for *West Side Story* embodies both cultural difference and cultural inter-relatedness. Bernstein's desire to compose 'American' music is an important consideration here. Deborah Jowitt's seminal text on the work of Jerome Robbins, and Nigel Simeone's study of *West Side Story*,[6] each provides essential and illuminating perspectives on the work of choreographer and composer.

Characterization of Gangs through Dance-Music Relationships

The gangs are characterized through the relationship of dance and music, and the interdependence of the aural and kinaesthetic is clear from the beginning. As Simeone observes:

> The role of music as one of the plot-developing elements of the work is at once apparent from the jagged dissonance in the Prologue, and setting the street scene with purely instrumental resources lends it starkness and brutality while also emphasizing the primacy of dance.[7]

Robbins and Bernstein both draw upon a variety of dance forms, interweaving the different popular forms with 'classical' (balletic or symphonic/operatic) structures. Choreographically, these movement 'flavours' are interwoven with the Broadway jazz and ballet styles in which Robbins was primarily trained and which also embody a set of cultural values. But the ways in which Robbins subtly ascribes contrasting movement qualities to the gangs serves to expose the values that underpin them, whilst the interchangeability of vocabularies for both gangs underlines their common humanity in important respects.

Various cultural influences are evident in Bernstein's score, in particular the rhythms of South and Central American dances, both in the explicitly named numbers such as 'Mambo' and 'Cha-cha', and through the score as a whole. Further, Wells argues that these 'rhythms and pulses' would be familiar to audiences and indeed had become 'part of a *lingua franca* that already engaged in a convivial

[5]   Elizabeth Anne Wells, 'West Side Story and the Hispanic', in *ECHO: a Music-Centered Journal* www.echo.ucla.edu, 2/1 (Spring 2000), S1-S41; Wells, *Cultural Perspectives*.

[6]   Nigel Simeone, *Leonard Bernstein: West Side Story* (Farnham, 2009).

[7]   Simeone, *Leonard Bernstein*, p. 84.

dialogue with concert and popular music style'.[8] In addition to these and other recognizable references (Simeone and Wells also refer to the Jewish influence in Bernstein's music), there are musical motifs embedded in the musical structure of *West Side Story* which run like connecting threads through the whole, animating the narrative. Important among these are the interval of a tritone, clashing keys (usually C and A), major-minor tension and hemiola rhythm patterns; all of these musical and choreographic ideas are set up in the Prologue.[9]

The Prologue: Setting the Scene

The contrast between the Jets' and Sharks' movement vocabulary during the 'Prologue' provides an important template for their distinctive characterizations. The two gangs execute virtually identical steps and gestures seemingly unaligned with their supposed class or racial descent: *ronds de jambe en l'air* from the classical ballet genre, step ball changes from the jazz genre, and *tours en l'air* and *grands battements* that exhibit elements of both genres. Each gang performs these with very different qualities: most noticeably in their relation to space and gravity. The Sharks' focus is predominantly down, and they dance with a more languid or gliding dynamic. Their movement tends to be more 'placed': for example, one arm is held behind the back to exaggerate *épaulement*, which also references flamenco. Jets meanwhile exhibit a more staccato dynamic in keeping with their laid-back status; their focus is either up or out, consistent with a greater level of confidence and 'ownership' of the surrounding space. But, here again, group identity becomes blurred in relation to the appropriation of 'cool' and pseudo-Africanist qualities by white, Western culture, and Brenda Dixon Gottschild's consideration of the Africanist presence in American dance forms is particularly relevant,[10] as we shall see.

Meaning is also carried in dance structure in the 'Prologue', with the idea of 'strength in numbers' conveyed via accumulation of steps, force, structure and complexity just as it is in the music through accumulation of instruments and

---

[8]   Wells, 'West Side Story and the Hispanic', S2.

[9]   The tritone is an augmented 4th interval which divides the octave exactly in half. Structurally it opens up the possibility of slipping easily between otherwise unrelated keys. It is frequently referred to as the 'hate motif' (or 'gang motif') because of its immediate association with the rivalry between the Jets and the Sharks. The two tonal areas of A and C major are frequently pitted against each other, and the conflict is centered in the clash of C natural and C sharp which also embodies a conflict of major and minor tonalities and resulting dissonance, and thence a direct connection to jazz influence in the tonal shading. The hemiola is a rhythmic structural pattern placing a division into two against a division into three.

[10]   Brenda Dixon Gottschild, 'Stripping the Emperor: The Africanist Presence in American Concert Dance', in Ann Dils and Ann Cooper Albright (eds), *Moving History/ Dancing Cultures. A Dance History Reader* (Middletown CT, 2001), pp. 332-41.

increase in dynamic. These themes are also reinforced visually in the set and camera angles, which shift from the abstraction of the New York skyline to the realism of the streets, and provide a relevant backdrop of enclosed tenements for the Sharks and open public space to accompany the Jets' dance. These spatial references too are interchangeable throughout, in terms of alignment of relatively closed or open spaces with Sharks or Jets respectively.[11]

The key musical elements employed by Bernstein carry historical and cultural significance, as well as great expressive potential. As Swain observes, they 'merge so naturally ... that in the end the listener notices not how weird they are, but how well they work together'.[12] Their integration in the manipulation of popular dance forms and classical symphonic structures results in musical 'tropes' that allow for a significant depth and complexity of meaning that goes far beyond any facile alignment of musical 'signatures' with characters or situations.[13] The shifting and colourful orchestration brings another dimension: on the one hand, the prominence given at times to saxophones, trumpets and varied percussion evokes jazz and Hispanic references; on the other, more 'classical' instrumental conventions, particularly in the use of strings, suggest a different cultural alignment.[14]

In their integration of so-called classical and vernacular influences, Bernstein and Robbins thus challenge conventions and values that are embedded within the different genres. In addition, the fusion of these disparate influences provides a combustible element that underpins the violence and clash of cultural values inherent in the narrative. Thus, the marriage of 'art' dance and music with 'popular' dance and music carries with it more than just incidental interest. Rather, it becomes fundamental to the story and meanings attached to it, enabling the musical to raise moral and ethical issues such as 'racism, gang warfare and disillusionment with the "American Dream"',[15] that hitherto were confined more usually to the legitimate theatre stage.[16]

---

[11]   For example, the low enclosed garage space for 'Cool' where the Jets regroup after the rumble and attempt to reassert their identity; the open rooftop for the Sharks' exuberant 'America', both of which contrast with and contradict the spatial associations set up in the Prologue.

[12]   Swain, 'Tragedy as Musical', p. 213.

[13]   Robert Hatten writes, 'Troping in music may be defined as the bringing together of two otherwise incompatible style types in a single location to produce a unique expressive meaning from their collision or fusion': see his *Interpreting Musical Gestures, Topics and Tropes. Mozart, Beethoven, Schubert* (Bloomington, 2004) p. 68.

[14]   Bernstein was himself closely involved in the orchestration of the dance numbers, a job often given to an assistant (Swain, 'Tragedy as Musical', p. 218).

[15]   Claims made by the film's publicity material.

[16]   However, *Show Boat* (1927) was a highly influential work in terms of dealing with serious contemporary social themes, as were later works such as *Carousel* (Rodgers and Hammerstein, 1945) and *Street Scene* (Weill, 1947).

Dance at the Gym: Mambo!

In 'Dance at the Gym' we can see references in dance and music to jitterbug, mambo and its derivative, cha-cha. To these sources we can add flamenco-style music and dance in reference to Puerto Rican cultural influences. Wells writes, 'The interpolated cries of "Mambo!" by the two gangs are a direct descendant of the flamenco tradition in which dancers are urged on by their enthusiastic onlookers.'[17]

Unlike the 'Prologue' or 'Cool', the studio had removed Robbins by the time 'Dance at the Gym' was filmed and the staging for this passed to his assistant Peter Gennaro, who had also set 'America' for the Broadway version. Although Gennaro's influence is important in terms of its energy and 'cool', as well as his expertise in Latin dance about which Robbins felt less secure,[18] it seems clear that it was Robbins, ultimately, whose vision ensured the overall success of the choreography.

Setting the Scene

From the lead-in to the dance, individual character and group identities emerge. It is clear from Robbins's notes to producer Robert Wise during the editing process that Robbins was intimately concerned with the way in which the drama builds visually:

> The Sharks (in a shot including the Jets) should be seen to withdraw and then take over the dance hall; then the Jets (in a shot including the Sharks) should be seen gathering and taking it back and dispersing the Sharks; then the Sharks reassemble and take it back, and the Jets re-counter. When Riff and Graciella [*sic*] are dancing competitively against Bernardo and Anita, the *total* picture, including both couples, isn't seen until the very last minute … Tony and Maria must meet at the *fiercest* moment of the gangs' crescendoing competitive dancing.[19]

The strong visual dimension includes colour symbolism in set and costume. But this 'translation' of visual and music clues is just one part of the whole. The choreography draws on more than dance motifs, but acknowledges and then deconstructs the conventions that are embedded within the disparate styles in order to subtly question the hierarchical values that are attached to them. This acknowledgement and deconstruction of conventions becomes apparent when we turn our attention to the detail of the dance and music.

---

[17]   Wells, 'West Side Story and the Hispanic', S34.
[18]   Wells, *West Side Story*, p. 147.
[19]   Robbins in Jowitt, *Jerome Robbins*, p. 290.

Maria declares to Bernardo that the dance will mark the beginning of her 'life as a young lady of America'. The music immediately following exploits the ubiquitous tritone, as Maria spins happily, dreaming of the coming evening and her first dance as 'a lady of America'. There is a characteristic ambiguity of key as well as chromatic dissonance, even though overall the mood is happy and optimistic. Significantly, the 'hate motif' introduces this scene as it heralds not only the 'dance-off' between Jets and Sharks, but also the eventual meeting of Maria and Tony and thus the great love motif of the musical, where hate is transformed and the tritone resolved in Tony's ecstatic reiteration of her name in 'Maria'. The tritone continually sustains the tension until this resolution.

On the Dance Floor

After Maria's spinning, the scene cuts to the dance floor on which Jets and Sharks are dancing in couples in a swing/jive style that are at first glance indistinguishable from each other. A tone of difference is set, however, after Maria's introduction, through the ways in which the groups interact socially amongst themselves and greet other group members. Social mores for the Sharks appear formal in comparison to the relaxed attitude of the Jets. For example, Bernardo's insistence on Maria being chaperoned at all times, hints at European nineteenth-century moral coding. Meanwhile the Jets have moved into the modern urban age, which, it is suggested in both movement and music, is informal and arrogant, albeit still manifesting sexual segregation.[20]

Jets couples and trios begin to stand out from the crowd as they dominate the centre space, each dancing 'in character'. The Sharks make their entrance and the gauche social worker Glad Hand averts confrontation between the gangs by attempting to organize a 'get together' dance. In the music the use of dissonance and reference to vernacular forms in a deeply ironic tone underpins Glad Hand's attempts to persuade the rival gangs to see each other as young people like themselves, not bitter enemies. A single dissonance in the bass-line (via the tritone) introduces the ironic tone, and distorts the rather pedestrian promenade music[21] provided for the adolescents to circle round each other and arrive at a new partner. The music's old-fashioned banality invites, and receives, a scornful response from the young people; its triteness highlights the dramatic idea, as if a communal dance could heal the deeply divisive wounds of gang warfare. The

---

[20]   An examination of the representation of women in *West Side Story* is beyond the scope of this chapter. Wells presents a complex and balanced analysis of gender and ethnic roles, arguing that, far from following Hollywood orthodoxy, the movie musical 'shows some of the tensions within both the theater and culture, between male and female roles and how these dovetail with ethnicity, voice and the demands of a story unlike any told in musical theater [*sic*] before' (Wells, *West Side Story*, p. 144).

[21]   Although marked 'Tempo di Paso Doble' in the score, the promenade is clearly polka-like, referencing 'Polack' heritage.

bumbling awkwardness of Glad Hand thus throws the barely contained simmering conflict into stronger relief.

Cultural Contrasts

Leader of the Jets, Riff, struts out to the centre of the room, then beckons his girl Graziella onto the floor with a mere nod of the head. Both pay more attention to the surrounding audience and the impression each is making than to each other. Their entrance is followed by Sharks' leader Bernardo and his girl Anita who, in contrast, make a big play of grace and formality by the extroverted use of their bodies, courtly hand gestures, partnered twirls and general embellishments: Bernardo leads Anita 'as though he were presenting the most magnificent lady in all the world'.[22] Thus differences in gender representation and gender relations are also flagged. Anita displays her skirt with her left hand as if she is entering a European ballroom of a bygone era, while at the hip her costume suggests the classical ballet tutu, a reference that connotes partnering, lifts and female on male dependency. Graziella is in a shorter shift dress with kick pleats, which, while displaying more of the body, permits less freedom of movement. It is worth noting however that Ice's girlfriend, Velma, wears a dress similar in style to Anita's costume, tight-fitting to the hip, from which it flares. Furthermore, both gangs take on the characteristics of each others' signature moves as the dance progresses, with the Jets adopting flamenco arm positions and the Sharks taking on jitterbug partnering just prior to Maria and Tony's first meeting. The messages here are complex in relation to ethnic stereotyping and gender representation.

Mambo: Jazz and Latin Flavours

The mambo begins, marked in the music by the rhythmic layers played simply but urgently on percussion alone, drawing attention to the generative rhythms. Simeone writes:

> Launched by a fusillade of Latin percussion (bongos, timbales, cowbells and traps), this is a violently confrontational and competitive dance, which leaves the Jets marginalized. If the first three numbers introduced us, musically speaking, to the world of the Jets, here are the Sharks.[23]

However, we can discern in all of this some shifts between a stronger jazz element employing syncopation and more grounded movement, and a more obviously Latin dance element that privileges step for note moves, verticality, and a held torso clearly evident in the bodily carriage and dancing of the characters. Both

[22]   Ernest Lehman, 'West Side Story. Screenplay', Photocopy of typed film script, Burbank, CA, Screenplay Library Services (17 June 1960; revised 28 July 1960), p. 45.
[23]   Simeone, *Leonard Bernstein*, p. 98.

gangs, and both genders, perform similar movements: high kicks and hip wriggles as they move into position; fast partnered turns followed by *sissonnes* alternately crossing front and back; and spin turns ending arms up in flamenco-style 'bull's horns'. But all of these are identifiably Sharks' signature moves, established and developed later in 'America', only here danced by both gangs to blur the distinctions between them. Performance style differs in important respects though: the Sharks' dance style is speedy, punchy and sensuous but at the same time manifests a high degree of centred control, retaining their characteristic upright posture, flexible back arches and pronounced *épaulement*; the Jets appear athletic rather than dancerly, displaying a more 'modern' sensibility in contrast to the Sharks' formality and verticality. Sharks are paired male/female and expression is focused in the shoulder, neck and face, which is offset by a formality between the partners in other respects: in the acknowledgement of their partners, for example, and in delicate hand contact. Jets, on the other hand, demonstrate 'cool' and 'laid back' with movement that is either exaggeratedly slow and languid, or fast and furious; and with weight that is predominantly into the ground with emphasis on bent knees. The torso is typically relaxed and expression tends to be carried by gesture. There is also a general informality, even lack of respect, between male/female Jets partners.

At the beginning of 'Mambo!', the Sharks' women present a formidable line as they edge forward using small shifts of weight with pronounced hip movement, skirts held in one hand and the other raised flamenco style above the head, palm facing up and out, chin raised, suggesting pride in their cultural identity. Their movement is contained and sensuous, emphasizing the body with hip wriggles and partnering, when it occurs, that maintains close body contact, before they cut loose with high kicks and swishing skirts. In response, the Jets perform long low runs towards the Sharks to reclaim their space, then funky chicken head bobs towards each other; their stag leaps with bull's horns arms are a more stylized version of the Sharks' signature moves. Jets have male and female placed further apart, which belies their otherwise less formal gender relations.

The 'Dance Off'

In the 'dance off' between Bernardo/Anita and Riff/Graziella, the differences become even more pronounced. Bernardo and Anita develop intricate footwork and precise placement; Riff and Graziella, on the other hand, develop their dance in terms of acrobatic moves, athleticism, high energy and risk. Anita performs a low backbend with one leg extended behind while Bernardo displays her as he would in a popular paso doble. Their partnered lift, however, is reminiscent of a classical *pas de deux* finale, with Anita held triumphant on Bernardo's shoulder. Meanwhile, Riff performs cartwheels and back flips; Graziella multiple *chaîné* turns. In their respective duets, emphasis is on Anita in her couple and on Riff in the Jets couple.

The music, as it shifts from Maria's spinning into the dancing, is strongly rhythmical and harmonically harsh. The clash of major and minor triads, set up in the 'Prologue', creates dissonances that can be seen to relate to the gang rivalry itself: each is strong and persistent, neither is decisively dominant. The major/minor dichotomy underlies the dialogue after this, ensuring that the sense of threat, instability and conflict is kept very much alive through the background music.

The mambo music itself is characterized by the constant shifting of tonality, exemplified by the conflict between the keys of C and A and the resulting dissonances produced through the harmonic clashes between C natural and C sharp. While the different key areas could be aligned with the different gangs, it is rarely that straightforward. More often, a shift in key denotes a shift in mood, an increase in dramatic tension, and in totality embodies a sense of the precarious balance of power between the gangs, thus suggesting the equally unstable and ambiguous position of adolescence.

The orchestration mirrors these inflections quite subtly. Brass and percussion are prominent during the Jets' dance; strings and, to a lesser extent, orchestral woodwinds (flute, oboe, clarinet and bassoon, which are more stereotypically 'classical' in connotation) accompany the Sharks, at least at first. As the dance progresses, however, solo virtuoso trumpet figures accompany the Sharks' increasingly virtuoso dance, reminiscent of both jazz with its 'Latin tinge' and Hispanic popular dances. The 'hate' theme, in various instantiations, frames the entire scene. Dance equivalents of the tension, conflict and aggression evoked through the music may be seen in syncopation and abrupt changes of dynamic; however, both dance vocabulary and music demonstrate unequivocally that both groups are essentially the same adolescents, exhibiting their human frailty as well as positive, albeit misplaced, youthful energy.

High-Low Inversions

We have argued that the movement vocabulary of the gangs, and the music that accompanies them, have similarities and differences that are manipulated in order to advance the narrative, but also blur the distinctions between cultural boundaries in significant ways. If we look more closely at the movement styles that Robbins draws on, we see that the clash of embodied value systems leads to complexity and ambiguity and to conclusions that may challenge our assumptions still further.

In the late 1940s and 1950s, mambo music played by bands such as those of Machito and his Afro Cuban Band and Puerto Rican Tito Puente became popular, first in Mexico then in New York.[24] Big bands, sheet music and dance instruction booklets became commonplace as the 'craze' for mambo dancing

---

[24] But Wells notes 'As white bands had started taking over Latin music, many of the bandleaders and musicians were Jews, notably Alfredo Mendez, whose real name was Mendelsohn' (Wells, 'West Side Story and the Hispanic', S28).

blossomed, and everyone wanted to learn the latest version. As Wells relates, 'the 1950s provided the broadest consumer market yet for pleasure dancing and its attendant romance'.[25] The widespread popularity of the dance led to variations and developments, with faster beats, and the use of side steps which formed the basis of cha-cha. Both mambo and cha-cha were extremely popular in the 1950s and 1960s and are characterized by 'Cuban' hip motion which accentuates the change of weight forward and back, and the expressive use of arms, legs, head and hands.

But another dance craze, the jitterbug, was significant to Robbins, and used as a basis for the Jets' movement style. The jitterbug had developed in Harlem during the late 1920s and 1930s and had later been popularized all over Europe via American GIs.[26] Constance Valis Hill describes it as:

> [m]ore than a step, the jitterbug was a style, a state of mind: a violent, even frenzied athleticism made it hazardous, exciting, sexual, cathartic; the jitterbugger became synonymous with the 'hepcat', a swing addict.[27]

The jitterbug, with its sense of physical abandon and loss of control, implicitly questioned the inherited social order and traditional value system of the old world; with the post-war era 1945-55 becoming known as the 'jitterbug years'.[28] Nadine George Graves argues that ragtime's adoption of African-influenced dance, and the appropriation of black music and dance by a white audience, was a way of relaxing Victorian strictures in the early part of the twentieth century, whilst still maintaining power of the dominant class and ethnic group.[29] The adoption of jitterbug, jive and jazz by 1950s youth can be seen then to mirror this appropriation: with the dominant group adopting 'black dance' in order to relax post-war austerity, while nonetheless maintaining the status quo in terms of racialized power structures. The European immigrant Jets embrace jitterbug dance moves such as back flips and hip swings together with a loss of inhibition demonstrated both in a relaxed use of the body and informal gender relations and these moves derive from Afro-Caribbean dance. In contrast, when the competition intensifies, the Sharks at first increase their virtuoso 'classical' style, suggesting a desire on their part to return to a European aesthetic. This may be interpreted as a desire to assimilate into the dominant culture (echoing the sentiments of Anita and friends in 'America') or

---

[25]   Wells, 'West Side Story and the Hispanic', S11.

[26]   Marshall and Jean Stearns, *Jazz Dance. A Story of American Vernacular Dance* (London, 1968).

[27]   Constance Valis Hill, 'From Bharata Natyam to Bop: Jack Cole's "Modern" Jazz Dance', *Dance Research Journal*, 33/2 (Winter 2001), p. 29.

[28]   Adrian Padmore, dir. *The Jitterbug Years*, Bristol (2005).

[29]   Nadine George Graves, '"Just Like Being at the Zoo": Primitivity and Ragtime Dance', in Julie Malnig (ed.), *Ballroom, Boogie, Shimmy Sham, Shake: A Social and Popular Dance Reader* (Urbana, IL, 2009), pp. 55-71.

as an ironic reversal of New World values. That both gangs in the end share and freely exchange these values speaks of their shared humanity, energy and frailty.

Critique of Hierarchical Values

Throughout *West Side Story*, we have seen that Robbins tends to characterize the Sharks by referring to flamenco, with its expressive use of the shoulders, feet stamps, hand claps marking hemiola rhythms and use of the skirt. We also see the hip-accentuated weight changes that are typical of mambo. However, the similarity between flamenco's upright use of the body and ballet technique that is also Robbins's staple technique means that the Puerto Ricans fuse the characteristics of popular dance forms with a dominant European aesthetic. And this link is supported further through the musical orchestration at moments throughout the story, when a more classical emphasis on strings and woodwind coincides with key points in the Sharks' drama.[30]

In contrast, the Jets' movement characteristics include a relaxed torso intermingled with extreme bursts of energy; rounded torso with shoulders forward and a frequently hunched 'what's your problem?' gesture; and finger clicks, which are just behind the beat and therefore links them to a jazz aesthetic, with its roots in Afro-Caribbean (albeit appropriated) and European immigrant culture. Dixon Gottschild contrasts Afro-Caribbean and European dance qualities in relation to their respective aesthetic value: 'In a broad sense, the Africanist aesthetic can be termed an aesthetic of contrariety, while the European perspective seeks to remove conflict through efficient problem solving. The Africanist aesthetic embraces difference and dissonance, rather than erasing or resolving it',[31] and these are interesting connections to make in relation to Jets' and Sharks' movement vocabulary when seen in the context of each group's social aspirations. Jets' moves are interspersed with fast multiple turns, vertical jumps and acrobatic moves. But their movement strikes a strong contrast between physical control and explosive, destructive anger, characteristics that are later developed in 'Cool', the Jets' signature piece. Again, the musical emphasis on brass and varied percussion gives an insolently extrovert effect at times, in comparison with the Sharks' music. Sharks, on the other hand, speak almost invariably of elegance and control interspersed with smouldering passion rather than anger, and these elements are developed further in their signature piece, 'America'. Dixon Gottschild develops her thesis in relation to American identity: 'The Africanist presence is a defining

---

[30]   In the 'Prologue', after his first humiliating meeting with the Jets, Bernardo's sharp turn to the wall, fist clenched, is accompanied by *sforzando* tremolo strings, a new musical idea which differs from the brass and percussion jazz-inflected rhythmical material up to this point, and is strongly evocative of a late-romantic symphonic sensibility.

[31]   Dixon Gottschild, 'Stripping the Emperor', p. 332.

ingredient that separates American ballet from its European counterpart'.[32] In other words, Bernstein and Robbins aligned their gangs with American values, values that included African and European influence among others, but that sought to assimilate all these influences into an identifiably American culture.

It comes as no surprise then that Bernstein and Robbins give the 'Polacks', the poor second-generation European immigrants, the characteristics of black dance for their group and individual identities, but they give the Puerto Ricans the cultural characteristics of the European court in what we argue is a knowingly ironic inversion, because their overriding concern is to express an inclusive American identity. These features are reinforced and echoed in the deeper structures of the musical. Robbins and Bernstein were not only playing with national identity and power relations, but also subverting notions of national identity and renegotiating the tension between European and Cuban/Puerto Rican cultural identity.[33] This point is made all the more cogent when we remember that all the collaborators on *West Side Story* were of Jewish émigré stock, so that addressing questions of belonging and presenting a challenge to the status quo becomes an even more critical project.[34]

Added to which, Robbins was acutely aware as a bisexual of his 'otherness' and, in relation to police hostility and brutality throughout the film, Frances Negrón-Muntaner reminds us that 'the force was a constant enemy of the gay community of New York during the 1950s',[35] just as the police throughout *West Side Story* are presented as a common enemy to the gangs.

Through it all, Robbins and Bernstein offer a perspective that is both sympathetic to the passions of the liminal post-war generation and able to recognize and draw attention to the tragic irony of a situation in which the protagonists share so much more than divides them. Common movement sources (ballet, especially, but also the 'Latin' aspect that infuses both Puerto Rican Spanish heritage and modern American jazz), and a cultural blend, (albeit different blends for each) are what the gangs share, as each gang draws on its own heritage and on modern/contemporary trends in a quest for identity. Both disdain the 'establishment', whether in the form of the police or the social worker Glad Hand. Central to the film's plot is the issue of American identity: an identity that, despite superficial appearances, is far more inclusive than exclusive.

[32]   Dixon Gottschild, 'Stripping the Emperor', p. 336.
[33]   As Wells argues, '[the music] sounds American while still allowing for "difference" between the warring factions', 'West Side Story and the Hispanic', S39.
[34]   On Jewish assimilation and African American appropriation, see Negrón-Montaner, 'Feeling Pretty', p. 90.
[35]   Negrón-Montaner, 'Feeling Pretty', p. 97.

Chapter 10

Talking Machines, Dancing Bodies: Marketing Recorded Dance Music before World War I[1]

Susan C. Cook

In February of 1914, the Victor Talking Machine Company hired white social dancers Irene and Vernon Castle (1893-1969 and 1887-1918, respectively) as spokespersons for its growing catalogue of dance recordings. The Castles had already achieved a national presence through popularizing new kinds of African American-derived dancing. Seeking to capitalize on over three years of growing consumer demand for syncopated music and one-step dances, company executives wrote enthusiastically to their local dealers about this partnership of celebrity dancing bodies and recorded popular music:

> This is a diplomatic 'coup' which must have a very pronounced effect on business. The Castles have a national fame and Victor dance records a national reputation. Imagine what the combination means to you.[2]

By 1914, recording technology had produced unexpected possibilities for the consumption of popular musics previously dependent on live entertainments, mass-marketed sheet music and factory-produced instruments. Ragtime, in particular, was the first widely popular social dance activity to be able to utilize the availability of recorded sound. As ragtime dance and the recording industry's coming of age converged, the technology provided new modes of agency for the popular and its bodies to circulate through both increasing access and legitimating desire. Victor's likening of their business arrangement to an act of political diplomacy, however, reveals continuing tensions between those dancing bodies and musical technology. Through a close reading of recording industry primary sources in conjunction with the Castles' career, I seek to interpret this act of embodied diplomacy and with it the constitutive and contested practices of dance, music and technology.

---

[1]   I could not have written this essay without a Hagley-Winterthur Fellowship for Arts and Industry and access to The Radio Corporation of America/Victor Division Records (hereafter RCA/Victor Records) in the Hagley Museum and Library, Wilmington, DE.

[2]   'Victor Letters to the Trade', *The Voice of the Victor*, 9/4 (1914), p. 76. The letter quoted here is dated 24 February 1914.

From Minstrelsy to Ragtime

The co-generative point of departure for ragtime dance and music was the nineteenth-century blackface minstrel show whose depictions of plantation slavery had become a transatlantic export by 1850.[3] According to Jeffrey Magee, the terms 'rag' and 'ragtime' did not appear in print as musical terms until 1896.[4] Many of the piano 'rags' published in the late 1890s and into the first decade of the twentieth century, including those by foremost contributor Scott Joplin, carried additional subtitles such as 'cakewalk', 'march', 'two-step' and 'slow drag', generic labels that clearly embed the music within movement and dance.

Central to the popularity of these repertories was syncopation, an aural sign of racial difference, whose rhythmic energy produced new kinds of movements articulated through an increasing number of body parts. Like the African American culture from which it came, ragtime remained simultaneously exciting and fearful to white practitioners and cultural observers. As early as 1900, *Etude*, a music publication long associated with middle-class norms, referred to ragtime as 'an insane craze', a 'virulent poison' and 'a musical impurity', terms that reflect the deep-seated fears behind racialized difference and especially racial mixing.[5]

Fears, notwithstanding, within a decade, the term 'ragtime' denoted a sub-genre of popular songs available in sheet music, featured in live entertainments and recorded by popular white performers. These songs, such as Irving Berlin's best-selling *Alexander's Ragtime Band* (1911), featured self-referential texts that drew attention to their syncopated vitality and celebrated the music's popularity across race, class and even national lines as an accompaniment for social dancing. Unlike the 'coon songs' that had preceded them, these songs suggested that ragtime could be more inclusively 'American' than African American, a position often made clear in accompanying illustrations. Whereas sheet music covers for rags and 'coon songs' often featured minstrelsy-like caricatures of African American couples performing the cakewalk or other dances, the covers of ragtime songs depicted youthful, frequently upper-class, white Americans engaged in dance. Ragtime, these songs implied, was an embodied, widespread and desirable practice.[6]

---

[3]   On blackface minstrelsy in England, see Derek B. Scott, 'Blackface Minstrels, Black Minstrels, and their Reception in England', in Rachel Cowgill and Julian Rushton (eds), *Europe, Empire, and Spectacle in Nineteenth-Century British Music* (Aldershot, 2006), pp. 265–80; Rachel Cowgill, 'On the Beat: The Victorian Policeman as Musician', in Martin Hewitt and Rachel Cowgill (eds), *Victorian Soundscapes Revisited* (Leeds, 2007), pp. 191–214; and Michael Pickering, *Blackface Minstrelsy in Britain* (Aldershot, 2008).

[4]   Jeffrey Magee, 'Ragtime and Early Jazz', in David Nicholls (ed.), *The Cambridge History of American Music* (Cambridge, 1998), p. 389.

[5]   'Musical Impurity', *Etude*, 18 (January 1900): p. 16. See also W. F. Gates, 'Ethiopian Syncopation', *Musician* 7 (1902): p. 341.

[6]   For additional interpretations of these complicated racialized practices and discourses, see Danielle Robinson, 'Performing American: Ragtime Dancing as Participatory

The trotting one-step dances and the ragtime songs that extolled them, emerged into the public sphere through transnational staged entertainments and localized participatory practices. By 1910, according to historian Kathy Peiss, in New York City alone, over 500 dance halls regularly provided opportunities for participation.[7] In 1911, Louise de Koven Bowen, writing as head of the Juvenile Protective Association in Chicago, estimated that as many as 86,000 individuals regularly attended some 300 dance venues available in that city.[8] The vast majority of the participants were teenage working-class boys and girls for whom dancing was a central pleasure in lives spent in tedious low-paid factory work. This dancing activity provoked comment from progressivist social reformers, like Bowen, her Chicago colleague Jane Addams and others, for its wiggling and shaking movements, its closed partner hug holds, and the commercialized venues in which it took place. Along with Bowen, New York City-based reformer Belle Israels argued that this new dancing, especially when presented in unchaperoned urban spaces in proximity to commercialized vice, held real dangers for the sexually-emergent, pleasure-seeking, working-class women who might choose prostitution as an alternative to factory work.[9]

While first associated with working-class 'girl' culture, the new dancing proved to be socially mobile, across both class and regional lines. By January 1914, Ethel Watts Mumford asked the readers of *Harper's Magazine*, 'Where Is Your Daughter this Afternoon?'[10] Daughters of the middle and upper classes, Mumford maintained, now attended afternoon tea dances at upscale hotels that increasingly resembled the informal spaces of working-class dance halls. Unchaperoned daughters, Mumford cautioned, had taken to 'the careless forming of undesirable acquaintances, the breaking down of barriers of necessary caution'; without guidance or the constraints previously present in the family-controlled ballroom, these dancing daughters literally threatened to overstep social boundaries. The inherent repeatability and portability afforded by talking-machine technology both created new modes and practices of dancing and contributed to ragtime dance's desirability.

Minstrelsy', *Dance Chronicle*, 32 (2009): pp. 89-126 and Nadine George-Graves, '"Just Like Being at the Zoo": Primitivity and Ragtime Dance', in Julie Malnig (ed.), *Ballroom, Boogie, Shimmy Sham, Shake: A Social and Popular Dance Reader* (Urbana, 2009).

[7] Kathy Peiss, *Cheap Amusements: Working Women and Leisure in Turn-of-the-Century New York* (Philadelphia, 1986), p. 88.

[8] Louise de Koven Bowen, *Our Most Popular Recreation Controlled by the Liquor Interests. A Study of Public Dance Halls* ([Chicago], 1911).

[9] One of Israels's earliest reports is 'The Dance Hall and the Amusement Resorts', *Transactions of the American Society of Sanitary and Moral Prophylaxis*, 3 (1910): pp. 46-50.

[10] Ethel Watts Mumford, 'Where is Your Daughter this Afternoon?' *Harper's Weekly*, 17 January 1914, p. 28.

Talking Machines: From Penny Arcade to Parlour

Historians of technology credit Thomas A. Edison with the invention of the phonograph, a term he patented in the US along with his cylinder-playing machine in 1877.[11] Alexander Graham Bell, his cousin Chichester A. Bell and Charles Tainter, as well as Emile Berliner, developed the possibilities of recorded sound beyond Edison's initial experiments. By 1885, the Bells and Tainter had perfected Edison's cylinder with their graphophone. Berliner's gramophone, patented in 1887, abandoned Edison's cylinder altogether for the disc and lateral movements within stabilizing grooves, the technology that dominated the market by the teens and remained in place until the advent of the compact disc. After complex patent battles among subsidiaries, licensees, patent-sharers, managers and agents, recorded sound technology became a commercially viable industry by the turn of the twentieth century. Machinist Eldridge R. Johnson, who had worked with Emile Berliner and had patented his own disc machine innovations, created the Victor Talking Machine Company in 1901 which became the industry giant in the US and forged powerful European connections.

Although with hindsight we can see how influential this technology would become, those involved at the time were not so sure. What was a talking machine, be it phonograph, graphophone, or gramophone, good for? More importantly, who would buy it and why? Edison's telegraph had found immediate utility in an increasingly geographically displaced, industrialized US society, and he prioritized business applications for his recording invention, through the preservation of speech, something his cylinder technology uniquely allowed.[12] Edison's company marketed the phonograph, the name itself derived from the earlier technologies of telephone and telegraph, to record, reproduce and preserve important talk; hence the generic term for the machines as 'talkers'. For home use, Edison envisioned preserving the voices of loved ones as a kind of aural photograph.[13]

---

[11]   For decades, Roland Gelatt's *The Fabulous Phonograph 1877-1977*, 2nd rev. ed (New York, 1977), remained the sole social history of recorded sound. More recent studies include André Millard, *America on Record: A History of Recorded Sound* (Cambridge, 1995); William Howland Kenney, *Recorded Music in American Life: The Phonograph and Popular Memory, 1890-1945* (Oxford, 1999); David Morton, *Off the Record: The Technology and Culture of Sound Recording in America* (New Brunswick, 2000); and David Suisman, *Selling Sounds: the Commercial Revolution in American Music* (Cambridge, MA, 2009). I also benefited from Marsha Siefert's 'The Audience at Home: The Early Recording Industry and the Marketing of Musical Taste', in James S. Ettema and D. Charles Whitney (eds), *Audiencemaking: How the Media Create the Audience* (Thousand Oaks MI, 1994), pp. 186-214, and 'Aesthetics, Technology, and the Capitalization of Culture: How the Talking Machine Became a Musical Instrument', *Science in Context*, 8/2 (1995): pp. 417-49.

[12]   Gelatt, *That Fabulous Phonograph*, pp. 29; 45. See also Frederick J. Garbit, *The Phonograph and Its Inventor, Thomas Alvah [sic] Edison* (Boston, 1878), pp. 9-10.

[13]   The unnamed author of the *The Phonograph and How to Use It* provides as an example of this home use, a grieving mother listening to a recording of her deceased child

In contrast, by 1894 Emile Berliner predicted 'whole evenings will be spent at home going through a long list of interesting performances'.[14] He and others recognized the talking machine's commercial potential within the entertainment industry. In venues from travelling shows to penny arcades, talking machines offered consumers novel aural experiences for a low price. With the development of increasingly simpler and less expensive machines, companies saw that the future lay in creating a demand for musical experiences in the private home. Recordings now acquired greater significance as a means to keep consumers engaged and encourage the purchase of higher-priced machines. As the talking machine entered a domesticated market associated with leisure, it competed with the piano and parlour organ for dominance. Victor capitalized on the domestic market with the development of its Victrola whose cabinet construction hid its machinery, rendering it, as its Vice President and General Manager Leon F. Douglass noted, more suitable to the parlour and to the women who were largely in charge of domestic consumption.[15] Shut out from industrial use, talking machines thus became intrinsically linked to the feminine domestic sphere, mass marketed novelty and the quotidian popular.

Marketing 'Good Music'

In the early years of the twentieth century, the recording industry in the US along with its European partners and subsidiaries utilized the growing possibilities of advertising by harnessing what Holly Kruse describes as, 'the expectations, aspirations, and fears of potential phonograph buyers'.[16] As early as 1903, Victor's Douglass launched aggressive promotional campaigns, such as double-paged advertisements in the *Saturday Evening Post*.[17] Companies built upon a pre-existing discourse of 'good music', developing a position that conferred legitimacy

---

(New York: National Phonograph Company, 1900), p. 137.

[14] Emile Berliner, 'The Gramophone: Paper Read before the Franklin Institute, May 16, 1888 by its inventor', Washington DC, 1894, p. 19.

[15] Leon F. Douglass, 'Memoirs', unpublished manuscript, excerpts in RCA/Victor Records, series II/50, chapter VIII, p. 1, in the Hagley Museum and Library, Wilmington, DE. See also 'Catering to Women', *The Talking Machine World*, 9/3 (1913): p. 12. Kenney also explores aspects of women consumers in 'The Gendered Phonograph', in *Recorded Music in American Life*.

[16] Holly Kruse, 'Early Audio Technology and Domestic Space', *Stanford Humanities Review*, 3/2 (1993): p. 6.

[17] Victor frequently advertised the amount of money it spent on advertising, and later company histories identify advertising as central to Victor's success and one of the company's contributions to twentieth-century business practices. See Robert Frothingham, 'Little Advertising Stories: The Victor', *Everybody's Magazine*, July 1910, 80d-80h; William H. Jenkins, *The Romance of Victor* ([n.p.], 1927), pp. 7-8; and B. L. Aldridge, 'Victor's First Contributions to Recorded Music', RCA/Victor Records, series III/58, II/78.

on their technology as a purveyor of edification and distanced it from suspect leisure entertainment. Talking machines became a technology of betterment, of moral uplift, of social refinement and respectability.

Nowhere is the concern for talking machine legitimacy and reliance on musical goodness more apparent than in *The Talking Machine World* (hereafter *TMW*), an industry-wide trade publication that appeared in January 1905 under the editorship of Edward Lyman Bill (1862-1916). While the main editorial office was in New York City, with branches in Boston, Chicago and San Francisco, by the second year of publication, Bill celebrated the increasingly transnational nature of the industry and opened an office in London. *TMW* reported on the uses of talking machines and the activities of individual dealers, discussed patents, promoted marketing and advertising techniques, offered information about the care and repair of machines, and provided advance lists of recordings. Bill's editorials championed industry-wide advances and addressed the emerging technology's place in twentieth-century consumer culture.

For the first five years of *TMW*'s existence Bill's editorials largely defended talking machines against perceptions that they were a frivolous novelty associated with cheap entertainments. While he often included abstract statements about the value and nature of good music, related stories provided evidence of the ideology in action. In the second issue of *TMW*, for example, the article 'Exercises a Moral Influence' demonstrates how the talking machine became an instrument of civilization:

> The best part of it all is that such instruments [talking machines] are a decided moral benefit to those on shipboard. The lives of sailors are lives of dreary solitude and hard work, and this is the reason why, as soon as they reach land, they made for some low dance hall, where there is a barrel organ, a cracked piano or accordeon [sic] grinding out music of a character more villainous even than the surroundings in which it is played.[18]

As this quotation makes clear, good music's morally superior position, now aided by the talking machine, requires a dichotomous Other here specifically associated with the dancing body and its disreputable music. In similar stories appearing throughout the run of the journal, white, Anglo-European males introduce talking machines and good music recordings, rarely identified by name, to foreign natives with predictable and profitable outcomes: the natives enjoy 'our' good music and thus willingly provide the natural resources or labour desired by the white businessmen.[19]

---

[18] 'Exercises a Moral Influence', *The Talking Machine World* [hereafter *TMW*], 1/2 (1905): p. 21.

[19] A brief sample of such stories includes: 'Talking Machine a Civilizer: C. P. Sterns Tells of Trip Through the Philippine Islands in Which a Talking Machine Played a Star Part', *TMW*, 1/8 (1905): p. 7; 'Helps to Spread Civilization', *TMW*, 2/7 (1906): p. 5; 'Music

Whether described as teacher, comfort, cultivator or 'decided moral benefit', the trope of the civilizing talking machine relied on beliefs about the affective power of 'good' music on a receptive listening subject through a mediating technology that replaced actual performing bodies. Not surprisingly, pre-existing and inequitable power relations of race, class and gender further shaped this technological mediation. Hierarchical listening relationships existed in Edison's initial formulations where he identified his invention as both preserving and creating the important business talk of the presumptive white male: 'I am sure [it] makes men more brief, more business-like, and more straightforward'.[20] In a 1907 pamphlet touting the use of his business phonograph, the relationship between powerful talk and a responsive listening subject was explicitly raced and gendered. As the pamphlet subtitle 'From Brain to Type' suggested and the accompanying cover illustration clearly showed, the mindful white businessman talked while the white female stenographer listened and responded as directed.[21]

Differential power relationships became central to the corporate image of the Victor Talking Machine Company through its trademark of Nipper the dog listening to 'His Master's Voice'.[22] Nipper is obedient to and tamed by the sound of power. Other illustrations from the Victor corporate archives and used on occasion in early advertisements replaced Nipper with images of the passive female consumer and the feminized male alien reflecting again racialized and gendered power relations between sound and sounded upon.[23] Talking machines not only reproduced the power relationships of the master's voice but through the master's good music provided the sound of civilization.

Beginning in 1903 Victor exploited the possibilities of the 'good' music market further through its Red Seal recordings of European opera singers.[24] Heavily

---

at the North Pole', *TMW*, 1/2 (1905): p. 10; and 'Chinese Phonograph Records', *TMW*, 1/1 (1905): p. 6.

[20]   Thomas A. Edison, 'Introduction', in George E. Tewksbury, *A Complete Manual of the Edison Phonograph* (Newark, 1897), p. 12.

[21]   *The Edison Commercial System Conducted with the Business Phonograph* (Orange, NJ, 1907): pp. 8-9. This relationship could remove the troublesome female body altogether, as an earlier Edison publication noted: 'Instead of talking to a giddy and unreliable young lady stenographer ... the letter is talked, just the same, into the specially prepared cylinders' (*The Phonograph and How to Use It*, p. 140). See also Morton, 'Girl or Machine?: Gender, Labor, Office Dictation, and the Failure of Recording Culture', in *Off the Record*, pp. 74-107.

[22]   Victor celebrated Nipper, based on a painting by Francis Barraud and first used by Emile Berliner's Gramophone Company before being registered by Victor in 1900, as 'the best-known trademark in the world' and protected it against the claims of Berliner's descendants that they had unfairly appropriated the image. See copies of correspondence between Oliver Berliner, Emile's grandson, and B. L. Aldridge dated from 2 December 1955 to 27 February 1956 in RCA/Victor Records, series II/35.

[23]   Illustrations found in RCA/Victor Records, series III/49.

[24]   For more on Red Seal recordings, see my essay '"In imitation of my negro mammy": Alma Gluck and the American Prima Donna', in Rachel Cowgill and Hilary Poriss (eds),

advertised, Red Seal recordings cost more as befitted their luxury status. However, as Victor acknowledged to the inner circle readers of *TMW* in 1905, popular recordings regularly outsold Red Seal offerings but there was 'good advertising in Grand Opera'.[25] Higher-priced Red Seal records conferred refinement upon both consumers and an industry refashioning itself from purveyor of novelties to purveyor of prestige. Victor's advertisements continued to present distinctions between the kinds of entertainment it offered, especially when illustrating the idealized Victor consumer. One lavish full-colour advertisement from 1913 shows an obviously well-to-do white couple in evening dress seated in front of a Victrola.[26] As if conjured from the machine, diminutive versions of the Red Seal recording stars appear before them while caricatures of popular recording stars, including a character in blackface, lurk behind the well-appointed furnishings of the private parlour; at best, popular music offered entertainment from the margins.

Not surprisingly *TMW*, with its editorial rejection of novelty, carried stories about 'discordant ragtime' and the need to educate listeners beyond their 'ruinous' popular music tastes.[27] Just as ragtime dancing emerged more fully in public venues of all kinds, a front-page story from April 1911 claimed: 'the only way to develop musical taste is to give people what they can take in and then gently lead them to better things'. The article argued further that even those 'in the deepest stage of ragtime' would eventually come to greater self-respect through access to good music provided by talking machines.[28]

'Loud Enough for Dancing'[29]

Industry discourse aside, company catalogues from the beginning reveal how early recordings, like live entertainments in the US overall, remained linked to the performance of racial, ethnic and class difference. Popular material harking back to the nineteenth-century minstrel show appears in abundance. Recordings of dance music were available virtually from the beginning as well. An 1899 Edison catalogue, for example, offered more than 75 dance selections that, although

---

The Arts of the Prima Donna, 1720-1920 (Oxford, 2012), pp. 290-307.

[25]   Victor Talking Machine Co. Advertisement, *TMW*, 1/10 (1905): p. 36. The advertisement states: 'There are four Victor pages in this issue. Three show pictures of operatic artists; one shows pictures of popular artists. Three to one-our business is just the other way, and more, too; but there is good advertising in Grand Opera.'

[26]   Supplement to *The Music Trades*, 7 June 1913. The caption indicates that it would be used in the *Saturday Evening Post, Collier's* and elsewhere. RCA/Victor Records, series IX, Advertising Scrapbook, 1913-1915, p. 64.

[27]   'The Talking Machine as a Musical Educator', *TMW*, 4/5 (1908): p. 51; and 'The "Talker" as an Educator', *TMW*, 4/5 (1908): p. 3.

[28]   'Developing Musical Taste', *TMW*, 7/4 (1911): p. 3.

[29]   Victor advertising caption appearing on the back cover of the *Saturday Evening Post*, 177 (24 September 1904).

dominated by waltzes included several two-steps such as 'Ragged Williams Two-Step', derived from Rossini's opera *William Tell*, and an early example of what would later be referred to as 'ragging the classics'.[30] A 1903 Victor catalogue prominently featured Sousa's Band and its recording of the cakewalk 'At A Georgia Camp Meeting' popularized through its worldwide tours. The company also acknowledged 'an increasing demand for records for dancing' and the creation of a specialized dance orchestra.[31] The following year Victor published a separate list of recordings made by its Dance Orchestra, including 25 selections suitable for the two-step or cakewalk. The cover illustration of a large well-dressed dancing crowd and a prominent talking machine carried the caption, 'What could be more charming than a social dance on the porch or lawn with a Victor to furnish the music!'[32]

Companies increasingly used dance music to sell machines, advertising their products with images and stories that, like the example above, demonstrated how talking machines replaced live ensembles and created private dance events at the control of the consumer. As the duple-metre trotting dances gained popularity, industry advertising continued to circulate images of the upper-class dancing couple and their modern private leisure activities made possible by high-priced talking machine technology.[33] By 1913, even as *TMW*'s editorials and feature stories still touted musical goodness, reports from distributors across the US and Europe provided additional evidence of the potent realities of talking machines, popular music and ragtime dance. In February, *TMW*'s London editor reported that 'distributors [of a line of ragtime recordings] have reaped a rich harvest of sales, and the boom is still on'.[34] Two months later a report from Detroit noted that the 'demand for "tangoes" and "turkey trot" records continues unabated'.[35] In August, a Philadelphia merchant reported strong sales of dance records made all the more newsworthy because his store was 'one of the closest to the aristocratic district of the city and enjoys an exclusive trade'.[36]

In September 1913, Columbia advertised recordings from *The Sunshine Girl*, a show that first achieved success on the London stage and had opened in New York City during the previous season. Starring Vernon Castle as the comic secondary male lead, the show featured both Castles, fresh from success in Paris,

---

[30]   *Edison Records* (Boston, 1899), pp. 14-16.
[31]   *Record Catalogue: Victor and Monarch Records*. RCA/Victor Records, series III/28.
[32]   *Victor Dance Records* ([n.p.: n.d.]), p. 76. Trade catalogue in the Hagley Museum and Library Collection; based on the record numbers listed and Steve Barr's *The Almost Complete 78 RPM Record Dating Guide* (Huntington Beach, CA, 1991), the recordings were issued in January and June of 1904 and thus the catalogue likely appeared in the second half of 1904.
[33]   *The Voice of the Victor*, 2/1 (1907): p. 12.
[34]   'From Our London Headquarters', *TMW*, 9/2 (1913): p. 40.
[35]   'From Our Chicago Headquarters', *TMW*, 9/4 (1913): p. 21.
[36]   'August a Productive Month in Philadelphia', *TMW*, 9/9 (1913): p. 50.

demonstrating syncopated trotting dances. Vernon also performed a tango with the leading lady Julia Sanderson and, within weeks of the premiere, newspaper stories recounted his talent as a dance instructor charging as much as $1 a minute.[37] Within months the Castles, through a variety of live performance venues and careful use of print media, became active proponents of new modes of 'refined' participatory social dancing even as criticism about its racially-marked ragtime music and accompanying practices continued.[38]

By January of 1914, *TMW* noted the overall strength of Christmas sales of dance records, and Columbia announced an innovative series of dance instruction recordings that emphasized the repeatable and domesticated nature of talking machine technology:

> You know very well that there are hundreds of thousands of people in this country who would be dancing if only they could learn all alone in their own homes without going to the expense of private lessons or the publicity of class lessons.[39]

The featured dances – the one-step, tango, hesitation waltz and maxixe – included those regularly demonstrated by the Castles, although Columbia drew on the expertise of teacher G. Hepburn Wilson.[40]

Ever more portable and cheaper machines made dancing available, so advertisements claimed, to practically anyone at any time, even to consumers outside urban areas. Trade journals increasingly carried stories that celebrated how talking machines created dance venues in hotel lobbies, at summer resorts, in private homes, in offices or workplaces over lunch or after hours, and in college dorms where coeds alternately studied and practised the latest steps.[41] Dealers far removed from big cities utilized talking machines to put on their own dance exhibitions and provide their rural customers with the latest popular, urban fare.[42]

[37] 'How to Dance the Tango,' *The Atlanta Georgian*, 27 March 1913; 'Teaching Dancing at $1 a Minute', *Atlanta Journal*, 16 March 1913; 'How to Dance the One Step', *Toledo News-Bee*, 2 April 1913; 'Tango According to Castle', *Metropolitan*, June 1913.

[38] For additional interpretations of the life and career of Vernon and Irene Castle, see my 'Watching Our Step: Embodying Research, Telling Stories', in Lydia Hamessley and Elaine Barkin (eds), *Audible Traces: Gender, Identity, and Music* (Zurich, 1999), pp. 177-212, and 'Passionless Dancing and the Passionate Reform: Respectability, Modernism, and the Social Dancing of Irene and Vernon Castle', in William Washabaugh (ed.), *The Passion of Music and Dance: Body, Gender, Sexuality* (Oxford, 1999), pp. 133-50.

[39] Advertisement, *TMW*, 10/6 (1914): pp. 30-31.

[40] Julie Malnig, 'Athena Meets Venus: Visions of Women in Social Dance in the Teens and Early 1920s', *Dance Research Journal*, 31/2 (1999): p. 39.

[41] 'Making the Vacation 99 9/10% Fun', *The Voice of the Victor*, 10/8 (1915): p. 154 featured a photo with the caption 'Lunch hour – Dancing the Tango'; 'Cincinnati Co-Eds Use Victrola," *The Voice of the Victor*, 10/10 (1915): p. 194.

[42] For example, *Voice of the Victor*, 9/6 (1914): p. 119, carried a photograph showing an outdoor dance floor created in Waco, Texas.

And dance instruction itself became an unexpected and profitable development stimulating sales of both machines and recordings. Talking machine technology reshaped spaces and created participatory opportunities by providing sounds previously unavailable or even impossible to have had otherwise.

While Columbia and Victor, and to a lesser extent Edison, consciously and even creatively marketed ragtime dance music and as their salespeople reported on sustained, unexpected and profitable demand for dance records, Bill's own *TMW* editorials betray a continuing ambivalence about the popular presence of ragtime dance. Not until April 1914, with the Castles on board for Victor and a full year after his own *TMW* reported on the growing demand for ragtime recordings, did he acknowledge the obvious: 'There is no part of America, so far as we are able to learn, where the dance craze has not appeared', and he agreed that the 'tango mania' had benefited the industry enormously.[43] His choice of the terms 'craze' and 'mania', while commonly used by other social critics, still betray the irrational, temporary and secondary status of social dance and the popular.

The Castles owed much of their success as live performers to the 'authentic' music supplied by their music director, the composer and conductor James Reese Europe and his 'Superior Colored Musicians', as his own letterhead proclaimed.[44] Already an established figure in the New York City entertainment world before his relationship with the Castles, Europe established the Clef Club in 1910 as an alternative booking agency for African American performers much sought after for their syncopated music but barred from membership in the official musicians' union. Europe's Society Orchestra appears to be the first African American ensemble to record, and they released eight sides on the Victor label from December 1913 to February 1914, including the popular one-steps *Too Much Mustard* and *Down Home Rag*.[45]

The Castles consciously marketed the refinement of their 'modern dancing' in opposition to 'rougher' working-class versions. Their 'suggestions for correct dancing' contained in Victor's instructional pamphlet *Three Modern Dances* provides a list of what *not* to do (such as wriggle the shoulders, twist the body, or stand too close together as a couple) as part of their movement aesthetic of 'dancing gracefully' and remaining in control of the movement, in contrast to the ragtime songs that extolled the improvisatory and 'out of control' possibilities seemingly inherent and desirable in the racially-marked music.[46] Well aware of the pervading discourse of racialized dance pathology and its fearsome social effects, the Castles and their apologists, notably their agent Elisabeth Marbury, relied on yet another discourse of uplift found in earlier nineteenth-century dance tutors and

---

[43] 'Editorial', *TMW*, 10/4 (1914): p. 13.

[44] Letters from James Reese Europe to Lee Shubert, 2 January 1915 and 15 March 1915, in the Shubert Archive, General Correspondence File, 1910-26: 1360.

[45] Reid Badger, in his definitive biography of Europe, provides a complete discography: see *A Life in Ragtime: A Biography of James Reese Europe* (New York, 1995), pp. 235-40.

[46] *Three Modern Dances* (Camden, NJ, 1914).

etiquette manuals.[47] Whereas talking machines provided access to good music, the Castles and their likeminded supporters claimed that dancing was a social 'good' because it afforded healthy exercise.

The Castles updated their health argument by drawing on then current understandings of neurasthenia, a disease that had been identified in the late nineteenth century as attacking society's 'brain-workers' – typically male, upper-class, white protestants.[48] Nervous, anxious neurasthenics suffered from the ill-effects of industrialized society; they were overly-civilized, overly-rational, sapped of strength and vitality. Their desk-based jobs threatened to render them both passive and impotent, and their enervated condition raised anxieties about low birth rates and racial suicide that were central to the Eugenics and anti-immigration discourses of the time.[49] Neurasthenics, like Theodore Roosevelt and Victor's own marketing executive Douglass, sought to balance the effects of over-cultivated rational white manhood with experiences of primitive nature, such as through the physical challenges of big game hunting.[50] However, while the male neurasthenic might restore his virility through the thrill of a carefully choreographed hunt, he did not give up his rights to race, class or gender privilege. Douglass, who celebrated the prowess of his hired, lower-class, hunting guide, did not seek to trade places with him after the hunt. Instead, following trips to Arizona and California, Douglass returned to corporate life renewed, invigorated and restored to rational mind and physical potency. Likewise, the Castles argued, when executed properly, ragtime dance and its syncopated music revitalized enervated white bodies. Their 'modern' dance practices harnessed syncopated 'coloured' vitality through their performance of rational self-control.

With the Castles on the cover, Victor's 1916 list of dance recordings demonstrates the considerable growth in its recorded dance offerings. Whereas their 1913 catalogue listed 20 one-step titles, three years later the number of one-step selections had grown to 133, of which 62 commanded the top fee of $1.25, and they provided an additional 54 selections for the newer fox trot. By 1916, however, Vernon Castle, a British citizen, had returned to England to join the RAF in a war that had already taken its toll. When the US entered the war the following year, James Reese Europe volunteered as well and recruited other

---

[47]   See in particular their *Modern Dancing* (New York, 1914).

[48]   George Beard's *American Nervousness: its Causes and Consequences. A Supplement to Nervous Exhaustion (Neurasthenia)* (New York, 1881) is a classic text. For a more recent treatment of the phenomenon, see Tom Lutz, *American Nervousness, 1903: An Anecdotal History* (Ithaca, 1991).

[49]   See Christina Cogdell, 'The Futurama Recontextualized: Norman Bel Geddes's Eugenic World of Tomorrow', *American Quarterly*, 53 (2000): pp. 193-245.

[50]   Three folders of personal correspondence between Leon Douglass and Eldridge R. Johnson, housed in the Johnson Victrola Museum, Dover, DE, document Douglass's nervous ill health and hunting trips the men took together. Letters from Douglass to Johnson, dated 11 September, 19 September, 20 October and 5 December of 1911; letter from Douglass's secretary to Johnson, 10 June 1915.

African American musicians to join him. Victor now turned its factories over to making rifle fittings, detonator cases and airplane wings. The industry boasted that fighting men took talking machines with them into battle where music once again served the cause of moral uplift, now marked by nationalism.[51]

'Imagine What the Combination Means to You'

To return to the opening quotation from Victor's letter to its dealers, what *did* the combination of the Castles' fame and Victor's reputation mean then, and what might it mean still today? Given the industry's reliance on the discourse of 'good music', Victor's identification of a company 'reputation' and the Castles' 'fame' maps once again onto a pernicious high/low dichotomy, one that doubly marked ragtime dance through its connection to the body and the culture of second-class African Americans. As the talking machine industry acknowledged on rare occasions though, being 'morally uplifting' did not guarantee success within a market-driven capitalist economy. In actuality, Red Seal recordings attracted fewer consumers. Ragtime dance, on the other hand, reinvigorated the industry both in sales of recordings and of the machines themselves. Yet even as the industry reaped unforeseen commercial success from dance music, it continued to perpetuate ideologies that music associated with embodied 'crazes' and leisure entertainment was of lesser value.

As it responded to consumer demand, however, the talking machine industry legitimated ragtime dancing in ways that ultimately challenged its own 'good music' binary. Ragtime dance could not have attained the unprecedented popularity it did without the new means of consumer access, control and artistic legitimation afforded by talking machines and an industry discourse of uplift. As advertisements constantly reminded the public, talking machines were purveyors of moral good and ownership of them conferred not only class status but provided the means to create and control the aural experience and, by extension, dance practices. Talking machine goodness thus resonated with the refinement discourse voiced by the Castles and others, redefining and reframing ragtime dance as a practice of white modernity. The technology provided a way for owners, listeners and dancers to rehearse and prepare for live events and to shape their own dance experiences in private homes or other semi-private spaces as an alternative to or in combination with public ones. In the presumptive middle-class home, the technology could both signal class prestige and effectively remove dance from its potentially disreputable connections with urban spaces where unchaperoned men and women of all classes might meet, mingle and touch. It likewise distanced the racialized bodies who made the music or were understood as originary to it, from

---

[51]   For a discussion of issues of social dance and masculinity surrounding Vernon Castle, James Reese Europe and others, see Cook, 'Passionless Dancing and Passionate Reform'.

the white dancing body. Talking machine technology acted as a kind of modern, industrial eraser, removing ragtime's most troubling bodies from the social dance experience.

While perpetuating the hierarchy of 'good' music, recording technology simultaneously provided new means for the popular and its bodies, both absent in recording and very real in what those recordings could signify, to circulate. And its moralizing technology ultimately disrupted the very hierarchy its creators sought to claim. In a way perhaps that Edison and others feared, recordings provided new accessibility to the affective power of a racially-marked music. In Edison's desire to preserve and reproduce important talk, his technology gave to those racially-marked objects of faddish entertainment a timelessness supposedly the preserve of 'good' music. Talking machines literally gave the power of the master's voice to African Americans whose appropriated music privileged the power of the dancing body. Consumers might be removed from actual physical contact with the Other, but by bringing James Reese Europe's ragtime music and its dance into their homes, they also made themselves newly vulnerable to the musically affective power and practices of those same threatening Others.

The contradictory and ambivalent response of the recording industry concerning ragtime dance echoes the larger discursive ambiguities of 'whiteness', 'manhood' and modernity itself. Like the neurasthenic modern, white male, talking machine culture relied upon a discourse of rationality, moral good and control while seeking commercial vitality in the supposed primitive. Soaring sales of dance recordings and machines, with their promises of participatory pleasure, acted like a restorative tonic for the industry. Regardless of what *TMW*'s Bill and others wrote, moral uplift and ragtime dance's racialized vitality were equally for sale; Victor and its fellow companies thus marketed both the modern disease and its necessary cure.

The talking machine industry unceasingly argued for its importance, but I would emphasize here that it has yet to acquire the 'manly' business legitimacy it so desired in its embrace of musical goodness. Recorded sound technology remains under-explored even by those of us it most serves, and the history of recorded sound is not yet central to a story of twentieth-century modernity, of skyscrapers and automobiles, of the captains of industry and their important business. Talking machines could not escape being judged on their own limited criteria of value. Like popular music and dance, white womanhood and people of colour, they occupied a place and a function, but with limited claims to cultural prestige. As the convergence of ragtime and recorded sound reveals, though, the much proclaimed power of the timeless is often no match for the embodied timely and its popular dance.

PART IV
Politics of the Popular

Chapter 11
Superficial Profundity: Performative Translation of the Dancing Body in Contemporary Taiwanese Popular Culture

Chih-Chieh Liu

Dance, arguably, is one of the most prominent phenomena in contemporary popular culture. From international superstars ranging from Madonna, Beyoncé and the late Michael Jackson, to the more regionally-based dance icons such as Namie Amuro of Japan and Jolin Tsai of Taiwan, and to those numerous self-recorded videos posted online by fans, the prevailing visibility of the dancing body is both undeniable and inescapable. Yet the dancing body in popular culture, despite not being entirely ignored, receives relatively little academic attention compared with its actual significance. This neglect could result from dance's corporeal nature which, in terms of Western philosophy, is considered 'inferior' to the mind;[1] possibly because these bodies are located in a field which, in Taiwan for instance, is traditionally considered the opposite of 'serious high culture'; possibly because popular dance is often marketed under the categories of popular music, a field where corporeality has always been overlooked;[2] and possibly because these 'popular bodies' are categorized as dance, a relatively marginalized discipline in the arts and humanities.[3] In other words, the dancing body in the popular field is often alluded to as naive or superficial. Counter to this persistent view towards these highly visible dancing bodies, my aims are two-fold: first, to stress the popular dancing body's importance in terms of culture, politics, music, economics and aesthetics; and, second, to formulate an analytical framework which has

---

[1] See Susan Bordo, *Unbearable Weight: Feminism, Western Culture, and the Body* (Berkeley, 1993), pp. 1-11.

[2] As McClary states, 'music theories and notational systems do everything possible to mask those dimensions of music that are related to physical human experience'. See Susan McClary, 'Towards a Feminist Criticism of Music', *Canadian University Music Review*, 10/2 (1990): p. 14. Also see Hans T. Zeiner-Henriksen, 'The "PoumTchak" Pattern: Correspondences Between Rhythm, Sound, and Movement in Electronic Dance Music' (PhD dissertation, Oslo, 2010), pp. 12-29.

[3] See Jane C. Desmond, 'Embodying Difference: Issues in Dance', in Jane C. Desmond (ed.), *Meaning in Motion: New Cultural Studies of Dance* (Durham and London, 1997), p. 29.

the theoretical capacity to capture its high-speed transmission and mutation. Consequently, I set out to excavate the profundity of these bodies alongside their commonly misunderstood appearance of superficiality. I will argue for a contradictory sense of the significance of these bodies in everyday life through what I refer to as 'superficial profundity'. Using Homi Bhabha's idea of 'cultural translation'[4] in tandem with Judith Butler's notion of 'performativity',[5] I embark on a reinvention of a new analytical method for these bodily practices, which I term 'performative translation', to examine these highly-mutable bodies in the (online) encounter between sound and image.

To pursue this argument, I choose to focus on a chain of events in three case studies centred on a spectacular concert opening of Jolin Tsai (hereafter Jolin): first in her live performance and then moving into two online fan videos. Jolin is one of the best known superstars in the genre of Mandarin pop (hereafter Mandopop). Based in Taipei, Mandopop is a vibrant music genre in East Asia with a history traceable to the 1920s jazz period in Shanghai.[6] It is transcultural in construction with strong foreign influences in terms of its musical features, performing styles and modes of production, and features an infusion of commonly referred to music categories such as rock, hip hop and rap. Its international associations affect the way it is perceived and 'foreignness' is arguably its embedded logic of spectacle. The success of the genre has led to foreign investment by major international companies.[7] Michael Keane, a media scholar, states that 'it is now the developed "Western" media economies that are talking of catching up with East Asia'.[8]

There are multiple reasons to focus on Mandopop, especially in Jolin's performances. First, compared to other music genres in the Anglophone world, there exists a disproportionate lack of scholarly attention. Second, Mandopop has been condemned through a discourse of superficiality[9] and therefore provides an ideal testing ground for the hypothesis of 'superficial profundity'. Third, a local and active fan culture called *kuso* (parody)[10] parasitically follows and interrupts the

---

[4] See Homi K. Bhabha, *The Location of Culture* (New York, 1994); and 'The Third Space (an Interview)', in Jonathan Rutherford (ed.), *Identity: Community, Culture, Difference* (London, 1990), pp. 207-21.

[5] See Judith Butler, *Gender Trouble: Feminism and the Subversion of Identity* (London and New York, 1990).

[6] Marc L. Moskowitz, *Cries of Joy, Songs of Sorrow: Chinese Pop Music and Its Cultural Connotations* (Honolulu, 2010), pp. 16-18.

[7] These companies include EMI, Polygram, Sony BMG, Universal and Warner Brothers: see Moskowitz, *Cries*, pp. 6-7.

[8] See Michael A. Keane, 'Once were Peripheral: Creating Media Capacity in East Asia', *Media Culture Society*, 28/6 (2006): p. 848.

[9] There is, however, a tendency in existing scholarship to draw away from this remark in recent years. Mandopop, in the view of Moskowitz, 'has surprisingly complex cultural implications' (see Moskowitz, *Cries*, p. 1).

[10] The word *kuso* originates from a minor swear word in Japanese, 'shit' (糞), but has taken on the new, localized meaning of 'parody' in the translation process. Initially being

production of Mandopop, constituting a rich and vibrant context for investigating the mutation of the body.

These features can be found in Jolin's star image. Starting her career in 1999 as a local Taipei girl, Jolin's 'local-ness' is the opposite to the genre's logic of spectacle, and her performances are often tinted with the idea of superficiality. Her early star image is marked by an intense love-hate relationship with her spectators, leading to abundant *kuso* reproductions based on her performances. The mimetic practices revolving around Jolin's dance performances surged with the development of her star image, creating an alternative online *mediascape* characterized by a proliferation and circulation of the dancing body. Thus, although she is now a trans-Asian superstar, scholars have surprisingly awarded little attention to her performance work.

Against this context, I have chosen to focus on the highly-acclaimed opening of her 2006 concert, *Dancing Forever*, where she descended onto the stage in a spectacular straddle splits posture, articulating a sense of virtuosity. Calling upon Richard Dyer's notion of authenticity,[11] I analyse the way cultural discourses and body politics are deployed in her virtuoso display of the dancing body and how this posture is used to create a 'corporeal signature' to authenticate her image (Case 1). Parallel to this analysis, I prioritize the dancing body in the nexus between sound and image to explore the embedded economic and musical tensions. This example is followed by two online 'fan videos' in which the practitioners toyed with this posture by replacing Jolin's legs with prostheses (Case 2 and Case 3). I analyse the mutation of cultural discourses and body politics, paying specific attention to its musical and economic implications. Comprehending these three examples as a whole, I contest a specific aesthetic issue through the deployment of the dancing body: the construction of 'originality' in Case 1, parodying the 'original' in Case 2 and an ambiguous performing event with multiple interpretative potentials that challenge the previous two examples in Case 3. I conceive these three examples as a 'performative translation' of corporeality taking place in a contemporary online *mediascape*. This theoretical reformulation will be used to highlight the importance of popular dancing through its challenge to cultural discourse, body politics, musical articulation, commercial strategy and aesthetic categories.

Performative Translation: Contesting 'Original', Imitation and Parody

Aesthetic categories concerning mimetic practices, including imitation and parody, have long been contested issues since the initiation of Western philosophy.

---

based on BBS (Bulletin Board System), *kuso* has penetrated cyberspace in recent years, joining what Jenkins terms the 'participatory culture'. See Henry Jenkins, *Confronting the Challenges of Participatory Culture: Media Education for the 21st Century* (Cambridge, MA, 2009).

[11] See Richard Dyer, 'A Star is Born and the Construction of Authenticity', in Christine Gledhill (ed.), *Stardom: Industry of Desire* (London, 1991), pp. 132-40.

Mimesis, derived from the Greek with a meaning of 'to imitate', has never been clearly defined. When Arne Melberg defines mimesis as the meeting place for similarity and difference, [12] it can be argued that its meaning shifts ambiguously between these two poles. However, modern scholars tend to regard imitation and parody as two distinguishable categories within this spectrum, in that parody keeps a 'critical distance' from repetition and imitation.[13] Contemporary theorists characterize parody as an 'ironic inversion',[14] which denotes a 'comic refunctioning of performed linguistic or artistic material'.[15]

In contrast to imitation and parody, the idea of an 'original' is considered as the opposite to these two categories; it is defined as 'pertaining to the origin or beginning', 'not derived copied, imitated, or translated from anything else' and 'creative'.[16] These definitions perceive 'originality' with a closed boundary as a *sui generis* entity. It is a boundary which, according to Walter J. Ong, emerged with the technological advances of print culture, giving birth to 'the romantic notions of "originality" and "creativity"'.[17] In this sense, originality is understood as a stable and unchangeable entity, often equated with unique-ness and authenticity, and therefore renders any form of mimesis as reproducible and 'inferior'. The relationship between 'original', parody and imitation can therefore be signified as the three distinct vertices in that each of the concepts cannot be reduced to any other.

These three concepts are manifest in many forms. In the realm of popular culture, the division between pop stars and fan practices is based on the dichotomies between 'original' and copy. When Henry Jenkins defines the fan as 'textual poacher',[18] the act of 'poaching' implies an 'origin' and therefore suggests a sense of authenticity for the pop stars. In studying star image, Dyer also stresses the importance of authenticity.[19] From Western philosophy to contemporary popular culture, the division between 'originality' and mimetic practices of imitation and parody continues to operate in a most profound yet mundane way, involving a stable dichotomy in that 'originality' carries an epistemological superiority to that of mimesis.

Counter to this classic understanding, I propose a reverse view in that 'originality' is acquired through the very process of reproduction of mimesis.

---

[12]   Arne Melberg, *Theories of Mimesis* (Cambridge, 1995), p. 3.

[13]   Linda Hutcheon, *A Theory of Parody: The Teachings of Twentieth-century Art Forms* (Urbana, 1985), p. 6.

[14]   Hutcheon, *Theory*, p. 6.

[15]   Margaret A. Rose, *Parody: Ancient, Modern, and Post-modern* (Cambridge, 1993), p. 52.

[16]   *Chambers English Dictionary* (7th edn, Edinburgh, 1988), p. 1013.

[17]   Walter J. Ong, *Orality and Literacy: The Technologizing of the Word* (1982; London, 2001), p. 133.

[18]   Henry Jenkins, *Textual Poachers: Television Fans and Participatory Culture* (London, 1992).

[19]   Dyer, 'A Star is Born'.

In this line of argument, the triangular relationship of 'originality', 'mimesis' and 'parody' is never a self-evident fact, but *is achieved* through an inversion of cultural practices which are initially considered opposite. That is to say, 'originality' acquires its full definition as an authentic, superior category through the very existence and the continual re/production of mimesis. In order to delineate the process of inversion, I turn to Homi Bhabha and Judith Butler, with a specific focus on the notion of cultural translation and the concept of performativity. This selection is based on their internal theoretical similarities. Both theorists directly engage with the ambiguous conceptual constructions of 'originality', imitation and parody and argue for their open-ness and mutability. Moreover, both highlight the force of displacement in everyday life and stress that this force is a drive to stimulate the fluidity of cultural identities and aesthetic categorization.

Emerging from an anthropological tradition, Bhabha's idea of translation denotes 'the performative nature of cultural communication'[20] and a way of:

> imitating, but in a mischevious, displacing sense – imitating an original in such a way that the priority of the original is not reinforced but by the very fact that it can be simulated, copied, transferred, transformed, made into a simulacrum and so on: the 'original' is never finished or complete in itself.[21]

Thus, Bhabha directly argues against the traditionally understood idea of 'original': 'original' is mimetic in construction with its form shifting between imitation and parody. In this sense, translation, as a performative act of communication, is understood as an ambiguous practice of cultural displacement, which has the potential to challenge any form of rigid definition.

The act of displacement also characterizes Butler's theory of performativity. Arguing against gender essentialism, Butler asserts there exists no ontological basis for gender identity; rather, it is performatively constructed in and through repetition. What used to be upheld as 'original', according to Butler, is a naturalized copy. In the process of repetition, Butler highlights the transformative potential, arguing the importance of parody as a strategy to '*displace* the very norms that enable the repetition itself'.[22] In other words, parody reveals itself as being '*of* the very notion of an original'; the original identity after which gender fashions itself is therefore 'an imitation without an origin'.[23] Butler specifically stresses the subversive potential of drag performances: as a form of parody, these acts have the ability to open gender identity to acts of resignification, revealing gendered bodies as many 'styles of the flesh'.[24]

---

[20] Bhabha, *Location*, p. 326.
[21] Bhabha, *Location*, p. 210.
[22] Butler, *Gender Trouble*, p. 148.
[23] Judith Butler, *Undoing Gender* (New York, 2004), p. 112.
[24] Butler, *Gender Trouble*, p. 139.

Both Bhabha and Butler emphasize the displacement of the 'original' in and through mimetic practices, and thus question the validity of its classic division. To analyse the interrogative potential of the dancing body, I tentatively coin the notion of 'performative translation' to comprehend the transmission and mutation of the dancing body, and provisionally define it as 'a performative way of corporeal communication, which imitates the "original" in a mischevious, displacing sense'. However, the nexus between Bhabha and Butler is characterized by a lack of attention to corporeal practices, especially dance, reflecting the blind spot of cultural studies. As Jane C. Desmond points out:

> Cultural studies remains largely text-based or object-based … Even excursions
> into popular culture are concerned largely with verbal or visual cultural products,
> not kinaesthetic actions.[25]

Specifically taking into account Butler's emphasis on body and identity, her avoidance of dance, according to Sarah R. Cohen, is 'surprising' taking into account 'how closely she invokes its process as she brings a critique of pure physicality to her consideration of performed identity'.[26] Ann Cooper Albright further questions Butler in her prioritization of gendered categories by pointing out her seeming unawareness of other parameters such as race or physical ability.[27]

Taking the dancing body as 'a site of discourse and of social control',[28] the following three case studies pay special attention to what Susan Bordo terms the 'politics' of these performing bodies. In Bordo's view, the body is 'a site of political struggle' which is shaped by cultures through 'the practices and bodily habits of everyday life'.[29] The notion of performative translation takes into account the politics of the dancing body in the process of displacement in everyday events. By analysing the three dancing bodies in Mandopop, I examine the theory of performative translation as a potential analytic model for exploration of the transmission, proliferation and mutation of the dancing body in a contemporary online *mediascape*.

Case 1: Constructing 'Originality': Dancing Virtuosity

Descending from above the stage to floor level in a splits posture across a pair of gymnastic rings, Jolin, under a pencil of light against the pitch-dark stage,

---

[25]   Desmond, 'Embodying Difference', p. 30.
[26]   Sarah R. Cohen, 'Performing Identity in the Hard Nut: Stereotype, Modeling and the Inventive Body', *The Yale Journal of Criticism*, 11/2 (1998): p. 486.
[27]   Ann Cooper Albright, *Choreographing Difference: The Body and Identity in Contemporary Dance* (Middletown CT, 1997), p. 9.
[28]   Helen Thomas, *Dance, Modernity, and Culture: Explorations in the Sociology of Dance* (London, 1995), p. 20.
[29]   Bordo, *Unbearable*, p. 16.

articulates virtuosity through a spectacular display of her dancing body (see Figure 11.1). Performed without the aid of a safety device and with minimal synthesizer accompaniment, the production prioritized her body, resulting in intense media attention over her virtuosity and courage. This is the opening of Jolin's much-acclaimed 2006 concert tour *Dancing Forever*, which premiered in Hong Kong, followed by a two-and-half year progress across China, Australia, Taiwan and Malaysia, ending in New York. Critics described the Hong Kong premiere as 'astonishing', 'breathtaking' and 'a new page of history' and reported the price of the insurance cover as being one billion Taiwanese dollars.[30] Jolin's virtuosity was utilized by her record company as a market strategy through a coined term, *the acquired talent* (地才), highlighting that genius can be acquired through arduous practice. With intensive promotion through DVD, poster and online circulation, this phrase has subsequently become a recognized neologism in contemporary Mandarin.

Figure 11.1   *Dancing Forever* (2006): Jolin's concert opening.

This moment, central in the development of Jolin's star image, transformed her from a 'cute' star with limited dance ability into a fully-fledged 'sexy' dance star. Starting her career in 1999 while a high school student in Taipei, Jolin was initially marketed under the title of 'the young boy killer' (少男殺手), which follows the mode of production of 'cuteness'. Despite releasing albums showing the influence of electronic dance music, she was known for her rigid body and as the one whose hand 'cannot reach the floor when bending forwards'.[31] This awkwardness in dance reflects Taiwan's post war body discipline, especially in the Martial Law era

---

[30]   Approximately two million pounds sterling, see *United Daily News* (聯合報), 16 September 2006.

[31]   *Cheers Magazine* (快樂工作人雜誌), 1 August 2006.

(1949-87) where public displays of the dancing body were banned. With Mandopop's logic of spectacle historically shaped by the notion of foreignness, Jolin's local identity and rigid body were considered counter spectacles, resulting in her image being tainted with criticism from her spectators and the alternative nickname of 'the queen of copycat'.[32] In Dyer's study of star image, the idea of authenticity is a key element in the successful construction of a star's charisma;[33] in Jolin's case, this idea was not pronounced in her early image. Between 'originality' and copy, Jolin's audiences have polarized, generating a love-hate relationship the intensity of which was demonstrated in 2000 when she simultaneously won the title of 'the best popular star' and a booby prize for 'the worst pop star' in Taiwan.[34]

Between 2002 and 2003, owing to a contract dispute, Jolin was 'frozen' by her record company, which resulted in a subsequent change of management. The one-year gap triggered a media-constructed 'transformation', which re-introduced Jolin as follows:

> Jolin Tsai … has always been fearless. [This spirit] has supported her *transformation* from an outdated teen idol, who can only stand obediently while singing, to a rhythmic sexy dancing queen.[35] [my emphasis]

This 'transformation' denotes a dramatic paradigm change from immature to mature, from obedient to confident, from 'cuteness' to 'sexiness', from outdated to spectacular and, most importantly, from motionless vocal performance to kinetic dance presentation. From a 'local' cute girl to an 'international' sexy star, gendered, corporeal and linguistic discourses and body politics were simultaneously reconfigured through a temporal and geographic switch: temporally, there is an update from the Martial Law period to the contemporary moment, whilst, geographically, there is a process of expansion in that Jolin's local-ness is internationalized. In the process of displacement, the dancing body functions as a 'corporeal signature', authenticating Jolin's star image, reaffirming her musical interpretation and validating the reinvention of her image.

The opening scene of Jolin's 2006 performance, in the transitional development of her star image, is therefore one of the most important events in the continual process of performative translation through the trope of 'transformation'. Through the very act of dancing, the idea of power is exercised, both in the sense of physical strength and in the sense of body politics. It is a moment of corporeal communication, which constructs 'originality' through displacing Jolin's early corporeal configuration and reformulates body politics according to the idea of

[32] *Now News* (今日新聞), 17 March 2009.
[33] Dyer, 'A Star is Born'.
[34] *Business Weekly* (商業週刊), 15 October 2007.
[35] Author's translation: '蔡依林 […] 總是永遠有種Fearless能量，支持著她從一個只會站著乖乖唱歌的過氣候少男偶像，轉型成為動感性感的天后。' See *Cosmopolitan* (柯夢波丹), 10 April 2008.

virtuosity. In this sense, Jolin's dancing body forms 'a site of discourse'[36] for 'struggles over the shape of power';[37] it is a focal point through which originality and charisma are gradually produced and naturalized to be one of her 'authentic' features. Through the display of this 'corporeal signature', Jolin gradually realizes Dyer's notion of authenticity after 2006.

Most important of all, in the process of achieving authenticity, two significant features occur: first, bodily display is prioritized over music and, second, the status of 'originality' is paradoxically achieved by the emergence and the proliferation of mimetic practices. First, as a commercial event where Jolin's music is at the centre of the promotional process, the opening moment surprisingly lacks any identifiable musical features. Instead, her bodily display is set against the general backdrop of sparse synthesizer beats, which gradually intensify with the progression of her performance. Moreover, at the start of the concert, the dancing body plays a much more important role than the music itself in that it *leads* the entrance of the music, the actual object for promotion. In this sense, corporeality cannot be denied its musical and economic significance: it allows a commercial event to be staged and the sale of the music to be stimulated.

Second, parallel to Jolin's realization of authenticity, a sudden surge of interest proliferates in the vernacular field, especially in the *kuso* subculture, to reproduce Jolin's performance into fan video. Most noticeably, from the music video of *Dancing Diva* (2006), the trend extends to *Agent J* (2007) and her recent release, *Honey Trap* (2010), forming a parasitical *mediascape*. Considering the timing of the mass emergence of fan video and Jolin's gradual establishment of authenticity, the mimetic practices paradoxically reaffirm Jolin's 'originality', uplifting her image from the realm commonly considered as being fake/inferior to the status of authentic/superior, as the one to be imitated.

The following sections examine two widely circulated fan videos, one on *YouTube* and the other on *Facebook*. I will continue to analyse the mutation of cultural discourse and body politics in the process of corporeal displacement, at the same time interrogating the aesthetic entanglement of issues surrounding 'original', imitation and parody. Taking the three examples as a whole, I question the definition of the three concepts, indicate the impossibility of a stable categorization, and suggest that performative translation is a productive theoretical model with the ability to capture the rapid fluidity of the bodies in the process of online re/production.

Case 2: Parodying the 'Original'

Uploaded by *justredtw* [ID] and circulated on *YouTube*, the first fan video came from a group of 14 clips. Each of the clips targets a regional / international icon.

---

[36]   Thomas, *Dance*, p. 20.
[37]   Bordo, *Unbearable*, pp. 16-17.

In this collection of performances, Jolin was the most popular, being reproduced four times.

Beginning almost in blackout with lights twinkling and cheerful noises in the background, this fan video starts with a close resemblance to the opening of a concert. As the lights suddenly illuminate, the performer appears in the middle of a medium-long shot in a room full of Christmas decorations. Adopting Jolin's famous posture, the performer looks into the camera confidently with his/her hands spreading sideways to support a pair of gymnastic rings and his/her 'legs', shod in blue heels, split through the ring holes in a straddle pose. Dressed in a sparkling blue camisole and a matching mini skirt, the performer indistinctly displays a pair of white trousers below the outfit. Imitating Jolin's concert opening, the role of music is non-existent; sound gives priority to visual effect as a means to highlight the dancing body, which is constructed according to the logic of spectacle.

Figure 11.2   *Kuso* Example 1: Jolin's concert pose reproduced at a private party (2007).

As argued in Case 1, the lack of any of Jolin's indicative music in such a signature moment constitutes a musical interruption and commercial paradox. This complex issue continues in this example, as there is eventually no music, only a mixture of applause and laughter, which gradually intensify when the performer turns round to 'leave the stage'. Walking away holding the same posture, the split 'legs' are revealed to be prostheses and the gymnastic rings are on movable sticks. On the way to exit, the performer tries to 'squeeze' through the space, causing the prostheses to flop. The video ends with a small dog running after the false legs, generating more laughter which characterizes the soundscape of the video. The video features an encore where the performer reappears on the stage with the same posture to recite, in a female voice, Jolin's much-cited statement: 'there is no true genius, but I have proved how talent can genuinely be acquired through hard work'.

In many ways, this *kuso* reproduction intentionally toys with Jolin's virtuoso dancing body through performative translation. Having closely simulated Jolin's opening scene through a careful construction of concert ambience, outfit, camera framing and body posture, cultural discourses and body politics embedded in Jolin's virtuosity are mutated by revealing the 'legs' as prostheses and the posture as a sham. As false legs are associated with disability, it disrupts the idea of the virtuoso dancing body as a signifier of ability: the gymnastic rings are no longer a testing ground for the dancing body to 'conquer', but a tool which helps the performer to 'pick up' the legs. Most importantly, as virtuosity defines Jolin's star image, the *kuso* video renders the symbol of Jolin's subjectivity as merely an object, which can be chased around by a dog, turning Jolin's triumphal construction of image into a joke. Jolin's virtuosity, often constructed as 'difficult' and 'dangerous' (as the price of the insurance indicates), is performatively displaced in this fan video with ease through the deployment of the prostheses, fake rings and camera framing.

Characterized by differences constructed on the basis of similarities, this *kuso* performance clearly reflects Melberg's definition of mimesis.[38] To be precise, marked by Hutcheon's sense of 'ironic inversion'[39] and Rose's notion of 'comic refunctioning' of the source material,[40] this fan video resembles parody more closely than imitation. Indeed, when Butler argues the significance of the parody in the process of transgressive reinscriptions, Osborne and Segal point out that this procedure operates most effectively within 'critical subcultures';[41] the practice of *kuso* seems to demonstrate this view fully. Moreover, this fan video shows the importance of the dancing body in the process of performative translation in that the body is the centre for the displacement of cultural discourse and body politics, offering the theoretical configurations of Bhabha and Butler a somatic dimension. In this sense, the dancing body corporeally responds to enquiries emerging from the field of dance studies to the dominant, still largely literary-centred, cultural approaches.

Most important of all, this fan video testifies to the theoretical potential of performativity to go beyond the solo focus on gender categories. In Butler's theory, drag is highlighted among various forms of parody. With the strong affiliation to drag in *kuso* subculture, the performer offers an unsubstantiated implication as a man in drag. However, with the performer voicing Jolin's statement in the encore, she 'gives away' her gender identity not as male but, surprisingly, as female. From a suspected drag performance to a non-drag practice, the transgressive reinscription Butler highlights does not come from drag, but from the rebuttal of drag. Destabilizing Jolin's construction of virtuosity and foreignness through vernacular practices, this video therefore offers an example to demonstrate the way that physical ability and foreignness can be destabilized in the process of

---

[38]   Melberg, *Theories*, p. 3.
[39]   Hutcheon, *Theory*, p. 6.
[40]   Rose, *Parody*, p. 52.
[41]   Peter Osborne and Lynne Segal, 'Gender as Performance: An Interview with Judith Butler', *Radical Philosophy*, 97 (1994): p. 38.

performative translation *without* subverting gender identity, offering a way to answer Albright's critique. This *kuso* performance thus provides an excellent case study to exemplify performative translation, forming a parody which has the potential to interrogate cultural discourses and body politics constructed in a mass-mediated context. The dancing body is therefore 'the focal point for struggles over the shape of power':[42] it is 'a primary not secondary social "text"'[43] where performative translation is staged, having the potential to expand at the same time challenging contemporary cultural theory.

Case 3: Parodying the 'Original', Imitating the Parody or Parodying the Parody?

With Jolin continuing to articulate the idea of virtuosity through her dancing body with her new releases over the years, the authenticity of her star image became more established and attempts to reproduce her work have become increasingly prevalent. In 2011, a series of *kuso* videos emerged on *Facebook* of the recording of the annual party of a hair salon in Taipei, featuring reproductions of various stars and fictional personae. This series paid special attention to Jolin, featuring an almost full range reproduction of her work, in pastiche, including *Dancing Diva* (2006), *Agent J* (2007) and her recent release, *Honey Trap* (2010). Her famous concert opening likewise opened the series (see Figure 11.3).

Figure 11.3   *Kuso* Example 2: Jolin's concert pose reproduced at Flux Hair Boutique's annual celebration (2011).

Starting with a covered screen of a makeshift white 'curtain', the cloth is gradually lowered with the intensification of the musical prelude of *Agent J*, featuring increasingly sharp synthesizer beats. The performer appears with the

---

[42]   Bordo, *Unbearable*, pp. 16-17.
[43]   Desmond, 'Embodying Difference', p. 31.

alteration of soundscape: the music suddenly fades out, to be replaced by the sound of an audience cheering and screaming. The absence of the music gives the dancing body maximum visibility in the nexus between sound and image, readdressing issues of commercial opportunities and musical interpretations that the body can possibly create. Fashioned in a similar blue outfit and a corresponding hairstyle, the performer poses in Jolin's straddle posture with split 'legs' replaced by prostheses, secured by a pair of made-up gymnastic rings. Compared with the previous *kuso* video where the real legs of the performer are disguised by trousers, which blend into the background, the 'real' legs of this performer are blocked by the 'curtain'. Towards the end of the video, the performer clears his throat to announce, in a male voice, Jolin's statement of an 'acquired talent'. The similarity between this performer and Jolin is constantly reinforced by a hand-held concert poster of Jolin, where her opening posture is magnified.

Deploying an almost identical strategy of corporeal displacement with the previous example, this video is first and foremost a parody in that the performance is characterized by ironic inversion, comically refunctioning the 'original' to denaturalize its cultural discourses and body politics. However, despite the performance self-consciously targeting Jolin (Case 1), it is nevertheless at the same time displacing the previous parody (Case 2) by using drag. In this sense, to suggest that this fan video displaces the 'original', the expression of 'original' is characterized by ambiguity as it can simultaneously represent Jolin's dancing body (Case 1) and its parody (Case 2). This performance therefore shifts between uncertain aesthetic categories: it parodies the 'original' (as the poster denotes), imitates the parody (through the use of prostheses) or parodies the parody (through the use of drag). The dancing body in this performance is therefore intrinsically unstable, allowing a variety of potential interpretations to invert ironic edges into itself.

To focus on Case 2, it can be argued that, with the emergence of a new mimetic reproduction (Case 3), the existing parody gradually achieves the status of 'originality'; it becomes the origin for other parodies to copy. 'Originality' is, therefore, paradoxically constructed through the emergence of other mimetic practices and, in this case, through the performative translation of corporeality. This contradiction, to a certain extent, explains the phenomenon that Jolin's authenticity is achieved in a similar period to the mass emergence of *kuso* videos. While the emergence of *kuso* can be a result of Jolin's growing fame, Jolin's 'upgrade' to the realm of 'originality' has been officially, albeit tacitly, confirmed by the spectators through the emergence of *kuso* video. 'Originality' is thus a status to be achieved with the emergence of other mimetic practices; in return, mimesis can suddenly become 'original' with the surfacing of other mimetic articulations of, in this example, the dancing body.

The dancing body, in this sense, can denaturalize the cultural discourses and body politics, at the same time questioning the aesthetic category which constitutes itself. By inverting the parody onto itself, it interrogates the very definition of the aesthetic category. Aesthetic categories are therefore movable concepts, which are characterized by their fluid nature, ready to be switched, twisted and turned in every act of corporeal articulation. Hence, in these aesthetic categories, performing events cannot be viewed in an isolated manner, but have to be considered in a continuous chain of performative translations taking into account the emergence of other new works. Through performative translations, 'originality' proves to be a construction, mimesis can become 'original' and parody can imitate/parody other parodies, forcing the classic triangular model between 'original', imitation and parody to implode. Aesthetic categories are therefore constantly on the move, performatively contesting their own meaning through different cultural contexts.

Superficial Profoundity: The Dancing Body in the Contemporary World

Revolving around the circulation of popular dance, contemporary popular culture is decidedly body-centred and visually-oriented. Existing in the multimedial intersection between sound and image, the dancing body has a primary importance over other media. Whilst the dancing body forms a corporeal signature, which has the ability to authenticate Jolin's image and her musical interpretation (Case 1), it also serves as a medium through which her body configuration can be mutated in the vernacular practice (Cases 2 and 3). All three case studies are characterized by a minimization, if not a lack, of music. The dancing body, therefore, is the major means of communication through which cultural discourses can be reformulated, body politics can be contested, musical articulation can be interrupted, commercial sales can be stimulated and aesthetic categories can be challenged.

By addressing the importance of the dancing body, I formulate the idea of performative translation as a means to capture these fast-changing and highly mutable corporealities. I define the idea of performative translation as 'a performative way of corporeal communication, which imitates the "original" in a mischievous, displacing sense'. This idea offers a productive model in that the dancing body can contribute a critical insight to examine and expand cultural theories, and illuminate cultural, political, musical, economic and aesthetic aspects of the contemporary world.

Situated in the genre of Mandarin pop, with a focus on Jolin's performance and her online fan videos, all of which have long been viewed as both trivial and superficial, I argue for the significance of these seemingly depthless corporealities and through the 'superficial profundity' of the dancing body. Most importantly, this significance is achieved through articulations of the body in everyday life. The dancing body in popular culture is a contagious, widely circulated, parasitical phenomenon of contemporary culture urgently in need of further scholarly attention. In the busy junction between sound and image, the dancing body is irreducible to other parameters: it is an important and complicated physical platform for the staging of performative translation and for the analysis of popular phenomena, facilitating cultural communication in a most mundane yet effective way.

Chapter 12

Keeping the Faith: Issues of Identity, Spectacle and Embodiment in Northern Soul

Laura Robinson

In 2007, British blue-eyed soul singer Duffy rose to chart success with her hit single *Mercy* (2007).[1] The accompanying music video featured black-and-white shots of predominantly white young men executing intricate foot shuffles, tight heel spins and athletic drops to the floor; a striking intertextual reference to a distinct but relatively unexplored era of British music and dance history that continues to thrive within conventions, weekenders, blogs, websites and theme nights.

Coined in 1968 by London-based blues and soul journalist and record shop owner Dave Godin, the term 'Northern Soul' identified the music and dance nightclub scene that developed in the North of England and the Midlands in the late 1960s to mid-1970s, in which enthusiasts celebrated rare and long-forgotten 1960s African American soul records. Godin's term thus provided both a British geographical pinpoint for the scene's development, and a reference to the transatlantic revival and appropriation of obscure and commercially unsuccessful North American soul music.[2] Produced by small independent Detroit-based record labels (for example, Golden World, Shrine and Champion), tracks such as *Instant Heartbreak* by The Precisions (1967) recreated the popular 1960s Motown sound, but remained largely unknown due to poor quality recordings, sparse distribution and the influx of Motown hits produced by the larger labels of Tamla, Motown and RCA.[3] British DJs uncovered and imported the Motown scene's 'lost' tracks from US record shops and revived them on the turntables of Northern England nightclubs. Northern Soul devotees travelled considerable distances to visit the few clubs in the UK that played their music: the Twisted Wheel in Manchester, The Golden Torch in Stoke-on-Trent, the Blackpool Mecca and, most famously, Wigan Casino. These clubs held 'all-nighter' events, which attracted predominantly young white working-class men who wanted to let off steam, swap and buy rare records, take amphetamines and, most importantly, listen and dance to soul music.

---

[1]   Duffy is a Welsh singer-songwriter whose debut album sold 1.68 million copies (http://www.iamduffy.com/).

[2]   David Nowell, *Too Darn Soulful: The Story of Northern Soul* (London, 2001).

[3]   Tim Wall, 'Out on the Floor: The Politics of Dancing on the Northern Soul Scene', *Popular Music*, 25/3 (2006): pp. 431-45; Nowell, *Too Darn Soulful*.

In this chapter, I explore the complex shift between community and individual identity in both the original scene of the late 1960s to early 1970s and Northern Soul's contemporary practice through the lens of post-subcultural analysis. In particular, I examine constructions of identity and embodiments of the music on the dance floor. Furthermore, I argue for a link between the construction of self and notions of spectacle, and draw upon Guy Debord's 'society of spectacle'.[4] I build on Keith Kahn-Harris's study of subcultural spectacle and the mundane within the Global Extreme Metal Music scene to reveal how spectacle is muted and shunned within ageing Northern Soul subcultural practices to protect the integrity and value of the practice.[5] I examine both the 1970s and the contemporary Northern Soul scene through participant interviews, reference to scholarly and popular literature, and textual analysis of film footage, fan websites and Northern Soul records.[6]

A once under-researched area, Northern Soul's increased visibility in both academic journals and popular media reflects the growing consciousness of its historical and contemporary significance.[7] Alongside narrative accounts that chart the scene's development, academic studies have focused on the politics of subcultural identity, as well as the participants' relationships to the music, drugs and affiliation with African American culture.[8] While these studies offer a nuanced post-subcultural understanding of the scene, there still remains an emphasis on the

---

[4]   Guy Debord, *Society of the Spectacle*, trans. Ken Knabb (London, 2004).

[5]   Keith Kahn-Harris, 'Unspectacular Subculture?: Transgression and Mundanity in the Global Extreme Metal Scene' in Andy Bennett and Keith Kahn-Harris (eds), *After Subculture: Critical Studies in Contemporary Youth Culture* (Basingstoke and New York, 2004).

[6]   Interviews were conducted in Higham Ferrers, Northamptonshire, England, on 20 April 2011 with Richard 'Gilly' Gilbert, a regular Northern Soul attendee for over 40 years; Karen Bridges, a Northern Soul dance enthusiast; and Nicola Anderson, a fan of Northern Soul music and dance for over 20 years. Participants were sourced through family friends and their extended social groups, and their interviews were transcribed from taped recordings.

[7]   Music video adaptions of Northern Soul dance are featured in Moloko's *Familiar Feeling* (2003) and Plan B's *Stay too Long* (2009). Northern Soul television documentaries include *Dance Britannia*, Episode 3, BBC4 Documentaries (2008) and *This England: Wigan Casino*, Granada Colour Production (1977).

[8]   Narrative accounts include Russ Winstanley and David Nowell, *Soul Survivors: The Wigan Casino Story* (London, 1996); and Nowell, *Too Darn Soulful*. Subcultural studies include Andrew Wilson, *Northern Soul: Music, Drugs and Subcultural Identity* (Cullompton, Devon, 2007); Nicola Smith, 'Beyond the Master Narrative of Youth: Researching Ageing Popular Music Scenes', in Derek Scott (ed.), *The Ashgate Research Companion to Popular Musicology* (Farnham, 2009); Paul Hodkinson, 'Ageing in a Spectacular "Youth Culture": Continuity, Change and Community Amongst Older Goths', *The British Journal of Sociology*, 62/2 (2011): pp. 262-82. A recent popular music study is David Sanjek, 'Groove Me: Dancing to the Discs of Northern Soul', in Jill Terry and Neil A. Wynn (eds), *Transatlantic Roots Music: Folk, Blues, and National Identities* (Jackson, 2012).

music-related practices of Northern Soul, while the vibrant movement vocabulary of Northern Soul stands neglected. In his ethnographic research on contemporary Northern Soul, Tim Wall highlights the strange omission of the dance considering its centrality within the scene.[9] In his analysis of Northern Soul dance styles, Wall comments how Northern Soul television programmes, such as *Soul Nation* (2003), reduced the dance form to its gymnastic elements and overlooked the core rhythmic slide patterns.[10] While I agree that Northern Soul dance is more nuanced than media representations suggest, I maintain that these spectacular elements are significant in that they capture the attention of the public consciousness of the Northern Soul scene, thus resulting in new or renewed interest in its participatory practice. I would acknowledge, however, that this interest is not always welcomed amongst original participants, resulting in a defensive adaption of Northern Soul style. Therefore, the significance of mediated representations of subcultural styles, such as Duffy's borrowing of Northern Soul, lies in the unexplored issue of how such images impact on the contemporary vernacular scene.

Duffy's music video neatly reflects some of these contestations present within the scene and consequently reveals the rationale for my research. First, the ideals of the British Centre for Contemporary Cultural Studies (CCCS) for an organized and tight-knit subcultural community are swiftly juxtaposed in the video by close-up camera shots that frame the individual dancer's standalone solo performances.[11] The struggle between the development of both self-identity and a sense of community is indicative of a post-subcultural reading of the scene, and raises the question of how individualism and affiliation are constructed on the Northern Soul dance floor and within the scene's related social network. Secondly, the video enhances the athletic and explosive elements of the dance style rather than focusing on the steady and rhythmic side-to-side foot slides of the dance form; slow-motion back drops, splits and back flips mediated through slow-motion editing enhance the spectacle and visual elements of the form. As the performances build in skill and pace, the dancers' feet are set alight, a mediated effect to visualize metaphorically their speed and intensity. While the virtuosic elements of the dance style create an exciting viewing experience, they also reflect society's fascination with the visual and raise the question of how practising members of contemporary Northern Soul both celebrate and conceal its spectacular and commercialized elements. Thirdly, the chosen dancers in the video are representative of Hebdige's subcultural model of young, working-class white

---

[9]   Wall, 'Out on the Floor'.

[10]   Helen Littleboy, *Soul Nation* (2003), cited in Wall, 'Out on the Floor'.

[11]   Stuart Hall and Tony Jefferson (eds), *Resistance through Rituals: Youth Subcultures in Post-War Britain* (London, 2006); Dick Hebdige, *Subculture: The Meaning of Style* (London, 1979). Post-war youth subcultural theory was born out of the neo-Marxist approach of the CCCS that interpreted youth subcultures as homogenous groups of predominantly young, white, working-class males, who demonstrated resistance against hegemonic institutions through the consumption of commodities.

males and do not reflect the evolution and expanse of the contemporary ageing subcultural movement.[12] Both Smith's and Hodkinson's post-subcultural research cite Northern Soul as an example of significant adult participation in subcultural practice away from the restrictive category of youth, therefore looking beyond a static subcultural movement to examine instead a fluid and evolving practice.[13]

Northern Soul Dance

Karen, a regular Northern Soul attendee for fourteen years, describes the moment when a favourite track comes on and how she gets 'soul blinkers' that compel her to dance.[14] While not a dancer himself, Richard shares in the euphoria of Northern Soul:

> Dancing for some is a way of expressing their love and I mean pure love of the record spinning at the time. It goes into the ear, spins around the head and exists through the movements of the dancer. There are many people who I know who dance to the records and by watching their expressions from their face all the way through their bodies you can feel the love and enjoyment they are feeling for the music.[15]

Such passion for the embodiment of the music is common amongst Northern Soul participants, who describe the dancing as exhilarating and link the activity with notions of escapism and joy.[16] Both Richard's and Karen's responses equate with Christopher Small's notion of 'musicking' in that Northern Soul music is not a passive experience but an activity that demands physical participation.[17] The stomping, driving beat of such soul tracks as Toni Clarke's *Landslide* (1966) or Sandi Sheldon's *You're Gonna Make Me Love You* (1967) propels this argument and, consequently, my interest in the Northern Soul club scene lies in the embodiment of Northern Soul music through its distinctive movement vocabulary; the sliding foot patterns, sharp claps and tight spins, which evolve into more energetic and athletic steps such as back drops, hand springs, splits and high kicks. Using Stuart Cosgrove's documentation of the dance, Wall describes the posture and movement character of the repetitious horizontal gliding:

---

[12] Hebdige, *Subculture.*
[13] Smith, 'Beyond the Master Narrative of Youth'.
[14] Karen Bridges, Interview Transcript.
[15] Richard Gilbert, Interview Transcript.
[16] See Sherril Dodds, *Dancing on the Canon: Embodiments of Value in Popular Dance* (Basingstoke, 2011), pp. 172-85.
[17] Christopher Small, *Musicking: the Meanings of Performing and Listening* (Middletown, CT, 1998).

Rigid upper torso, eyes up and looking forward; weight back and pushing down through the hips on to the heels; moving mostly with feet, with fairly straight legs, to propel oneself across the floor (almost always sideways); arms and hands tend to follow the shifting weight of the dancer, or push against it for expressive counterpoint.[18]

This steady side-to-side sliding of the feet mirrors the pounding 4/4 metre of the upbeat soul tracks, and the steady shifting of weight allows for improvised freedom on the interjections and flourishes in the music, including knee lifts and high kicks, drops to the floor, tight spins and a return into the stable gliding pattern. Using the dance as the central axis for my analysis, I now investigate the contestation between the construction of self-identity and subcultural community on the Northern Soul dance floor.

Community vs. the Individual

In the documentary *This England: Wigan Casino*, the hovering top shot of the Casino reveals a sea of dancers, all gliding in perfect unison.[19] This communal overview is then placed adjacent to images of the individual dancers performing nuanced versions of the gliding step, as well as athletic back drops and multiple sharp spins. One male dancer in particular executes a rapid quadruple spin and then sharply comes to a halt, casually blows his hair out of his face, and rejoins the community of gliders around him as if nothing had happened. As Nicola Smith reveals, 'Northern soul participants do dance alone, together'.[20] This rapid transition from the personal to the communal demands an analysis of the issues behind the construction of self-identity within the community practice of Northern Soul.

> From the moment I [Richard] began with this music I have never changed my perspective on it from the beginning to the present day and I am still listening and attending venues whether it be all-nighters or soul nights around the country.[21]

As Richard suggests, membership in the Northern Soul community is conceived as a lifelong and encompassing commitment, which extends further than listening to music within the home. The need to experience 'our music', as Richard maintains, in a social context with fellow enthusiasts implies ideas of ownership and community belonging, and draws similarities with Kahn-Harris's

---

[18] Wall, 'Out on the Floor', p. 436.
[19] *This England: Wigan Casino.*
[20] Smith, 'Beyond the Master Narrative of Youth', p. 433.
[21] Richard Gilbert, Interview Transcript.

concept of 'scene' – an inclusive space which encompasses music, lifestyle, behaviour, community practices and values.[22]

As a critique of the CCCS approach to subcultural research, Wilson argues against the essentialist notion that white working-class youth attended the 1970s Northern Soul scene only as a process of resistance to the dominant culture.[23] He states that working-class involvement in Northern Soul was instead centred around community and friendship groups rather than in the hierarchical order of social class. This sense of community was strengthened through the acceptance of diverse backgrounds and cultures, as well as through the celebration of African American music and culture. In particular, the community affiliation with black culture was achieved through listening to and buying obscure soul records from the 1960s, as well as through the assimilation of black argot and the 'right on' badges featuring the clenched black fist.[24] By listening to North American soul music, Northern Soul devotees constructed an imaginary partnership with African American culture to produce a sense of community and belonging across the North of England and the Midlands.[25]

This construction of a Northern geographical identity was also key to the development of the Northern Soul community. Brewster and Broughton observe that the scene was 'ignored or treated with contempt by the sophisticates of music journalism and London club land, allowing it to develop largely undisturbed and unobserved'.[26] Therefore, the Northern youth community was able to construct resistance over the musical nucleus of the South of England by creating an exclusive cultural hub away from the mainstream media influences of London. Conversely, Wall argues that 'the scene was not initially based upon a self-conscious articulation of a sense of northern-ness' and the geographical and commercial term 'Northern Soul' only became popular through media intervention when it became a commercial vehicle for selling pop music.[27] Hence, Northern Soul's constructed geographical community was eventually challenged by the South through commercial exploitation.

The incorporation of African American culture can also be seen in the dance repertoire of Northern Soul; as Brenda Dixon Gottschild states, 'the European attitude suggests centeredness, control, line-arity, directness; the Africanist mode suggests asymmetry (that plays with falling off center, looseness (implying flexibility and vitality), and indirectness of approach'.[28] This emphasis on looseness

---

[22]   Kahn-Harris, 'Unspectacular Subculture'.

[23]   Wilson, *Northern Soul.*

[24]   Wilson, *Northern Soul.*

[25]   Hollows and Milestone cited in Wall, *Out on the Floor.*

[26]   Bill Brewster and Frank Broughton, *Last Night a DJ Saved My Life: The History of the Disk Jockey* (London, 1999), p. 85.

[27]   Wall, 'Out on the Floor', p. 441.

[28]   Brenda Dixon Gottschild, *Digging the Africanist Presence in American Performance: Dance and Other Contexts* (Westport, CT, 1996), p. 17.

and falling off-centre can be seen in the back drops and use of gravity in the Northern Soul repertoire; movements far removed from the upright and controlled dance style evident in mainstream discothèques at the time, fuelled by the film release of *Saturday Night Fever* (1977).[29] Northern Soul members differentiated themselves against this perceived 'mass culture' and found an alternative identity by listening to previously released 1960s rare soul records from Detroit. Yet, Sarah Thornton questions this construction of power against the elusive mainstream through the appropriation of African American music, stating that Northern Soul members instead were far more concerned with increasing their subcultural capital in Northern Soul clubs through the appropriation of black cultural style in order to increase their 'hip' and 'cool' status.[30]

On the dance floor, this sense of community is not only referenced through the shared experience of music appreciation, but embodied through the uniformity and simplicity of the side to side gliding step. In particular, Wall observes how the 'soul clap', the piercing sound made by dancers clapping their hands wide in unison at the bridge of the music, brought together this 'sense of community of the scene ... and the collective experience of the dance'.[31] Richard confirms this embodied experience, stating that 'the dancing is very individual and formational; however, at particular times in a song such as (let's say) a crescendo or a saxophone break moves can be seen (but not timed) in sync. There are also times in certain songs that everyone would clap altogether.'[32] Karen concurs, stating 'I guess most people think they are individualists in some way or another but when we are all gathered in the same venue we are all the same'.[33] An analysis of these experiences suggests that, while Northern Soul dance is a solo practice, it is this physical embodiment of the music that generates a strong sense of community and belonging within its participants. Collective responses to the music, such as the soul clap, demonstrates an unspoken understanding of track knowledge and rhythmic phrasing between participants, and reveals how the somatic experience of the music expands to the Northern Soul community as a whole and is released as an explosive physical response.

As Richard explains, though: 'I am not a follower and prefer to be the individual that I am. The people on the soul scene are for the most part individuals but share the same music interests.'[34] Smith's study of the ageing Northern Soul subcultural movement recognizes this desire for identity construction away from the homogenous overarching label of community, stating that 'individuals acquire

[29] John Badham, *Saturday Night Fever* (1977).
[30] See Sarah Thornton, *Club Cultures: Music, Media, and Subcultural Capital* (London, 1995).
[31] Wall, 'Out on the Floor', p. 441.
[32] Richard Gilbert, Interview Transcript.
[33] Karen Bridges, Interview Transcript.
[34] Richard Gilbert, Interview Transcript.

an aspect of self via scene participation'.[35] She argues that the Northern Soul scene creates a space for the acquisition of self-identity through individual performances of knowledge, competency and skill, providing an initial explanation for continuous scene involvement. In addition, David Muggleton argues that subcultural identity construction is far more individualistic than collective, due to the instability of an overall community identity.[36] Therefore, I would conceive Northern soul as an individual practice sitting within a wider community context.

With regard to the importance of music and identity construction, Thornton states that 'when original performers are remote in time or place, as is the case with foreign imports and revived rarities, records can acquire prestige and authority'.[37] Here, she suggests that, instead of Northern Soul members solely choosing rare soul as a shared reaction to the popular funk and disco music, members were in fact constructing their own individual identities and status in the scene through the acquisition of 'subcultural capital'.[38] Wilson notes that DJs, club owners and bootleggers controlled the rarity of the records by charging over a week's worth of wages if a record was in particular demand, but that this construction of power could be reversed; if a bad track was played, the dance floor would clear, and could mean the end of a DJ's career.[39] As Northern Soul music was not available through mainstream radio, enthusiasts had to attend Northern Soul events in order to hear the music, with club owners maintaining 'this is what the kids want, it isn't something we want, it's something they want. All we've done in this particular location is met demand.'[40] This demand was often to the detriment of club owners and DJs alike; in 1975, Wigan Casino had to suspend membership temporarily as it had over 100,000 members and DJs had to 'cover-up' rare records with fake labels to protect them from being copied or 'bootlegged' by enthusiasts.[41]

As referenced, one of the most striking features of individualism within Northern Soul dance is its solo execution. Richard comments that 'rare soul dancing has always been a singular event on the scene, dancing with a partner is a no no.'[42] Although numbers were marginal in the 1970s, female members had the opportunity to construct individual identity on the dance floor, as the focus of the male attendees was on the music and dance rather than courtship.[43] This personal expression included the more intricate movement vocabulary of Northern Soul, such as the detailed footwork and tight spins, which when performed at the right

---

[35]   Smith, 'Beyond the Master Narrative of Youth', p. 432.
[36]   David Muggleton, *Inside Subculture: The Postmodern Meaning of Style* (Oxford, 2002).
[37]   Thornton, *Club Cultures*, p. 66.
[38]   Thornton, *Club Cultures*, p. 66.
[39]   Wilson, *Northern Soul*; Thornton, *Club Cultures*.
[40]   Nightclub owner, *This England*, 1977.
[41]   Nowell, *Too Darn Soulful*.
[42]   Richard Gilbert, Interview Transcript.
[43]   McRobbie cited in Wall, 'Out on the Floor'.

time, allowed the women's long, weighted skirts to whip around them at the end of a musical break to great visual effect. Richard observes that 'men and women's dance routines are I guess very similar, although you tend to find that the men are more energetic and the ones that do aerobatics are more forceful'.[44]

Men in the 1970s Northern Soul scene competed against each other for individual superiority by using their ability and skills as a means of creating a hierarchy amongst the club participants. Male Northern Soul dancers asserted their masculinity and dominance through the athletic nature of the movement and the in-depth knowledge of the individual tracks. The physical risks required of Northern Soul dance placed the male ego on trial, with men aiming to outperform each other to earn respect within the scene. Another method of asserting individuality and status was through the acquisition of knowledge. Wall and Wilson comment on how the knowledge of the relationship between the movement vocabulary and the music of Northern Soul was vital in carving out membership within the scene.[45] A spectacular athletic display of spins and back drops may attract attention, but Wall observes that these gymnastic elements often had to be executed within the instrumental break of the music, which again highlights the importance of track knowledge and keeping within the regulated structure of the music.[46]

These examples of identity construction still demonstrate an embodied link to the music, but also assert a desire to stand out through the creation of spectacle; the highest kick, the fastest spin, the rarest record. I would argue, however, that participants in the contemporary Northern soul scene have a greater desire to sit between the binary extremes of community and individual; a middle ground where individuality can be explored through creativity and interpretation, but not necessarily demonstrate showmanship and prowess. Karen explains how 'in any scene you get your sheep and your shepherds. For me I definitely am not a sheep nor want to be a shepherd.'[47] Both Richard and Karen reflect on how they both have shunned the conventions of Northern Soul fashion and dance style, and have carved out their own identity against the homogenous style of the scene:

> Early Wigan people would wear what I thought were hideous clothing i.e. extra, extra wide legged trousers called baggies. Some had badges sewn on and for some reasons multiple amounts of zips and pockets all over them, this was not for me. A lot of people wore bowling shirts, I thought these looked ok but again not for me … Carrying a niter bag, again with badges sewn on, also seemed to be popular. For me, and I know I have always been different, all of this attire was not something I wanted to have anything to do with.[48]

---

[44] Richard Gilbert, Interview Transcript.
[45] Wall, 'Out on the Floor'; Wilson, *Northern Soul*.
[46] Wall, 'Out on the Floor'.
[47] Karen Bridges, Interview Transcript.
[48] Richard Gilbert, Interview Transcript.

My dancing isn't the same as most peoples! I don't even know 'how' I learned the basic side to side steps, it's as though it was part of my DNA! I receive a lot of compliments though![49]

Both these accounts of individual practices and tastes highlight the possibility for fluidity and individuality away from the expected style of the scene, which displaces the subcultural ideal of a resistant and homogenous community. I would also maintain that this opens up a creative space for Northern Soul dancers where they neither have to conform to the repetitive gliding step nor the virtuosic components of the dance, but embody the music in their own way. This is particularly true of the new participants to the contemporary Northern Soul scene, who bring their individual musical and dance influences to their interpretation of Northern Soul music. Consequently, if Northern Soul does not merely comprise of a series of back flips and quadruple spins, but instead creates a fluid space for participants to discover and select new embodiments and affiliations to their beloved soul music, what is the relevance of the virtuosic and spectacular images represented in the televisual media, and how do these impact on contemporary Northern Soul practice?

The Spectacle of Soul

Spectacle is a multi-faceted term that points towards the visual, the extreme, the unexpected, the impressive and the superficial, sparking both outrage and delight in its audiences. In his book, *The Society of the Spectacle*, Debord posits that due to the prevalence of images within consumer society, social life has moved beyond a state of 'having' to a state of 'appearing', where there are no longer originals and real life has become a constant wash of images.[50] Such emphasis on the visual can be realized through both the historic and contemporary movements of Northern Soul, especially within the media appropriation of Northern Soul style.

In Hebdidge's reading of subcultural activity, spectacle is located at the level of style and viewed as both a symbolic form of membership and as an encompassing form of resistance against the dominant class culture.[51] Northern Soul's 'spectacular style', as Karen noted above, consisted of bowling shirts and baggy trousers for men, with long weighted skirts for the women, as well as sports holdalls that contained spare clothes for the morning, rare soul records to sell and swap, and large quantities of 'gear' to keep the night going.[52] These bags were also covered in numerous club badges that showed participants' allegiance to the venues and the Northern Soul movement. Kahn-Harris observes that

---

[49]   Karen Bridges, Interview Transcript.
[50]   Debord, *Society of the Spectacle*.
[51]   Hebdige, *Subculture*.
[52]   'Gear' is a British colloquialism that describes amphetamine drugs.

post-subcultural readings have re-examined the notion of subcultural spectacle, considering both the importance of unspectacular elements within a subculture, as well as members who demonstrate spectacular style but may not be wholly committed to the scene.[53] In addition, whereas classic subcultural readings focused on how subcultural spectacle related to the hegemonic culture, Kahn-Harris instead argues that the importance of subcultural spectacle lies in its relation to 'the experience of mundanity' in everyday life.[54]

In terms of media intervention, the popularity of the Northern Soul music was built upon collected archival records that had previously been released, which gave the 1970s scene an intrinsic defence against commercialization as the music industry failed to hold any economic power over the production or consumption of the records. The stylized image of the 1970s Northern Soul movement, however, was appropriated through the re-release and chart success of Northern Soul anthems, the appearance of Northern Soul dancers on *Top of the Pops*, clubs playing more soul records by white artists and the introduction of mainstream funk and disco music into DJ set lists.[55] This dissemination of Northern Soul's commercial image resulted in a more mainstream audience, which in turn created tensions between the original Northern Soul crowd and the 'newies'. In particular, Wilson comments that 'Wigan casino's representation of the scene had compromised the rare soul principle by playing up to the acrobatic dancing, badges and up tempo "stomper" image' as it chose up-tempo music of 100 beats per minute over traditional soul music.[56] New members to the scene wore club badges from different venues even if they had never attended the clubs before as a symbolic fast track into the subculture. As a reaction, original members began to remove the obvious symbols of Northern Soul, as they were 'a clear sign of the newcomer who was viewed as a sightseer, tourist or divvie, attracted to the scene by its glare of publicity'.[57]

In addition to Duffy, the contemporary remodelling of Northern Soul dance can be seen within Moloko's *Familiar Feeling* (2003) and most recently Plan B's *Stay too Long* (2009), British music videos that appropriate the notion of hip through the careful placement of Northern Soul dance repertoire. In addition, the trailer for the British film *Soul Boy* (2010), a coming-of-age drama set in the 1970s Northern Soul music scene, once again features spliced images of the spectacular elements of the dance form; en masse lateral sliding and clapping, split leaps and endless on-the-spot spins.[58] The question raised by these mediated versions of Northern Soul is the effect they have on the current Northern Soul scene and how

---

[53]   Kahn-Harris, 'Unspectacular Subculture'.
[54]   Kahn-Harris, 'Unspectacular Subculture', p. 112.
[55]   Hebdige, *Subculture*.
[56]   Wilson, *Northern Soul*, p. 33.
[57]   Wilson, *Northern Soul*, p. 36.
[58]   Shimmy Marcus, *Soul Boy* (2010).

participants react to both the increased interest and the emphasis on athleticism within the dance form.

The Contemporary Northern Soul Scene

Even though the original venues closed in the 1970s and 1980s, the Northern Soul dance scene still thrives in clubs and 'soul weekender' events across the United Kingdom, attracting a mix of 40-year-old followers as well as newcomers to the scene. Recent post-subcultural analysis of ageing music scenes dismisses the notion of subcultural participation as a purely youth activity and instead reveals significant levels of adult involvement. Smith argues that membership in the Northern Soul scene is more closely linked with identity formation rather than age and nostalgia, and that ageing participants can both leave and return to the scene at their will.[59] In his study of ageing goths, Hodkinson questions Smith's fixed and youthful description of Northern Soul, stating that it does not take into account the modifications made to the scene by its ageing participants.[60] While Richard considers himself a devotee of Northern Soul, his current situation and adult responsibilities restrict his commitment to the scene, which demonstrates how he has had to adapt his participation levels: 'I am more selective these days. I don't do every Friday and Saturday but try and attend at least three or four a month.'[61]

Other changes include the shift from buying and swapping rare records at club nights to the selling of nostalgic compilation albums and memorabilia; an example of the change in the value of rarity within the scene, as well as an indication of the collective move to web-based commercial outlets. Ageing Northern Soul devotees may no longer have the ability to perform the split leap and high kicks of the dance form, but they can continue to partake in the dance scene through the calmer side-to-side sliding and small spins on the break of the music. As Northern South participant Nicola Anderson reveals, her involvement was 'first about the dance and to hear the music. Now it is less about the dance and more about the music but obviously the social side is very important to me.'[62]

While the active removal of the athletic elements from the Northern Soul dance vocabulary appears to be a result of necessity, I would argue that removal of the visual and spectacular elements of the scene is a strategic device to keep the scene exclusive. In his analysis of the ageing punk movement, Andy Bennett reveals how the ageing subcultural community creates a new set of values by

---

[59]   Smith, 'Beyond the Master Narrative of Youth'.
[60]   Hodkinson, 'Ageing in a Spectacular "Youth Culture"'.
[61]   Richard Gilbert, Interview Transcript.
[62]   Nicola Anderson, Interview Transcript.

placing a positive emphasis on age and experience.[63] Whereas youth and virility used to be favoured, the original Northern Soul participants now construct a strong identity within the scene through the accumulation of years of attendance and commitment. Richard states:

> I think most people's views on our scene is to carry on playing, listening and dancing to our music but at the same time keep it exclusive and to keep it ours. That is unless you can introduce new people who will pick-up the same ideals.[64]

Here, Richard touches upon the politics and division between the dancers in their twenties, whose identities are based around a revival of the late 1960s scene and whose dance knowledge is formed through references to the aforementioned Northern Soul music videos, and the original Northern Soul attendants, now in their 30s to 50s, who link themselves far more with the late 1970s scene.[65] This wrangling of authority is negotiated through the varying embodiments of the music, with new participants favouring the spectacular elements of the style, while original participants favour the patterns of side-to-side shifts of the feet or a complete dismissal of the dance elements by choosing simply to watch and listen.

I would argue, however, that exclusivity is jointly achieved through the acquisition of knowledge and through the muting of Northern Soul's spectacular style, including the shunning of the overtly visual dance steps. Bennett's analysis of ageing punks reveals that due to work commitments and changing lifestyles, ageing punks transcend the need for the explicit spectacular style and instead chose to internalize their commitment to the punk subculture.[66] From this, I maintain that Northern Soul enthusiasts also maintain scene exclusivity through the silencing of visual display, in response to both the popular mediation of the dance form and the introduction of newcomers to the scene. Richard's interview response supports this argument: 'I personally don't like to see too much gymnastics/acrobatics and I would prefer to see old fashion foot work in time with the music.'[67] By reimagining Northern Style as a way of being through social discourse rather than a surface display of athleticism, ageing participants have in fact legitimated their involvement through knowledge and experience, and in turn created a new form of subcultural capital.

As I have argued, the construction of self-identity and community within the Northern Soul scene, and in particular on the dance floor, rests upon a series of embodiments: the music-dance connection, the proliferation of knowledge and expertise and the powerful connection between Northern Soul participants. As a

---

[63] Andy Bennett, 'Punk's Not Dead: The Continuing Significance of Punk Rock for an Older Generation of Fans', *Sociology*, 40/2 (2006): pp. 219-35.

[64] Richard Gilbert, Interview Transcript.

[65] Wall, 'Out on the Floor'.

[66] Bennett, 'Punk's Not Dead'.

[67] Richard Gilbert, Interview Transcript.

consequence of media intervention though, a greater emphasis is placed on the visual elements of the scene and the balance has shifted from a series of individuals carving out self-identity within a community, to a community protecting its practice from the spectacle of the individual. This communal concealment of Northern Soul's spectacular style through the shunning of dance-floor acrobatics is a consequence of the need to protect the core values of the scene and provides a way of maintaining exclusivity around a social practice that is becoming more popularized. This defensive reaction towards spectacle within the ageing members of the Northern Soul movement raises the question of shifting values, and whether future media intervention will influence the evolution of the practice or alternatively encourage its nostalgic retreat back to the past.

Chapter 13

Jazz, Dance and
Black British Identities[1]

Catherine Tackley

Robert Crease[2] has asserted unequivocally that 'Dance is an integral and indispensible part of jazz studies', yet its practices and meanings have rarely been given the attention they deserve. This may be because the manifestations of jazz as dance music highlight its popular status when, as I have argued previously, a 'high art' reading of the music is more compatible with conventional scholarly activity and has ensured that jazz has become a valid subject for study at educational institutions'.[3] Howard Spring, in the 'Dance' entry in *The New Grove Dictionary of Jazz*, has also suggested that 'it may simply be that jazz scholars don't usually dance'.[4] This lack of physical and therefore cerebral engagement with dance is regrettable, but perhaps not surprising given that the development of jazz criticism and scholarship has been intimately linked with the evolution of listening over dancing (not that the two are mutually exclusive) as the primary mode of reception. Perhaps there is an underlying feeling that the spectacle of dance (social or staged) is a distraction and incompatible with the ideal conditions for listening which might be considered necessary when the music is the primary focus of attention. Contemporaneously, the technological development of sound recording has provided a canon of jazz masterworks founded on the disembodied representation of performance. Recently, however, the dominance of this canon has been questioned, prompting consideration of previously excluded aspects of jazz.[5] At the most extreme, this scholarship

---

[1]   The research presented here forms part of the 'What is Black British Jazz?' project based at The Open University and funded by the Arts and Humanities Research Council's Beyond Text scheme.

[2]   Robert Crease, 'Jazz Dance', in Mervyn Cooke and David Horn (eds), *The Cambridge Companion to Jazz* (Cambridge, 2003), p. 80.

[3]   Catherine Parsonage, 'The popularity of jazz, an unpopular problem: the significance of Robbie Williams' *Swing When You're Winning'*, *The Source*, 2 (2004), p. 59.

[4]   Howard Spring, 'Dance', in *The New Grove Dictionary of Jazz*, 2nd edn, ed. Barry Kernfeld (Grove Music Online, Oxford Music Online, 2010) at http://www.oxfordmusiconline.com.libezproxy.open.ac.uk/subscriber/article/grove/music/J549000 (accessed 21 November 2011).

[5]   See Matthew Butterfield, 'Music Analysis and the Social Life of Jazz Recordings', *Current Musicology*, 71-3 (2002): pp. 324-52; and Jed Rasula, 'The Media of Memory:

involves musicians whose performances have not been made widely available on record, or in some instances not documented at all, often as a result of their race or gender.[6] Exclusion also extends to others who are involved in jazz performances but may not be represented sonically even on 'live' recordings such as the audience or, indeed, dancers.

The response (or even lack of response) to jazz through dance by listeners provides a fundamental indicator of the nature of the reception and understanding of the music in particular times and places. As such, dance is an important factor in the burgeoning area of research which focuses on jazz outside America, especially if an aim of such projects is to try to understand what jazz meant to people, rather than to simply document its manifestations. Previously, I have distinguished between jazz in Britain (imported, or closely derivative) and British jazz (native, with original elements).[7] Necessarily, understanding the latter requires a wider and pluralistic conception of 'jazz' than the established (primarily American) canon might suggest, and implies complex and varying interactions between foreign and native traditions. Indeed, jazz can provide both musicians and dancers with the potential to construct new styles as expressions of individual and collective identities:

> Popular dancing is an extremely important cultural activity, for bodily movement is a kind of repository for social and individual identity. The dancing body engages the cultural inscripting of self and the pursuit of pleasure, dancing events are key sites in the working and reworking of racial, class and gender boundaries.[8]

Undoubtedly, the divergent responses to jazz from the British population were intimately bound up with attitudes to race, especially as the African American contribution to jazz became more widely understood. Considering black participation provides further perspectives on the relationships between jazz, dance and race in Britain. This chapter focuses on two specific instances in which jazz and dance were linked with the expression of black British identities.[9]

The Seductive Menace of Records in Jazz History', in Krin Gabbard (ed.), *Jazz Among the Discourses* (Durham, NC, and London, 1995).

[6]   See Tim Brooks, *Lost Sounds: Blacks and the Birth of the Recording Industry, 1890-1919* (Urbana and Chicago, 2004); and Sherrie Tucker, *Swing Shift: 'All-Girl' Bands of the 1940s* (Durham, NC, 2000).

[7]   Catherine Parsonage, *The Evolution of Jazz in Britain, 1880-1935* (Aldershot, 2005), pp. 254ff.

[8]   Crease, 'Jazz Dance', p. 69.

[9]   In a section entitled 'Black and White on the Dancefloor' in Chapter 5 of *There Ain't No Black in the Union Jack* (1987; Abingdon, 2010), Paul Gilroy addresses similar issues, primarily focusing on the period between my two case studies.

Ken 'Snakehips' Johnson and his West Indian Dance Orchestra at the Café de Paris (1939-41)[10]

The formation of a black British band in 1936 whose success culminated with a residency at the Café de Paris in London's West End was timely. A clearer understanding of the African American contribution to jazz had developed in Britain during the latter part of the 1920s, as critics rejected Paul Whiteman's 'symphonic syncopation' which had previously been favoured, in racially loaded discourse, as an 'improved' form of jazz. The availability of records by African American jazz musicians, the visits of Duke Ellington and Louis Armstrong in the early 1930s and the development of critical frameworks for evaluating both live and recorded jazz performances in British periodicals such as *Melody Maker* and *Rhythm* were all important factors.[11]

However, the Ministry of Labour contemporaneously introduced increasingly restrictive policies on visiting musicians in response to pressure from the Musicians' Union.[12] Whilst this limited the opportunities for British jazz musicians to interact directly with their American colleagues, the popularity of African American entertainment in Britain fuelled a demand for black British musicians to provide apparently 'authentic' jazz performances. Leslie Thompson, from Jamaica, who had already benefitted from being 'the only coloured trumpeter in London when Louis's [Armstrong's] records became the talk of the music business', judged that the time was right to form a coloured swing band.[13]

The initial personnel of the band included recent immigrants from the British West Indies, who as citizens of the British Empire were not subject to the Ministry of Labour restrictions, some that had been born and bred in the UK and even white British musicians who blacked up.[14] Thompson's aim was clearly to emulate contemporary American swing bands:

> We did well over a month of rehearsing. No, nearly two months ... Eventually white boys would pop in to the rehearsal room, surprised at the sound we were getting. They thought it was an American band! I used the arrangements of Brons[15]

---

[10]   I gratefully acknowledge the generosity of Andy Simons, formerly of the British Library's National Sound Archive and an expert on Black British Swing, for sharing his knowledge and resources.

[11]   Parsonage, *The Evolution of Jazz*, pp. 57ff.

[12]   Parsonage, *The Evolution of Jazz*, p. 255.

[13]   Leslie Thompson with Jeffrey Green, *Swing from a Small Island: The Story of Leslie Thompson* (London, 2009), pp. 71, 92.

[14]   Thompson, *Swing from a Small Island*, p. 94.

[15]   Sidney Bron's Orchestral Service supplied arrangements to dance bands throughout the country. Caroline Westbrook, 'Gerry Bron Interview', at http://www.somethingjewish. co.uk/articles/2267_gerry_bron_interview.htm (accessed 27 January 2011).

[*sic*], all American: we had them all, so we got an American sound which British bands lacked.[16]

Thompson was encouraged in his venture by the dancer Ken Johnson, who was originally from British Guiana but had been schooled in Britain. Johnson first studied law but then sought dance tuition from Buddy Bradley.[17] Bradley, an African American, had come to Britain in 1930 and was in demand as a choreographer of stage shows and film musicals. Thompson credited him with:

> changing the whole style of dancing in Britain. Before Buddy Bradley there were 'hoofers', which was very much tap dancing. Buddy Bradley introduced movement, and new aspects of dance. There was no change in the music – it was not difficult for us to play. Bradley revolutionized choreography.[18]

Similarly, Marshall and Jean Stearns explain Bradley's style as 'a blend of easy tap plus movements from the Afro-American vernacular'.[19] Their chapter on Bradley begins with a description of his choreography for Clifton Webb in the *Little Show of 1929* in which he incorporated 'an imitation of Earl Tucker's Snake Hips dance'.[20] It is possible that Bradley's tuition similarly influenced Ken Johnson's dancing. After appearing in the British film *Oh Daddy!*, choreographed by Bradley, Johnson worked in British Guiana, Trinidad and the USA before returning to London in 1936.[21]

Thompson's band first played in cinemas in outer London from April 1936. The group had various names but Johnson often headed the billing since, according to *Melody Maker*, he was already 'well-known to British music-hall audiences'.[22] By September they were usually billed as 'Ken "Snakehips" Johnson and his Emperors of Jazz'.[23] The addition of the 'Snakehips' nickname suggests that Johnson's dancing had become a defining feature of the act. Jazz and dance bands, both British and American, had long been regular fixtures in theatres and cinemas,

[16]   Thompson, *Swing from a Small Island*, p. 94.
[17]   Andy Simons, 'Black British Swing Part One', *IAJRC Journal*, 41/3 (August 2008): p. 44.
[18]   Thompson, *Swing from a Small Island*, p. 74.
[19]   Marshall Stearns and Jean Stearns, *Jazz Dance: The Story of American Vernacular Dance* (1968; New York, 1994), p. 166.
[20]   Stearns and Stearns, *Jazz Dance*, p. 160.
[21]   Val Wilmer, 'Johnson, Kenrick Reginald Hijmans (1914-1941)', *Oxford Dictionary of National Biography*, (Oxford University Press, 2004); online edn (May 2006) at http://www.oxforddnb.com/view/article/74576 (accessed 21 November 2011).
[22]   Andy Simons, 'Black British Swing Part Two', *IAJRC Journal*, 41/4 (December 2008), p. 64; 'New British Coloured Band', *Melody Maker*, 18 April (1936), p. 1.
[23]   Howard Rye, 'Visiting Firemen 17: Valaida Snow', in *Storyville* (1998-9), p. 119; Mark Miller, *High Hat, Trumpet and Rhythm: The Life and Music of Valaida Snow* (Toronto, 2007), p. 93.

but they were usually most successful when there was a visual element to their presentation. Thus, Johnson's distinctive dancing aided the early success of the band in mainstream British entertainment as it conformed to British expectations of African American acts in its provision of high-quality musical performances with a dash of sensual exoticism.

At the end of the year, the band secured a residency at the Old Florida Club in upmarket Mayfair.[24] London's club scene had long been vital to the development of British jazz, since it provided spaces in which visiting American jazz musicians and their British colleagues could interact, largely free from musical, social or legal restrictions.[25] In the 1930s, clubs which were popular amongst the large numbers of visiting African American performers also attracted a white clientele who were keen to interact with them and possibly experience an impromptu cabaret of a more intimate and informal nature than was possible in a theatre.[26] Entrepreneurs exploited the fashion for black entertainment, providing opportunities for black British musicians that brought them to the capital from elsewhere in the UK and the British Empire. This musical migration produced a vibrant diversity of musical styles in Soho's clubs, including West Indian calypso and rumba as well as jazz, which were often played by the same musicians.

After six months at the Old Florida, Johnson renegotiated the contract with the management without Thompson's knowledge, assuming ownership of the group and cutting him out of any financial interest. This caused a split in the personnel as Thompson, and many band members who were loyal to him, left the band. Johnson then brought in new musicians directly from Trinidad.[27] Although Thompson dismisses Johnson as a 'stick wagger' who was 'no musician' in his memoir, the reminiscences of Bradley's pedagogy suggest that Johnson had a good knowledge of contemporary swing.[28] Bradley acknowledged the prime source of his inspiration: 'I bought rafts of records and listened carefully to the accenting of improvised solos'.[29] The classically trained dancer Chris Parry who studied with Bradley in the mid-twentieth century recalled:

> I found it amazing that Buddy would spend a whole class making us just sit
> and listen to music without doing one step. The way he pulled out the solos
> of different musicians from bands like Ellington's and Basie's, was a real 'ear

[24] 'Johnson's Resident Break', *Melody Maker*, 26 December (1936), p. 8.
[25] Criminal activity was rife in the underworld of London. Clubs were frequently raided and fined for not having the appropriate licences, but the police could also be bribed to turn a blind eye. It is unlikely that musicians contravening the terms of their work permits by 'sitting in' informally would have concerned many of the proprietors.
[26] Parsonage, *The Evolution of Jazz*, pp. 256-7.
[27] Simons, 'Black British Swing Part Two', pp. 64-5.
[28] Thompson, *Swing from a Small Island*, p. 97.
[29] Stearns and Stearns, *Jazz Dance*, p. 166.

opener', as distinct from an 'eye-opener', which made us acutely aware of what
was going on in the actual jazz band.[30]

Bradley's approach, in which close listening is the basis of the dancing
experience, exposes the inextricable links between listening to and dancing to jazz.[31]
This linkage complicates both a standard listening/dancing dichotomy found in
jazz histories, especially when discussing the transition from swing (popular dance
music) to bebop (art music for listening), and also the assumed associations of live
jazz performance with dancing and jazz recordings with listening. Therefore, the
complex ways in which the aural experience and kinaesthetic response to jazz are
intertwined demands proper consideration.

The band continued at the Old Florida until April 1939 when it transferred to
Willerby's, a new club.[32] Club engagements meant that, in addition to providing a
show, the band would also play for social dancing. *Melody Maker* alluded to this
crucial difference, noting optimistically: 'That Ken and his boys should do well
in this new departure is beyond doubt, as their music has a dance-inducing quality
which cannot fail to please, while, as an entertaining unit, the band ranks high'.[33]
Their success led to recordings, BBC broadcasts and eventually promotion to the
Café de Paris in October 1939.

The Café de Paris opened in 1924 as a high-class restaurant with entertainment.
Following the patronage of the Prince of Wales, it became a haunt for Royalty
and high society. The venue's name belies the influence of Parisian cabaret clubs
and, consistent with this, dancing seems to have been the main attraction initially,
both in opportunities for patrons to take to the floor, usually as couples, and to
watch exhibition dancers.[34] However, ballroom dancing 'had the disadvantage of
demanding much more floor space than was practical at the Café de Paris. The
more the tables encroached, the more profitable.'[35] Changing fashions and the
circumstances of the Depression influenced the introduction of a range of cabaret
acts, frequently involving African American performers. It is significant that
Johnson and his band were employed at the Café so soon after the outbreak of War.
Clearly, the steady supply of American cabaret acts would be disrupted, and also
British dance musicians would be called up, whereas native West Indians were not

---

[30]   Will Gaines, Frank Holder and Chris Parry, 'Rhythm Tap, Jazz Improvisation and
Buddy Bradley in 1950s and 60s London', in *Dancing at the Crossroads: African Diasporic
Dances in Britain*, Royal Festival Hall (London, 2002), p. 17.
[31]   The reliance on recordings rather than live performances as sources for dance music
anticipates later developments, including Jamaican sound system culture. See Gilroy, *There
Ain't No Black*, pp. 216ff.
[32]   Andy Simons, 'Black British Swing Part Three', *IAJRC Journal*, 42/1 (March
2009): p. 55.
[33]   'Johnson's Resident Break'.
[34]   Charles Graves, *Champagne and Chandeliers. The Story of the Café de Paris*
(London, 1958), p. 35.
[35]   Graves, Champagne and Chandeliers, p. 36.

subject to conscription. Johnson was ideal for the Café, in that he could provide the latest American swing music which both looked and sounded authentic.

Evidence suggests that the residency of Johnson's band at the Café de Paris had a significant impact on popular music and dance in Britain. Space restraints had already had an effect on social dancing which took place at such venues:

> Another fad of fashion, this time on the part of restaurateurs, was to convert the dance floors from what – with a touch of hyperbole – one might say was comparable to the space of Lord's Cricket Ground, into something the size of a cabbage patch. ... We keen dancers, who still had an affection for our West End bands and the haunts at which they played, were forced to invent another style to suit the speeded-up music and the small, crowded dance floors. We did it, our sense of rhythm guiding us, and the long glides and the flowing three-steps were usurped by short, lilting walks and condensed chassés. This conception of the foxtrot is still taught by teachers of dancing, to meet the requirements of pupils who only frequent this type of dancing rendezvous, and it is now called 'Rhythm Dancing' or 'Crush Dancing'.[36]

Alongside exclusive central London venues such as the Café de Paris, the Palais de Danse continued to be popular. Bradley notes that the Palais bands were there specifically to play for dancers, and tended to perform at slower tempos, leading to quick-step or slow foxtrot dancing.[37] A clear distinction developed between dancing in the large, suburban dance halls and in the smaller central venues which reflected a division along class lines. Bradley recalled that 'It was at this point that a sharp difference of opinion arose between the dancers and the bands, causing a breach which exists up to the present day'.[38] Dance teachers supported bands which played 'strict tempo' music to which it was easy to dance standardized steps. However, this style was branded 'farcical' by Stanley Nelson, who argued that it was the dance, and not the music, that needed to change:

> I have said until I am sick of saying it that Jazz is not suited to English-style dancing and that the sooner the English style is completely altered ... the sooner will there be some agreement between [band]leaders and teachers. ... I have said before and I say it again that all the changes in the ballroom have been brought about by the bands and not the dancers. Bands play for dancing today under sufferance. I met a dance musician only the other day who told me that he gave up his comparatively decently-paid palais job to play at a bottle party at half the money because he couldn't stand palais tempo![39]

---

[36]   Josephine Bradley, *Dancing Through Life* (London, 1947), p. 37.

[37]   Bradley, *Dancing Through Life*, p. 38.

[38]   Bradley, *Dancing Through Life*, p. 39.

[39]   Stanley Nelson, 'Swing – What are you teachers going to do about it?', *Dancing Times* (March 1938), p. 813.

However, just months after Johnson's debut at the Café de Paris, the *Dancing Times* published an article by the well-known dance teacher Monsieur Pierre on 'Dancing to Swing'. Pierre recommended the 'Continental Swing' as '*a principle which can be applied to most of the steps of the English "Rhythm" or "Crush" Dancing*' as 'an excellent foundation for the spectacular steps of the "Jitterbug" style.'[40] More specifically, Josephine Bradley noted in her column in the same publication in February 1940: 'So far [in wartime], I have not noticed a predilection for jitterbug dancing in the restaurants I have visited, with, perhaps, the exception of the Café de Paris.'[41] A vivid description of the moment on the evening of 8 March 1941 when a bomb fell on the Café suggests that trend for jitterbug dancing continued there during the War, although it was banned elsewhere:

> The girl-friend said, 'Let's dance' and down the stairs they walked to the dance floor, and as the band struck up 'Oh, Johnnie', the girl-friend stepped away from Howard Barnes, raised her right hand, executed a hep-step and cried, 'Wow, Johnnie!' The bomb fell at that exact moment.[42]

Although Barnes survived to tell his story many others were injured or killed. The lives and careers of two performers, the leader Ken Johnson and saxophonist Dave 'Baba' Williams, were tragically cut short and the incident brought this particular combination of music and venue to a close.

Just as swing dancing was adopted in a peculiarly English way, so Johnson's band recorded swing settings of quintessentially English Shakespearian texts. But hints of the inclusion of West Indian music in their live repertoire (although not in their known recorded output) suggest that Johnson and his band went beyond simply compensating for missing African Americans. Having advocated 'Continental Swing', Monsieur Pierre concluded his December 1939 article with an intriguing section on 'Swing Calypsos' which 'mostly come from Trinidad', commenting that 'there are really no basic steps danced to it, and the dancers in Trinidad seem to more or less improvise as they go on'. He continued: 'It would be interesting to import a Calypso Band into England and see the reaction of the dancing public, but we must get rid of the war nightmare first!'[43] Pierre's lack of awareness of such groups concurrently on the London scene is probably indicative of the presence of these bands in smaller clubs rather than venues like the Café de Paris.[44] In the same month, *Melody Maker* reported under the heading 'Ken Johnson has New Air Ideas':

[40]   Monsieur Pierre, 'Dancing to "Swing Music"', *Dancing Times* (December 1939), pp. 143-4.
[41]   Josephine Bradley, 'Random Reflections on War-Time Dancing', *Dancing Times* (February 1940), p. 292.
[42]   Graves, *Champagne and Chandeliers*, p. 121.
[43]   Pierre, 'Dancing to "Swing Music"', pp. 144-5.
[44]   See John Cowley, 'Cultural "Fusions": Aspects of British West Indian Music in the USA and Britain 1918-51', *Popular Music*, 5 (1985): pp. 81-96.

[Johnson] proposes to pursue a commercial swing policy, playing pop stuff in swing time and doing, for instance, a swing choir arrangement of *Boomps a Daisy*. There will also be those intriguing Calypso rumbas, and of course Ken's Swing Choir, which he features at the Café with enormous success.[45]

Although it is easy to read the inclusion of calypso and rumba, Trinidadian and Cuban respectively, as a specific articulation of cultural identity, it is important to note the confluence of these genres and American swing in contemporary descriptions. In this context, calypso and rumba acted generally as signifiers of the Caribbean and exoticism.[46] These descriptions of a hybrid repertoire suggest a generalized perception of black music commensurate with the blurring of the black identities of the musicians who performed them, which is perhaps characteristic of the black British experience at this time. The combination of dancers searching for new rhythms (Pierre discovered 'Swing Calypsos' from a dance teacher who had travelled to Trinidad), together with the obvious ability of Johnson's musicians to play in a wide range of styles, provided the opportunity for the reassessment of distinctions based on nationality, race, class, music and dance within the particular context of the Café de Paris in wartime, as illustrated in Bradley's description:

[at the Café de Paris] the leader of the band, a 'hot' dancer himself, commonly known as 'Snake Hips', breaks down barriers by descending from his bandstand and joining the dancers. I have seen even brass-hats [high-ranking military officers] throwing off restraint and following his lead to the strains of the dizzy blond in his arms warbling, 'My heart belongs to Daddy'.[47]

Paul Murphy at The Electric Ballroom (1982-1984)

In 1968, the Stearns concluded their survey of jazz dance with a section entitled 'Requiem', but nevertheless wrote optimistically:

There is little reason to believe that the great tradition of American vernacular dance has vanished forever, and much evidence to support the belief that a new and perhaps more remarkable age of highly rhythmic native dance will arrive in the not too distant future.[48]

---

[45] 'Ken Johnson has New Air Ideas', *Melody Maker*, 2 December 1939, p. 7.
[46] For further discussion, see Daniel Neely, '"Mento, Jamaica's Original Music": Development, Tourism and the Nationalist Frame' (PhD dissertation, New York University, 2008).
[47] Bradley, 'Random Reflections', p. 292.
[48] Stearns and Stearns, *Jazz Dance*, p 362.

The rise of bebop and adoption of new styles of popular music as vehicles for youthful self-expression is conventionally thought to have brought an end to the close association between jazz and dance:

> For many youths restlessly seeking a new bodily identity in the new cultural context of the turbulent post-war years, the break-up of the jazz music-dance alliance meant that jazz was no longer a tool of self-discovery.[49]

But this view ignores young people throughout Britain who began dancing to American popular music, including jazz, in the 1970s. The latter decades of the twentieth century were marked by the revival, resurgence and reinvention of swing-based social dancing as well as tap dancing on the stage. However, the UK club scene provides arguably more convincing examples of 'a new and perhaps more remarkable age of highly rhythmic native dance' in which dancers' interpretations of primarily American jazz records formed the basis of a British tradition of jazz dance, which in London was particularly connected with black British identities. Overshadowed in histories of jazz dance by the global swing revival, and neglected by scholars of contemporary club cultures in favour of genres such as House and Punk, jazz dance has also been largely written out of even *British* jazz history, presumably because, initially at least, this scene drew on recordings of imported American music, rather than live British performances. However, the jazz dance scene was not only influential on live jazz performance in Britain but also established jazz as significant for many black Britons, including musicians and dancers.

The UK's adoption of the American disco craze in the early 1970s included music which fused jazz elements with more popular styles, such as rock and funk, in various combinations and provided an alternative to mainstream chart music. Some DJs steered a path from jazz-influenced chart music towards more eclectic fusion tracks where jazz elements were more dominant. The adoption of jazz funk and fusion by DJs and dancers (of all races) was part of a counter-cultural music policy repeatedly referred to by Mark 'Snowboy' Cotgrove, DJ and Latin percussionist, and his interviewees[50] as 'black music'. Within this, jazz tracks became a significant part of many DJs' sets:

> The US Jazz Charts in 1977 were starting to look like the play-lists of the more adventurous clubs here in the UK (and there were many). Literally, of the 100 in the chart, I could think of at least one track off of most of the albums that had gotten played here on the dancefloor at some point – not that the artists would

---

[49]   Crease, 'Jazz Dance', p. 79.

[50]   Testimonies in this section are drawn from Mark Cotgrove's comprehensive collection of interviews with leading figures in the jazz dance scene: *From Jazz Funk and Fusion to Acid Jazz: the History of the UK Jazz Dance Scene* (London, 2009).

have made them with a dancefloor in mind – and it continued like this for the rest of the decade.[51]

Cotgrove's comment points to the essential dislocation between production and consumption of jazz in which the DJ plays a central mediating role. Jazz that was not intended for the dance floor created a scene distinct from the mainstream not only musically, but specifically through the challenge it presented to dancers, excluding those who lacked the technique or inventiveness to deal with it. DJ Robbie Vincent describes this alternative scene:

> I couldn't play some of those very fast Jazz Fusion records or some of the more esoteric jazzy records that the Jazz dancers were brilliant with. Most people couldn't dance to them, so what would be the point of wrecking my dancefloor? Because there was a market for that somewhere else, the jazzier side of our scene developed its own underground scene as rap did.[52]

Increasingly then, jazz was recognized as a specific genre within even the 'black music' club scene. In the late 1970s, club DJs incorporated 'jazz breaks' – 'maybe two or three sets of fifteen to twenty minute sections of Jazz of varying tempos and heaviness'.[53] 'Jazz Rooms' 'where all the DJs got a chance to play deeper Soul and Jazz than they would in the main ballroom' appeared at 'weekenders', dance parties which literally spanned a weekend. 'Jazz' had become a subcultural marker within a scene which was itself already distanced from the mainstream of chart music, and specific jazz nights at clubs had begun by the end of the 1970s. Although jazz dance had a national following, there were clear distinctions between North and South, with all-dayers and weekenders dominant in the former, and clubs in the latter. More specifically, within the southern scene that Cotgrove identifies, there was a clear difference between the 'Home Counties' and central London which reflected pre-existing social divisions based on race and class. This, in turn, influenced the music that was being played:

> Logic tells you that because of the sparse ethnic population in the home-counties, the scene was generally made up with a crowd of which the vast majority was White … In London however, just like any of the major cities around England, the scene was very black and liked a different sound.[54]

Increasing tension between young black people and the police, and the racialization of urban unrest in areas such as Notting Hill and Brixton in the media, were influential on door-policies which served to exclude black people from

[51] Cotgrove, *From Jazz Funk*, p. 19.
[52] Cotgrove, *From Jazz Funk*, p. 183.
[53] Cotgrove, *From Jazz Funk*, p. 22.
[54] Cotgrove, *From Jazz Funk*, p. 29.

London clubs. Although black dancers did attend some central venues in the 1970s, DJ Tony Hickmott recalled the limitations of this: 'I did *The Prince of Wales* in Hammersmith, but the management didn't like the crowd (too many Blacks).'[55] DJ George Power, who had a background in the Youth Club movement, had a major influence on the participation of black people in the London club scene.[56] Power tackled racism by simply refusing to play where discriminatory door policies were in operation.[57] Power's impact was dramatic; dancer Paul Anderson recalled that that a club called Crackers in Soho 'was more of a white scene then until George Power came in'.[58] When Power transferred to The Horseshoe in Tottenham Court Road in 1980, the dancers remained 'majority black'.[59] At this time, DJ Paul Murphy started another night at The Horseshoe called JAFFAS – 'Jazz and Funk, Funk and Soul' – which attracted many of Power's dancers. In 1982, the same pairing of Power and Murphy occurred again in Jazzifunk nights at The Electric Ballroom in Camden, North London, with Murphy providing jazz-focused sets in an upstairs room against Power's more mainstream soul and funk, all for a crowd that was 'almost entirely black'.[60] Although Murphy's contribution was the focal point for dancers, the strength of Power's social influence is shown by the dancers attempting to follow Murphy to a new club when he left the Ballroom in 1984, but being forced to return there by the continuation of racist door policies elsewhere.[61]

Cotgrove unequivocally defines Jazzifunk at the Electric Ballroom as 'the most important club night in this scene's history', a view confirmed by many of the interviewees in the second part of his book. A particular statement of a predominantly masculine black British style, expressed through dance, dress and music, with the increasingly jazz-dominated playlists at Crackers and The Horseshoe, which had developed alongside the growth of black participation, reached its apotheosis at The Electric Ballroom. The dance style drew on different influences, including contemporary ballet, disco and even martial arts, but dominant in the mix were elements drawn from the cultural roots of many of the dancers. DJ Ed Stokes commented: 'those fast movements of the Jazz Dancers, I can trace back to Ska. The original shuffle we used to do in the 60s was a lot of the very fast foot movements, the knee trembling effects.'[62] The 'shuffling' battles of West Indian dancers directly prefigured the distinctive competitive element in black British jazz dance where similar battles between individuals would

[55]   Cotgrove, *From Jazz Funk*, p. 187. Stan Beeler points out that 'racial quotas' were still in operation in the early twenty-first century: see his *Dance, Drugs and Escape: The Club Scene in Literature, Film and Television since the Late 1980s* (Jefferson, NC, 2007).

[56]   Cotgrove, *From Jazz Funk*, p. 184.

[57]   Cotgrove, *From Jazz Funk*, p. 29.

[58]   Cotgrove, *From Jazz Funk*, p. 251.

[59]   Cotgrove, *From Jazz Funk*, p. 34.

[60]   Cotgrove, *From Jazz Funk*, p. 36.

[61]   Cotgrove, *From Jazz Funk*, pp. 38, 49.

[62]   Cotgrove, *From Jazz Funk*, p. 196.

take place within a circle formed by the other dancers. Therefore, although the shuffle, circle and handkerchief are familiar tropes in African-derived vernacular dance including those associated with Jamaican dancehall, young West Indians specifically used jazz as a way of reinterpreting their heritage. Cotgrove relates anecdotally that 'it was quite dangerous being Black and into Soul or Funk in a Black area because the majority – the Reggae lovers – would call you a "Soul Head" – which although not sounding abusive, would be meant antagonistically – almost as if one were a traitor'.[63] Thus, dancers actively constructed multiple black British identities through deliberately distancing themselves from, but still referencing, their West Indian-ness.

Although both this process and the battles were essentially individual, as Paul Gilroy wrote in his essay on late twentieth-century black vernacular dance: 'Even in residual form, the conjunction of music and dance characteristic of African expressive cultures orchestrated the relationship between the individual and the group.'[64] The jazz dance 'crews' that began as groups representing particular areas and battling other crews collectively also had origins in West Indian dance. Travis Edwards comments that, in the early 1970s, 'I went to the *A-Train* [reggae club] in Mile End (London), which was a dangerous club. Different areas of London would come in and you'd know there'd be a battle.'[65] Gilroy, citing Carl Gayle, suggests that this violence led West Indians to seek a more tranquil alternative in the soul scene.[66] However, alongside the development of 'crews', jazz dance battles also became more intense. Michael Brown, a stalwart of Crackers and The Horseshoe, was 'proud of the Jazz scene, the dance, the integration of all colours; the innovations; the dancing, but [The Electric Ballroom] was too hot and sweaty and too many youngsters, and there were fights up there. It'd changed dramatically. Respect went out the window.'[67] A statement from dancer Gary Nurse relates this to the centrality of dance for young black Britons:

> If you got in front of someone, you'd be there to do battle. You're talking about people that have *got nothing in their life apart from their dancing* you know, so when that was at stake, if you beat him you'd better be prepared to get a slap. [my emphasis][68]

Despite and even because of this tension, a powerful collective identity developed around Murphy's session which was intimidating to outsiders. A significant dimension of this was racial, as even a relative insider, jazz dance DJ Gilles

[63]   Cotgrove, *From Jazz Funk*, p. 42.
[64]   Paul Gilroy, 'Exer(or)cising Power: Black Bodies in the Black Public Sphere', in Helen Thomas (ed.), *Dance in the City* (New York, 1997), p. 22.
[65]   Cotgrove, *From Jazz Funk*, p. 249.
[66]   Gilroy, *There Ain't No Black*, p. 220.
[67]   Cotgrove, *From Jazz Funk*, p. 253.
[68]   Cotgrove, *From Jazz Funk*, p. 261.

Peterson, described his first visit to The Electric Ballroom as 'a frightening experience. I was the only white person in there. It was hard core.'[69]

Ultimately, The Electric Ballroom thrived on the negotiation of hierarchy through the active construction of collective and individual style and identity. However, for many of those involved, the scene lost its vibrancy when the sense of the collective overwhelmed the potential for individuality:

> I went to The Electric Ballroom for the first year and a half and then stopped going. I got bored. Also, a lot of the individualism had gone. Everyone was copying each other and doing the same style and it was just about the music being as fast as can be.[70]

The Electric Ballroom dance style was subsequently disseminated in a number of ways including the performances of IDJ (I Dance Jazz) a successful professional dance crew which emerged from The Ballroom scene. However, Gary Nurse, a member of IDJ, articulates the essential difference between the crew's performances and dancing at The Ballroom:

> as soon as we went on stage you lose the root of what it was all about. At The Ballroom it's an individual thing, but you put it on stage and you're sharing it. … Challenging was what it was all about. Nowadays it's all clean fun but then, if you got burned you'd start wading into someone's face. It wasn't clean – that's what it meant to people back then.[71]

Conclusion: Individual and Collective Identities

These case studies of the Café de Paris and The Electric Ballroom show how black British identities were (re)presented in and constructed through dance as a kinetic response to the sounds of both live and recorded jazz. Although both scenes were notable for their eclecticism, Ken Johnson's presentation of black Britishness was attractive to white Britons, since it drew on their familiarity with African American culture and involved them as dancers, but the assertion of collective identity at The Electric Ballroom, itself characterized by virtuosic competitive display, served to largely exclude white Britons from participation. Johnson's performances were commensurate with confusion around the specificity of blackness in wider society prior to large-scale migration which brought such issues more to the fore, whereas dancers at The Electric Ballroom articulated an increasingly definite idea of black Britishness which, initially at least, provided individual freedom of expression for participants.

[69]   Cotgrove, *From Jazz Funk*, p. 231.
[70]   Cotgrove, *From Jazz Funk*, p. 253.
[71]   Cotgrove, *From Jazz Funk*, p. 259.

The development of both scenes can be broadly characterized by a shift from the peripheries towards the mainstream, mediated by the culture industry. Interestingly, in the 1930s and 1940s, this shift essentially involved the transference of a stage act into a social dance environment but the reverse was true of jazz dance in the 1980s. The dissemination of black British identities to a wider (white) audience was accompanied by a loss of specificity – in Johnson's case the conflation of musical styles and their origins and for the dancers of The Electric Ballroom the eradication of the competitive essence which had characterized it. Both scenes encouraged individualism in dance, but there were also explicit and implicit codifications of style and etiquette which led to a greater sense of the collective and might be regarded as a prerequisite for both mass mediation and further development.

Although both scenes discussed here began with the idea of jazz as imported (African) American music and dance, the geographical and cultural distance from this American identity allowed the British response to develop quickly from emulation via reinterpretation towards self-expression, resulting in manifestations which are distinctively black British. This chapter has shown that studying jazz and dance in cafés and ballrooms, and not only in the canonical heyday of the relationship between the two forms, is crucial to appreciating the social functions of jazz in different communities.

Epilogue: Terms of Engagement

Sherril Dodds and Susan C. Cook

As a physical collection of essays *Bodies of Sound* has a finite ending. The persistent impermanence of 'the popular', however, prevents any claims we could make here to offer a final word or bring closure. This epilogue provides instead an opportunity to reflect upon the transnational and transdiciplinary nature of this volume and its collective accumulation of ideas and revelations. In offering a frame of sorts to balance the introduction, we want to draw particular attention to how the collection stands as a whole and what emerges from this volume, itself a body of work.

The collection takes as its point of departure 'popular' 'music' and 'dance'. In their noun forms, 'music' and 'dance' as well as 'the popular' suggest stable objects or discrete practices. The essays in this collection, however, present the processes, actions and multiple agencies that surround dancing and 'musicking', to borrow sociologist Christopher Small's helpful and necessary gerund.[1] Through writerly performances of putting words on the page, the authors render music and dance active and activating in ways that demonstrate what these cultural forms 'do' as much as what they are. These 'doings' are themselves constitutive of the mobile, contingent and contested space of 'the popular', always in the process of making itself and being made.

In both the British and US academic environments that we have inhabited, interdisciplinary scholarship has become commonplace. Yet the actual nature of that scholarship and how it bridges or disrupts its disciplines and methodologies of origin frequently remains undefined. As editors, we sought to erode existing academic boundaries by privileging explorations of the popular that brought both the kinesthetic and the aural into play as equitably and as productively as possible. We challenged our contributors and ourselves to acknowledge and account for overlapping sonic and kinesthetic spaces and to identify the intrinsic linkages between the sensorial planes of sound and movement. While the terms 'trans-' or 'interdisciplinary' usefully describe the academic framework, the notion of 'engaged' better encapsulates what resulted. Like ideas of 'embodiment' and 'the popular', the verb 'engaged' and its noun form 'engagement' speak to a relational, participatory process enmeshed in the daily practices and meanings of self and other.

[1] Christopher Small, *Musicking: The Meanings of Performing and Listening* (Middletown, 1998), p. 9.

Engagement accounts as well for the dynamic interchange between moving and sounding, through the mobilizing relationships, negotiations, contestations and circulations that occur between and among dancers, musicians, DJs, spectators, instructors, judges, business owners, critics and everyone else who invests in popular sound and movement. As they excavated, theorized and interpreted localized and underexplored music and dance cultures, some authors reanimated past practices through examinations of archival sources, while others animated the contemporary lived experience through ethnographies and explorations of technological mediations, all of which embrace human endeavours and modes of embodiment. Thus the collection demonstrates an intellectual sharing and a strengthening of critical methodologies across the disciplinary domains and geographical locales where sound and movement typically reside.

The geographical breadth of *Bodies of Sound*, with engagements drawn from four continents, speaks to the transnational and globalized nature of the popular even as it is produced and understood at local, even personal, levels. In totality, the collection serves as a potent reminder of how vast the popular is and how much remains to be done to account for its very popularity, its ubiquity, its history and its variety. The individual essays repeatedly demonstrate how, within the quotidian popular sphere, moving and musicking go on repeatedly, regularly and rewardingly. The authors provide abundant evidence of the multiple ways popular, sonic embodiments interact, transform and transgress over time and place. More importantly, they remained attentive to what practitioners themselves made of these overlapping sensorial experiences and what meanings they created from them and attached to them.

These practitioners, past and present, and their fellow collaborators or observers are often articulate, reflective and instructive as they identify and rationalize the choices they make. Furthermore, there emerges a strong sense of where and how they come to move and engage with sound, or where they locate power and meaning for themselves or for those they observe and assist. The choices they make are many and nuanced. Some describe a need to move as a way to respond to a beloved's voice, while others actively musick or hear what they need in order to move. The variety of experiences presented in this volume suggests a continuum of codependent engagement, from listening to stimulate movement, moving to facilitate listening, and everything in between. What emerges overwhelmingly from the collection is the power these embodied engagements hold to shape individual and collective experiences both real and imagined. Or, more correctly, the multiple kinds of power that are potentially – and often simultaneously – available to attract and repel, to unite and divide, to construct and deconstruct, and to transform identities in ways that can transcend the space or time of the music-dance event itself.

In discussing a collection that celebrates bodies, we cannot help but note that the majority of contributors to this volume are female. What might this act of scholarly embodiment say about the space of the popular and its moving and musicking, about the processes of engagement, or about pleasure and power?

One response would seem to be that some scholarly investments remain of particular interest to some women. Many of us writing came to our work through a shared pleasure in performing and participating. Perhaps we share a need to understand meanings located within bodies, to reflect on the interface of pleasures and powers, or to explore what is done in the name of having fun. Identities, however, are complex, and gender is just one of many means available, along with – but not limited to – race, ethnicity, class, sexuality, national identity, religious affiliation, ability and age, through which we perform ourselves and our humanity is understood by others.

Not surprisingly, the individual essays reveal the complicated and highly contingent ways gender, as part of an unstable matrix of subjectivity and agency, works through the sonic and kinesthetic; in particular circumstances, men musick and men dance and women musick and women dance. The particularities of the circumstances matter in order to understand the choices, changes and contradictions by which and through which power circulates around moving and sounding bodies; the embodied experiences described herein may both gender and un-gender bodies in ways that remain to be explored. It bears repeating, though, that we need to remain attentive to gender not only within our research but as part of the conditions under which our scholarship is made and how it is valued.

It is perhaps the hope of all editors that the collections they create matter, that they provide a forum for new ideas and voices to emerge and provide models for subsequent like-minded projects. Our hope is that this collection matters because it speaks to the necessity of remaining engaged with the popular as conceived, practised and rendered meaningful within the sonic-kinesthetic space. Likewise, we hope that *Bodies of Sound* encourages others to seek in our histories and ask after in the present for the realities of moving minds, listening bodies, the meanings of their pleasure and the workings of their power.

Bibliography

Agulhon, Maurice, *Marianne au Pouvoir: L'imagerie et la Symbolique Républicaines de 1880 à 1914* (Paris: Flammarion, 1989).

Albright, Ann Cooper, *Choreographing Difference: The Body and Identity in Contemporary Dance* (Middletown: Wesleyan University Press, 1997).

Anthias, Floya, 'Social Stratification and Social Inequality: Models of Intersectionality and Identity', in Fiona Devine, Mike Savage, John Scott and Rosemary Crompton (eds), *Rethinking Class: Culture, Identities & Lifestyle* (Basingstoke: Palgrave Macmillan, 2005).

Antonetti, Guy, *Louis-Philippe* (Paris: Librairie Arthème Fayard, 2002).

Arkin, Lisa C., and Marion Smith, 'National Dance in the Romantic Ballet', in Lynn Garafola (ed.), *Rethinking the Sylph: New Perspectives on the Romantic Ballet* (Hanover: Wesleyan University Press, 1997).

Back, Les and John Solomos, eds, *Theories of Race and Racism: A Reader* (London: Routledge, 2000).

Badger, Reid, *A Life in Ragtime: A Biography of James Reese Europe* (New York: Oxford University Press, 1995).

Bakka, Egil, *Norske dansetradisjonar* (Oslo: Samlaget, 1978).

Bakka, Egil and Ingar Ranheim, eds, *Handlingsplan for Folkemusikk og Folkedans* (Trondheim: RFF-senteret, 1995).

Bakke, Marit, 'Cultural Policy in Norway', in Peter Dueland (ed.), *The Nordic Cultural Model* (Copenhagen: Nordic Cultural Institute, 2003).

Banerjea, Koushik, 'Sounds of Whose Underground? The Fine Tuning of Diaspora in an Age of Mechanical Reproduction', *Theory, Culture & Society*, 17/3 (2000): 64-79.

Barr, Steve, *The Almost Complete 78 RPM Record Dating Guide* (Huntington Beach, CA: Yesterday Once Again, 1991).

Barthes, Roland, *Image-Music-Text*, edited and translated by Stephen Heath (London: Fontana, 1977).

Beeler, Stan, *Dance, Drugs and Escape: The Club Scene in Literature, Film and Television Since the Late 1980s* (Jefferson: McFarland & Co., 2007).

Bennett, Andy and Keith Kahn-Harris, eds, *After Subculture: Critical Studies in Contemporary Youth Culture* (Basingstoke and New York: Palgrave Macmillan, 2004).

Bennett, Andy, 'Punk's Not Dead: The Continuing Significance of Punk Rock for an Older Generation of Fans', *Sociology*, 40/2 (2006): 219-235.

Bennett, Andy, Barry Shank, and Jason Toynbee, eds, *The Popular Music Studies Reader* (London: Routledge, 2006).

Bergeron, Katherine, 'Prologue: Disciplining Music', in Katherine Bergeron and Philip V. Bohlman (eds), *Disciplining Music: Musicology and its Canons* (Chicago: University of Chicago Press, 1992), pp. 1-9.

Bhabha, Homi K., 'The Third Space (an Interview)', in Jonathan Rutherford (ed.), *Identity: Community, Culture, Difference* (London: Lawrence & Wishart, 1990).

Bhabha, Homi K., *The Location of Culture* (New York: Routledge, 2004).

Bordo, Susan, *Unbearable Weight: Feminism, Western Culture, and the Body* (Berkeley: University of California Press, 1993).

Bosse, Joanna, 'To Lead and Follow: Gender, Dominance, and Connection in Ballroom Dance', paper presented at the Annual Meeting of the Society for Ethnomusicology (Atlanta, 2005).

Bosse, Joanna, 'Whiteness and the Performance of Race in American Ballroom Dance', *The Journal of American Folklore*, 120/475 (2007): 19-47.

Bosse, Joanna, 'Salsa Dance and the Transformation of Style: An Ethnographic Study of Movement and Meaning in a Cross-Cultural Context', *Dance Research Journal*, 40/1 (2008): 45-64.

Boyes, Georgina, *The Imagined Village: Culture, Ideology and the English Folk Revival* (Leeds: No Masters Co-operative, 2001).

Brabazon, Tara, *From Revolution to Revelation: Generation X, Popular Culture and Cultural Studies* (Aldershot: Ashgate, 2005).

Bradley, Barbara, 'Sampling Sexuality: Gender, Technology and the Body in Dance Music', *Popular Music*, 12/2 (1993): 155-76.

Brewster, Bill and Frank Broughton, *Last Night a DJ Saved My Life: The History of the Disk Jockey* (London: Headline, 1999).

Brocken, Michael, *The British Folk Revival, 1944-2002* (Aldershot: Ashgate, 2003).

Brooks, Tim, *Lost Sounds: Blacks and the Birth of the Recording Industry, 1890-1919* (Urbana and Chicago: University of Illinois Press, 2004).

Brunschwig, Henri, *French Colonialism, 1871-1914: Myths and Realities* (London: Pall Mall Press, 1966).

Buckland, Theresa Jill, *Society Dancing: Fashionable Bodies in England, 1870-1920* (Basingstoke: Palgrave Macmillan, 2011).

Buckley, David, *David Bowie: The Complete Guide to His Music* (London: Omnibus Press, 2005).

Burt, Richard, 'Shakespeare, "Glocalisation", Race and the Small Screens of Post-Popular Culture', in Richard Burt and Lynda E. Boose (eds), *Shakespeare, The Movie II: Popularizing the Plays on Film, TV, Video and DVD* (London: Routledge, 2003).

Butler, Judith, *Gender Trouble: Feminism and the Subversion of Identity* (New York: Routledge, 1990).

Butler, Judith, *Undoing Gender* (New York: Routledge, 2004).

Butterfield, Matthew, 'Music Analysis and the Social Life of Jazz Recordings', *Current Musicology*, 71-3 (Spring 2001-Spring 2002): 324-52.

Carvalho, José Jorge de, 'The Multiplicity of Black Identities in Brazilian Popular Music', in Larry Crook and Randall Johnson (eds), *Black Brazil: Culture, Identity and Social Mobilization* (Los Angeles: UCLA Latin American Center Publications, 1999).

Carvalho, Martha de Ulhôa, 'Tupi or not Tupi MPB: Popular Music and Identity in Brazil', in David J. Hess and Roberto DaMatta (eds), *The Brazilian Puzzle: Culture on the Borderlands of the Western World* (New York: Columbia University Press, 1995).

Çelik, Zeynep and Leila Kinney, 'Ethnography and Exhibitionism at the Expositions Universelles', *Assemblage*, 13 (December 1990): 34-59.

Chu, Petra Ten-Doesschate, 'Pop Culture in the Making: The Romantic Craze for History', in Petra Ten-Doesschate Chu and Gabriel P. Weisberg (eds), *The Popularization of Images: Visual Culture under the July Monarchy* (Princeton: Princeton University Press, 1994).

Clark, Maribeth, 'The Quadrille as Embodied Musical Experience in 19th-Century Paris', *The Journal of Musicology*, 19/3 (2002): 503-26.

Cogdell, Christina, 'The Futurama Recontextualized: Norman Bel Geddes's Eugenic World of Tomorrow', *American Quarterly*, 53 (2000): 193-245.

Cohen, Sandra, ed., *International Encyclopedia of Dance* (Oxford: Oxford University Press, 1998).

Cohen, Sarah R., 'Performing Identity in the Hard Nut: Stereotype, Modeling and the Inventive Body', *The Yale Journal of Criticism*, 11/2 (1998): 485-505.

Collin, Matthew, *Altered State: The Story of Ecstasy Culture and Acid House* (London: Serpent's Tail, 1987).

Cook, Pam, 'Transnational Utopias: Baz Luhrmann and Australian Cinema', *Transnational Cinemas*, 1/1 (January 2010): 23-36.

Cook, Susan C., 'Passionless Dancing and Passionate Reform: Respectability, Modernism and the Social Dancing of Irene and Vernon Castle', in William Washabaugh (ed.), *The Passion of Music and Dance: Body, Gender and Sexuality* (Oxford: Berg, 1998).

Cook, Susan C., 'Watching Our Step: Embodying Research, Telling Stories', in Lydia Hamessley and Elaine Barkin (eds), *Audible Traces: Gender, Identity, and Music* (Zurich: Carciofoli Press, 1999).

Cook, Susan C., '"R-E-S-P-E-C-T (Find Out What It Means to Me)": Feminist Musicology and the Abject Popular', *Women and Music: A Journal of Gender and Culture*, 5 (2001): 140-45.

Cook, Susan C., '"In Imitation of My Negro Mammy": Alma Gluck and the American Prima Donna', in Rachel Cowgill and Hilary Poriss (eds), *The Arts of the Prima Donna in the Long Nineteenth Century* (Oxford: Oxford University Press, 2012), pp. 290-307.

Cordova, Sarah Davies, *Paris Dances: Textual Choreographies of the Nineteenth-Century Novel* (San Francisco: International Scholars Publications, 1999).

Cotgrove, Mark, *From Jazz Funk and Fusion to Acid Jazz: The History of the UK Jazz Dance Scene* (London: Chaser Publications, 2009).

Cowgill, Rachel, 'On the Beat: The Victorian Policeman as Musician', in Martin Hewitt and Rachel Cowgill (eds), *Victorian Soundscapes Revisited* (Leeds: Leeds Centre for Victorian Studies and Leeds University Centre for English Music, 2007).

Cowley, John, 'Cultural "Fusions": Aspects of British West Indian Music in the USA and Britain 1918-51', *Popular Music*, 5 (1985): 81-96.

Crease, Robert, 'Jazz Dance', in Mervyn Cooke and David Horn (eds), *The Cambridge Companion to Jazz* (Cambridge: Cambridge University Press, 2003).

Crook, Larry N., *Focus: Music of Northeast Brazil* (New York: Routledge, 2009).

Csikszentmihalyi, Mihaly and Stith Benett, 'An Exploratory Model of Play', *American Anthropologist*, 73/1 (1971): 45-58.

Csikszentmihalyi, Mihaly and Isabella Selega Csikszentmihalyi, *Optimal Experience: Psychological Studies of Flow in Consciousness* (Cambridge: Cambridge University Press, 1988).

Csikszentmihalyi, Mihaly, *Flow: The Psychology of Optimal Experience* (New York: Harper and Row, 1990).

Debord, Guy, *Society of the Spectacle*, translated by Ken Knabb (1967; reprint, London: Rebel Press, 2004).

de Certeau, Michel, *The Practice of Everyday Life*, translated by Steven Rendell (Berkeley: University of California Press, 1984).

Deleuze, Gilles and Guattari, Félix, *Anti-Oedipus: Capitalism and Schizophrenia* (New York: The Viking Press, 1977).

Desmond, Jane, 'Embodying Difference: Issues in Dance and Cultural Studies', in Jane Desmond (ed.), *Meaning in Motion: New Cultural Studies of Dance* (Durham: Duke University Press, 1997).

Dixon Gottschild, Brenda, *Digging the Africanist Presence in American Performance: Dance and Other Contexts* (Westport: Greenwood Press, 1996).

Dixon Gottschild, Brenda, 'Stripping the Emperor: The Africanist Presence in American Concert Dance', in Ann Dils and Ann Cooper Albright (eds), *Moving History/Dancing Cultures: A Dance History Reader* (Middletown: Wesleyan University Press, 2001).

Dodds, Sherril, *Dancing on the Canon: Embodiments of Value in Popular Dance* (Basingstoke and New York: Palgrave Macmillan, 2011).

Drake, Philip, '"Mortgaged to Music": New Retro Movies in 1990s Hollywood Cinema', in Paul Grainge (ed.), *Memory and Popular Film* (Manchester: University of Manchester Press, 2003).

Dueland, Peter, ed., *The Nordic Cultural Model* (Copenhagen: Nordic Cultural Institute, 2003).

Dunn, Ginette, *The Fellowship of Song: Popular Singing Traditions in East Suffolk* (London: Croom Helm, 1980).

Dyer, Richard, 'A Star is Born and the Construction of Authenticity', in Christine Gledhill (ed.), *Stardom: Industry of Desire* (London: Routledge, 1991).

Ehrlich, Cyril, *The Music Profession in Britain since the Eighteenth Century* (Oxford: Clarendon, 1985).

Fanon, Frantz, *Black Skin, White Masks* (London: Pluto Press, 1986).

Farnell, Brenda, *Human Action Signs in Cultural Context: The Visible and the Invisible in Movement and Dance* (Metuchen: Scarecrow Press, 1995).

Farnell, Brenda, 'Metaphors We Move By', *Visual Anthropology*, 8 (1996): 311-35.

Fast, Susan, *In the Houses of the Holy: Led Zeppelin and the Power of Rock Music* (Oxford: Oxford University Press, 2001).

Filene, Benjamin, *Romancing the Folk: Public Memory and American Roots Music* (Chapel Hill: University of North Carolina Press, 2000).

Fine, Michelle, Lois Weis, Judi Addelston and Julia Marusza, '(In)secure Times: Constructing White Working-Class Masculinities in the Late 20th Century', *Gender and Society*, 11/1 (1997): 52-69.

Fiskvik, Anne, *Koreomusialsk Idealisering og Praksis: En komparativ koreomusialaks analyse av balletten Ildfuglen* (Trondheim: Tapir Akademisk Forlag, 2006).

Floyd, Samuel A., *The Power of Black Music: Interpreting Its History from Africa to the United States* (New York: Oxford University Press, 1996).

Folkedal, Halldis, 'Den kvinnelige hallingdansaren. Om kropp, kjønn og seksualitet i norsk folkedans', Master's thesis (Trondheim: Tapir Trykk, 2009).

Forrest, John, 'Morris Dance', in Selma Jean Cohen (ed.), *The International Encyclopedia of Dance: E-Reference Edition* (Oxford University Press, 1998, 2005), accessed 18 January 2012.

Foucault, Michel, *Discipline and Punish: The Birth of the Prison*, trans. Alan Sheridan (New York: Vintage Books, 1977).

Franks, A. H., *Social Dance, A Short History* (London: Routledge and Kegan Paul, 1964).

Frith, Simon, Will Straw, and John Street, eds, *The Cambridge Companion to Pop and Rock* (New York: Cambridge University Press, 2001).

Gaines, Will, Frank Holder and Chris Parry, 'Rhythm Tap, Jazz Improvisation and Buddy Bradley in 1950s and 60s London', in *Dancing at the Crossroads: African Diasporic Dances in Britain* (London: London Metropolitan University, 2002).

Galinsky, Philip, 'Co-option, Cultural Resistance, and Afro-Brazilian Identity: A History of the *Pagode* Samba Movement in Rio de Janeiro', *Latin American Music Review*, 17/2 (1996): 120-49.

Garratt, Sheryl, *Adventures in Wonderland: A Decade of Club Culture* (London: Headline, 1998).

Gasnault, François, *Guinguettes et lorettes: Bals publics à Paris au XIXe siècle* (Paris: Aubier, 1986).

Gelatt, Roland, *The Fabulous Phonograph 1877-1977*, 2nd rev. edn (New York: MacMillan, 1977).

George-Graves, Nadine, '"Just Like Being at the Zoo": Primitivity and Ragtime Dance', in Julie Malnig (ed.), *Ballroom, Boogie, Shimmy Sham, Shake: A Social and Popular Dance Reader* (Urbana: University of Illinois Press, 2009).

Gilbert, Jeremy and Ewan Pearson, *Discographies: Dance Music and the Politics of Sound* (London: Routledge, 1999).

Gilroy, Paul, 'Exer(or)cising Power: Black Bodies in the Black Public Sphere', in Helen Thomas (ed.), *Dance in the City* (New York: Macmillan, 1997).

Gilroy, Paul, *There Ain't No Black in the Union Jack* (1987; reprint, Abingdon: Routledge, 2010).

Gordon, Rae Beth, 'Natural Rhythm: La Parisienne Dances with Darwin: 1875-1910', *Modernism/modernity*, 10/4 (2003): 617-56.

Gordon, Rae Beth, 'The White Savage in the Parisian Music Hall', *Fashion Theory: The Journal of Dress, Body and Culture*, 8/3 (2004): 267-99.

Graves, Charles, *Champagne and Chandeliers: The Story of the Café de Paris* (London: Odhams Press, 1958).

Guillermoprieto, Alma, *Samba* (New York, 1990) *Samba* (New York: Vintage Books, 1990).

Hall, Joanna, 'House Queens and Techno Drones: The Social Construction of Gender in the House and Techno Club through Dance Movement and Other Embodied Practices', Master's thesis (University of Surrey, 2002).

Hall, Joanna, 'Mapping the Multifarious: The Gentrification of Dance Music Club Cultures', in Janet Lansdale (ed.), *Decentring Dancing Texts: The Challenge of Interpreting Dances* (Basingstoke: Palgrave Macmillan, 2008).

Hall, Joanna, 'Heterocorporealities: Popular Dance and Cultural Hybridity in UK Drum 'n' Bass Club Culture', PhD diss. (University of Surrey, 2009).

Hall, Stuart, 'Old and New Identities, Old and New Ethnicities', in Les Back and John Solomos (eds), *Theories of Race and Racism: A Reader* (London: Routledge, 2000).

Hall, Stuart, 'Notes on Deconstructing "The Popular"', in John Storey (ed.), *Cultural Theory and Popular Culture: A Reader* (London: Pearson Education, 2006).

Hall, Stuart and Tony Jefferson, eds, *Resistance through Rituals: Youth Subcultures in Post-War Britain*, 2nd edn (London: Routledge, 2006).

Hammer, Christopher, 'Sogne-Beskrivelse over Hadeland udi Aggershuus Stift i Norge, tilligemed et geographisk Kort og Tegning over de tvende Grans Hoved-Kirker paa en Kirkegaard', *Årbok for Hadeland*, 33 (2000): 14-223.

Hammergren, Lena, Karin Helander, Tiina Rosenberg, and Willmar Sauter, *Teater i Sverige* (Hedemora: Gidlund, 2004).

Hammergren, Lena, 'Dance and Democracy in Norden', in Karen Vedel (ed.), *Dance and the Formation of Norden* (Trondheim: Tapir Academic Press, 2011)

Hatten, Robert, *Interpreting Musical Gestures, Topics and Tropes: Mozart, Beethoven, Schubert* (Bloomington: Indiana University Press, 2004).

Hauser, Arnold, *The Social History of Art. Volume III: Rococo, Classicism and Romanticism* (London and New York: Routledge and Kegan Paul, 1951).

Hebdige, Dick, *Subculture: The Meaning of Style* (London: Methuen, 1979).

Hinchberger, Bill, 'Bahia Music Story', in Robert M. Levine and John J. Crocitti (eds), *The Brazil Reader: History, Culture, Politics* (Durham: Duke University Press, 1999).

Hobsbawm, Eric, 'Introduction: Inventing Traditions', in Eric Hobsbawm and Terrence Ranger (eds), *The Invention of Tradition* (Cambridge: Cambridge University Press, 1983).

Hodkinson, Paul, 'Ageing in a Spectacular "Youth Culture": Continuity, Change and Community Amongst Older Goths', *The British Journal of Sociology*, 62/2 (2011): 262-82.

Hooper, James, *Peirce on Signs: Writings on Semiotic by Charles Sanders Peirce* (Chapel Hill: University of North Carolina Press, 1991).

Hope, Donna, 'The Lyrical Don: Embodying Violent Masculinity in Jamaican Dancehall Culture', *Discourses in Dance*, 2/2 (2004): 27-43.

Huq, Rupa, *Beyond Subculture: Pop, Youth and Identity in a Post-colonial World* (London: Routledge, 2006).

Hutcheon, Linda, *A Theory of Parody: The Teachings of Twentieth-century Art Forms* (Urbana: University of Illinois Press, 1985).

Jenkins, Henry, *Textual Poachers: Television Fans and Participatory Culture* (New York: Routledge, 1992).

Jenkins, Henry, *Confronting the Challenges of Participatory Culture: Media Education for the 21st Century* (Cambridge, MA: MIT Press, 2009).

Jowitt, Deborah, *Jerome Robbins: His Life, His Theater, His Dance* (New York: Simon and Schuster, 2004).

Kahn-Harris, Keith, 'Unspectacular Subculture?: Transgression and Mundanity in the Global Extreme Metal Scene', in Andy Bennett and Keith Kahn-Harris (eds), *After Subculture: Critical Studies in Contemporary Youth Culture* (Basingstoke and New York: Palgrave Macmillan, 2004).

Keane, Michael A., 'Once were Peripheral: Creating Media Capacity in East Asia', *Media Culture Society*, 28/6 (2006): 835-55.

Keil, Charles, 'Participatory Discrepancies and the Power of Music', in Charles Keil and Steven Feld (eds), *Music Grooves: Essays and Dialogues* (1987; Chicago: Unversity of Chicago Press, 1995).

Kenney, William Howland, *Recorded Music in American Life: The Phonograph and Popular Memory, 1890-1945* (Oxford: University Press, 1999).

Kershaw, Baz, 'Curiosity or Contempt: On Spectacle, the Human, and Activism', *Theatre Journal*, 55/4 (2003): 591-611.

Kjølaas, Gerd, *Dans, ropte livet* (Skillingsfors: DGT, 1998).

Kruse, Holly, 'Early Audio Technology and Domestic Space', *Stanford Humanities Review*, 3/2 (1993): 1-14.

Lakoff, George and Mark Johnson, *Metaphors We Live By* (1980; reprint Chicago: Chicago University Press, 2003).

Lay, Howard G., 'Pictorial Acrobatics', in Gabriel P. Weisberg (ed.), *Montmartre and the Making of Mass Culture* (New Brunswick: Rutgers University Press, 2001).

Leme, Mônica Neves, *Que Tchan é esse? Indústria e produção musical no Brasil dos anos 90* (São Paulo: Anna Blume, 2003).

Lund, Sven, 'Jens Lolle. Komponisten til Amors og Ballettmesterens Luner', *Fund og Forskning I det kongelige biblioteks samlinger*, 13 (1966): 83-8.

Lutz, Tom, *American Nervousness, 1903: An Annecdotal History* (Ithaca: Cornell University Press, 1991).

McClary, Susan, 'Towards a Feminist Criticism of Music', *Canadian University Music Review*, 10/2 (1990): 9-18.

McGowan, Chris and Ricardo Pessanha, *The Brazilian Sound: Samba, Bossa Nova, and the Popular Music of Brazil* (Philadelphia: Temple University Press, 1998).

Mackinnon, Niall, *The British Folk Scene: Musical Performance and Social Identity* (Buckingham: Open University Press, 1993).

McLeod, John (ed.), *Beginning Postcolonialism* (Manchester: Manchester University Press. 2000).

McMains, Juliet, *Glamour Addiction: Inside the American Ballroom Dance Industry* (Middletown: Wesleyan University Press, 2006).

Magee, Jeffrey, 'Ragtime and Early Jazz', in David Nicholls (ed.), *The Cambridge History of American Music* (Cambridge: Cambridge University Press, 1998).

Magraw, Roger, *France 1815-1914: The Bourgeois Century* (Oxford: Fontana, 1983).

Malbon, Ben, *Clubbing: Dancing, Ecstasy and Vitality* (London: Routledge, 1999).

Malnig, Julie, *Dancing Till Dawn: A Century of Exhibition Ballroom Dance* (New York: New York University Press, 1992).

Malnig, Julie, 'Athena Meets Venus: Visions of Women in Social Dance in the Teens and Early 1920s', *Dance Research Journal*, 31/2 (1999): 34-62.

Malnig, Julie, 'Apaches, Tangos, and Other Indecencies: Women, Dance, and New York Nightlife of the 1910s', in Julie Malnig (ed.), *Ballroom, Boogie, Shimmy Sham, Shake: A Social and Popular Dance Reader* (Urbana: University of Illinois Press, 2009).

Malnig, Julie, ed., *Ballroom, Boogie, Shimmy Sham, Shake: A Social and Popular Dance Reader* (Urbana: University of Illinois Press, 2009).

Matoré, Georges, 'Cancan et chahut, termes de danse (1829-1845)', in Charles Bruneau (ed.), *Mélanges de linguistique française offerts à M. Charles Bruneau* (Geneva: Droz, 1954).

Meglin, Joellen A., 'Galanterie and Glory: Women's Will and the Eighteenth-Century Worldview in *Les Indes Galantes*', in Lynn Matluck Brooks (ed.), *Women's Work: Making Dance in Europe before 1800* (Madison: University of Wisconsin Press, 2007).

Melberg, Arne, *Theories of Mimesis* (Cambridge: Cambridge University Press, 1995).

Middleton, Richard, *Studying Popular Music* (Milton Keynes: Open University Press, 1997).

Millard, André, *America on Record: A History of Recorded Sound* (Cambridge: University Press, 1995).

Miller, Mark, *High Hat, Trumpet and Rhythm: The Life and Music of Valaida Snow* (Toronto: The Mercury Press, 2007).

Morton, David, *Off the Record: The Technology and Culture of Sound Recording in America* (New Brunswick: Rutgers University Press, 2000).

Moskowitz, Marc L., *Cries of Joy, Songs of Sorrow: Chinese Pop Music and Its Cultural Connotations* (Honolulu: University of Hawaii Press, 2010).

Muggleton, David, *Inside Subculture: The Postmodern Meaning of Style* (Oxford: Berg, 2002).

Munt, Sally, ed., *Cultural Studies and the Working Class: Subject to Change* (London: Cassell, 2000).

Myers, Edward, 'A Phase-Structural Analysis of the Foxtrot, with Tranformational Rules', *Journal for the Anthropological Study of Human Movement* (1979): 246-68.

Nahachewsky, Andriy, 'Once Again: On the Concept of Second Existence Folk Dance', *Yearbook for Traditional Music*, 33 (2001): 17-28.

Neal, Mark Anthony, *What the Music Said: Black Popular Music and Black Public Culture* (New York: Routledge, 1998).

Neely, Daniel, '"Mento, Jamaica's Original Music": Development, Tourism and the Nationalist Frame', PhD diss. (New York University, 2008).

Negrón-Montaner, Frances, 'Feeling Pretty: West Side Story and Puerto Rican Identity Discourses', *Social Text*, 18/2 (Summer 2000): 83-106.

Nora, Pierre, *Realms of Memory: The Construction of the French Past, Vol. 3: Symbols*, translated by Arthur Goldhammer (New York: Columbia University Press, 1998).

Nowell, David, *Too Darn Soulful: The Story of Northern Soul* (London: Robson Books, 2001).

Ong, Walter J., *Orality and Literacy: The Technologizing of the Word* (1982; reprint, London: Routledge, 2001).

Osborne, Peter and Lynne Segal, 'Gender as Performance: An Interview with Judith Butler', *Radical Philosophy*, 67 (1994): 32-9.

Packman, Jeff, 'The *Carnavalização* of São João: Forrós, Sambas, and Festive Interventions during Bahia, Brazil's June Party Season', *Ethnomusicology Forum*, 21/3 (2012): 327-53.

Parfitt, Clare, 'Capturing the Cancan: Body Politics from the Enlightenment to Postmodernity', PhD diss. (University of Surrey, Roehampton, 2008).

Parfitt-Brown, Clare, 'Popular Past, Popular Present, Post-Popular?', *Conversations Across the Field of Dance Studies*, 31 (2010): 18-20.

Parsonage, Catherine, 'The Popularity of Jazz, an Unpopular Problem: The Significance of Robbie Williams' *Swing When You're Winning'*, *The Source*, 2 (2004): 59-80.

Parsonage, Catherine, *The Evolution of Jazz in Britain, 1880-1935* (Aldershot: Ashgate, 2005).

Peirce, Charles Sanders, *Philosophical Writings of Peirce*, edited by Justus Buchler (New York: Dover, 1955).

Peiss, Kathy, *Cheap Amusements: Working Women and Leisure in Turn-of-the-Century New York* (Philadelphia: Temple University Press, 1986).

Penny, Patricia A., 'Contemporary Competitive Ballroom Dancing: An Ethnography', PhD diss. (University of Surrey, 1997).

Pessis, Jacques and Jacques Crépineau, *The Moulin Rouge* (Stroud: Alan Sutton Publishing, 1990).

Picart, Caroline, *From Ballroom to Dancesport: Aesthetics, Athletics, and Body Culture* (Albany: State University of New York Press, 2006).

Pick, Daniel, *Faces of Degeneration: A European Disorder, c. 1848-1918* (Cambridge: Cambridge University Press, 1989).

Pickering, Michael, *Blackface Minstrelsy in Britain* (Aldershot: Ashgate, 2008).

Pini, Maria, Club Cultures and Female Subjectivity: The Move from Home to House (Basingstoke: Palgrave, 2001).

Portis, Larry, *French Frenzies: A Social History of Pop Music in France* (College Station, TX: Virtualbookworm Publishing, 2004).

Price, David, *Cancan!* (London: Cygnus Arts, 1998).

Quinn, Michael, '"Never Shoulda Been Let out the Penitentiary": Gangsta Rap and the Struggle over Racial Identity', *Cultural Critique*, 34 (Autumn 1996): 65-89.

Rasula, Jed, 'The Media of Memory: The Seductive Menace of Records in Jazz History', in Krin Gabbard (ed.), *Jazz Among the Discourses* (Durham: Duke University Press, 1995).

Richardson, P. J. S., *A History of English Ballroom Dancing* (London: Herbert Jenkins, 1946).

Robinson, Danielle, 'Performing American: Ragtime Dancing as Participatory Minstrelsy', *Dance Chronicle*, 32 (2009): 89-126.

Robinson, Danielle, 'The Ugly Duckling: The Refinement of Ragtime Dancing and the Mass Production and Marketing of Modern Social Dance', *Dance Research*, 28/2 (2010): 179-99.

Robson, Garry, 'Millwall Football Club: Masculinity, Race and Belonging', in Sally Munt (ed.), *Cultural Studies and the Working Class: Subject to Change* (London: Cassell, 2000).

Rose, Margaret A., *Parody: Ancient, Modern, and Post-modern* (Cambridge: Cambridge University Press, 1993).

Rose, Tricia, *Black Noise: Rap Music and Black Culture in Contemporary America* (Hanover: Wesleyan University Press, 1994).

Rubin, Rachel and Melnick, Jeffrey, 'Broadway, 1957: *West Side Story* and the Nuyorican Blues', in Rachel Ruben and Jeffrey Melnick (eds), *Immigration and American Popular Culture* (New York: New York University Press, 2007).

Rye, Howard, 'Visiting Firemen 17: Valaida Snow' in Laurie Wright (ed.), *Storyville 1998-9* (Chigwell: Laurie Wright, 1999).

Said, Edward, *Orientalism* (New York: Pantheon Books, 1978).

Sandars, Diane, 'Highly Hybridic, Mostly Palimpsestic: Innovative Uses of Music Video in the Recent Australian Musicals, *Moulin Rouge* and *One Night the Moon*', paper presented at 'What Lies Beneath', Postgraduate Conference (University of Melbourne, 6 November 2003).

Sanjek, David, 'Groove Me: Dancing to the Discs of Northern Soul', in Jill Terry and Neil A. Wynn (eds), *Transatlantic Roots Music: Folk, Blues, and National Identities* (Jackson: University Press of Mississippi, 2012).

Savigliano, Marta, *Tango and the Political Economy of Passion* (Boulder: Westview Press, 1995).

Schiff, David, 'Bernstein, Leonard', in *Grove Music Online*, *Oxford Music Online*, accessed 14 February 2011.

Scott, Derek B., 'Blackface Minstrels, Black Minstrels, and their Reception in England', in Rachel Cowgill and Julian Rushton (eds), *Europe, Empire, and Spectacle in Nineteenth-Century British Music* (Aldershot: Ashgate, 2006).

Severiano, Jairo, *Uma História da Música Popular Brasileira: Das Origens à Modernidade* (São Paulo: Editora 34, 2008).

Shumway, David, 'Performance', in Bruce Horner and Thomas Swiss (eds), *Key Terms in Popular Music and Culture* (Malden, MA: Blackwell, 1999).

Siefert, Marsha, 'The Audience at Home: The Early Recording Industry and the Marketing of Musical Taste', in James S. Ettema and D. Charles Whitney (eds), *Audiencemaking: How the Media Create the Audience* (Thousand Oaks, MI: Sage Publications, 1994).

Siefert, Marsha, 'Aesthetics, Technology, and the Capitalization of Culture: How the Talking Machine Became a Musical Instrument', *Science in Context*, 8/2 (1995): 417-49.

Simeone, Nigel, *Leonard Bernstein: West Side Story* (Farnham: Ashgate, 2009).

Simons, Andy, 'Black British Swing Part One', *The IAJRC Journal*, 41/3 (August 2008): 35-44.

Simons, Andy, 'Black British Swing Part Two', *The IAJRC Journal*, 41/4 (December 2008): 59-68.

Simons, Andy, 'Black British Swing Part Three', *The IAJRC Journal*, 42/1 (March 2009): 55-66.

Sivertsen, Helge, 'Norsk kulturpolitikk 1945-1965', in Edvard Beyer et al. (eds), *Norsk kultur og Kulturpolitikk: Norsk Kulturråd, fortid og framtid* (Oslo: Cappelen Norsk Forlag, 1985).

Skeggs, Beverley, *Class, Self, Culture* (London: Routledge, 2004).

Skidmore, Thomas E., *Black into White: Race and Nationality in Brazilian Thought* (Durham: Duke University Press, 1998).

Small, Christopher, *Musicking: The Meanings of Performing and Listening* (Middletown: Wesleyan University Press, 1998).

Smith, Marian, *Ballet and Music in the Age of 'Giselle'* (Princeton: Princeton University Press, 2000).

Smith, Nicola, 'Beyond the Master Narrative of Youth: Researching Ageing Popular Music Scenes', in Derek Scott (ed.), *The Ashgate Research Companion to Popular Musicology* (Farnham: Ashgate, 2009).

Spring, Howard, 'Dance', in Barry Kernfeld (ed.), *The New Grove Dictionary of Jazz, Grove Music Online*, Oxford Music Online, accessed 21 November 2011.

Stearns, Marshall and Jean Stearns, *Jazz Dance: The Story of American Vernacular Dance* (London: Collier MacMillan, 1968; reprint, New York: Da Capo, 1994).

Storey, John, *Inventing Popular Culture: From Folklore to Globalization* (Oxford: Wiley-Blackwell, 2003).

Storey, John, *Cultural Theory and Popular Culture: An Introduction* (London: Pearson Education, 2006).

Streletski, Gérard, et al., 'Philippe Musard', in *Grove Music Online, Oxford Music Online*, accessed 27 October 2011.

Strinati, Dominic, *An Introduction to Theories of Popular Culture* (London: Routledge, 1995).

Suisman, David, *Selling Sounds: The Commercial Revolution in American Music* (Cambridge: Harvard University Press, 2009).

Swain, Joseph, P., *The Broadway Musical: A Critical and Musical Survey* (Oxford: Oxford University Press, 1990).

Sweers, Britta, *Electric Folk: The Changing Face of English Traditional Music* (Oxford: Oxford University Press, 2005).

Thomas, Helen, *Dance, Modernity, and Culture: Explorations in the Sociology of Dance* (London: Routledge, 1995).

Thompson, Leslie and Jeffrey Green, *Swing from a Small Island: The Story of Leslie Thompson* (London: Northway Publications, 2009).

Thornton, Sarah, *Club Cultures: Music, Media and Subcultural Capital* (Cambridge: Polity Press, 1995).

Tinhorão, José Ramos, *História Social da Música Popular Brasileira* (São Paulo: Editora 34, 1998).

Took, Barry, *Round the Horne: The Complete and Utter History* (London: Boxtree, 1998).

Tucker, Sherrie, *Swing Shift: 'All-Girl' Bands of the 1940s* (Durham: Duke University Press, 2000).

Turino, Thomas, 'Signs of Imagination, Identity, and Experience: A Peircian Semiotic Theory for Music', *Ethnomusicology*, 43/2 (1999): 221-55.

Turino, Thomas, *Music as Social Life: The Politics of Participation* (Chicago: University of Chicago Press, 2008).

Turner, Gordon and Alwyn Turner, *The History of British Military Bands*, 3 vols (Staplehurst: Spellmount Publishers, 1994, 1996, 1997).

Valis Hill, Constance, 'From Bharata Natyam to Bop: Jack Cole's "Modern" Jazz Dance', *Dance Research Journal*, 33/2 (Winter 2001): 29-39.

Vianna, Hermano, *The Mystery of Samba: Popular Music and National Identity in Brazil*, edited and translated by John Charles Chasteen (Chapel Hill: University of North Carolina Press, 1999).

Waddey, Ralph, 'Viola de Samba and Samba de Viola in the Recôncavo of Bahia (Brazil)', *Latin American Music Review* 1/2 (1980): 196-212.

Waksman, Steve, *Instruments of Desire: The Electric Guitar and the Shaping of Musical Experience* (Cambridge, MA: Harvard University Press, 1999).

Wall, Tim, 'Out on the Floor: The Politics of Dancing on the Northern Soul Scene', *Popular Music*, 25/3 (2006): 431-55.

Wells, Elizabeth Anne, 'West Side Story and the Hispanic', *Echo: A Music-Centered Journal*, 2/1 (Spring 2000), accessed 14 February 2011.

Wells, Elizabeth Anne, *West Side Story: Cultural Perspectives on an American Musical* (Lanham, MD: Scarecrow Press, 2010).

Wilmer, Val, 'Johnson, Kenrick Reginald Hijmans (1914-1941)', in *Oxford Dictionary of National Biography*, (Oxford University Press, 2004, online edn, May 2006), accessed 21 November 2011.

Wilson, Andrew, *Northern Soul: Music, Drugs and Subcultural Identity* (Cullompton, Devon: Willan Publishing, 2007).

Winstanley, Russ and David Nowell, *Soul Survivors: The Wigan Casino Story* (London: Robson Books, 1996).

Winter, Marion, *The Theatre of Marvels* (London: Benjamin Blom, 1962).

Zeiner-Henriksen, Hans T., 'The "PoumTchak" Pattern: Correspondences Between Rhythm, Sound, and Movement in Electronic Dance Music', PhD diss. (University of Oslo, 2010).

Published Primary Sources

Amateur, 'The Waltz and the Boston', *The Dancing Times* (December 1911): 57.

'An Invitation to SINGers, Skifflers, Choir Members', *Sing*, 4/1 (1957): 9.

'Are Ballroom Dancers Too Conservative?', *The Dancing Times* (September 1926): 530.

'A Singer's Notebook', *Sing,* 1/1 (1954): 11.

'August a Productive Month in Philadelphia', *The Talking Machine World*, 9/9 (1913): 50.

'A Waltz Dream', *The Dancing Times* (January 1911): 76-79.

'Ball-Room Dancing of To-day', *The Dancing Times* (April 1911): 164-5.

'Ball-Room Fashions', *The Ball Room*, 15/195 (November 1911): 9.

Barlet, *Le Guide des Sergens de Ville, et Autres Préposés de l'Administration de la Police* (Paris: chez l'auteur, 1831).

Beard, George, *American Nervousness: Its Causes and Consequences: A Supplement to Nervous Exhaustion (Neurasthenia)* (New York: G. P. Putnam's Sons, 1881).

Berliner, Emile, 'The Gramophone: Paper Read before the Franklin Institue, May 16, 1888 by its Inventor', (Washington, DC: The United States Gramophone Company, 1894).

Bournonville, August, *Mit teaterliv: erindringer og tidsbilleder* (1848; reprint, Copenhagen: Thaning & Appel, 1979).

Bradley, Josephine, 'Random Reflections on War-Time Dancing', *Dancing Times* (February 1940): 292.

Bradley, Josephine, *Dancing Through Life* (London: Hollis and Carter, 1947).

Bui, Ly Y., *Plan of the Champ de Mars, Paris 1889*, available online through the University of Maryland (2005), accessed 23 April, 2007, http://hdl.handle.net/1903.1/308.

Carter, Sydney, Ewan MacColl and Peggy Seeger, 'Going American?', *English Dance and Song* (1961): 19-20.

Castle, Vernon and Irene, *Modern Dancing* (New York: Harper and Brothers 1914).

'Catering to Women', *The Talking Machine World*, 9/3 (1913): 12.

'Chinese Phonograph Records', *The Talking Machine World*, 1/1 (1905): 6.

'Cincinnati Co-Eds Use Victrola', *The Voice of the Victor*, 10/10 (1915): 194.

Collinson, Francis, 'A Reminiscence', *Journal of the English Folk Dance and Song Society*, 8.3 (1958): 145-6.

Crompton, R.M., *Theory and Practice of Modern Dancing* (London: Willcocks, 1892).

Crozier, Gladys Beattie, *The Tango and How to Dance It* (London: Andrew Melrose, 1913).

D'Albert, Charles, *Dancing: Technical Encyclopaedia of the Theory and Practice of The Art of Dancing* (London, 1913).

de Koven Bowen, Louise, *Our Most Popular Recreation Controlled by the Liquor Interests: A Study of Public Dance Halls* (Chicago: Juvenile Protective Association of Chicago, 1911).

Desrat, G., *Dictionnaire de la Danse Histoire, Théorique, Pratique et Bibliographique* (Paris: Paris Librairies, Imprimeries Réunies, 1895).

'Developing Musical Taste', *The Talking Machine World*, 7/4 (1911): 3.

Dodworth, Allen, *Dancing and Its Relations to Education and Social Life* (New York: Harper & Bros, 1885).

Edison Records (Boston: Eastern Talking Machine Co., December 1899).

Edison, Thomas A., 'Introduction', in George E. Tewksbury, *A Complete Manual of the Edison Phonograph* (Newark: US Phonograph Co., 1897).

'Editorial', *Ethnic*, 1/4 (1959): 3.

Every Woman's Encyclopaedia (London: Amalgamated Press, 1910-12).

'Exercises a Moral Influence', *The Talking Machine World*, 1/2 (1905): 21.

Fox Strangways, A. H. and Maud Karpeles, *Cecil Sharp* (London: Oxford University Press and Humphrey Milford, 1933).

Fox Strangways, A. H. and Maud Karpeles, *Cecil Sharp*, 2nd edn (London: Geoffrey Cumberlege and Oxford University Press, 1955).

Freyre, Gilberto, *The Masters and the Slaves: A Study in the Development of Brazilian Civilization*, translated by Samuel Putnam (1933; reprint, New York: Knopf, 1964).

Frothingham, Robert, 'Little Advertising Stories: The Victor', *Everybody's Magazine* (July 1910): 80d-80h.

Gallini, Giovanni-Andrea, *A Treatise on the Art of Dancing* (1762; reprint, New York: Broude Brothers, 1967).

Garbit, Frederick J., *The Phonograph and Its Inventor, Thomas Alvah [sic] Edison* (Boston: Gunn, Bliss and Co., 1878).

Gates, W. F., 'Ethiopian Syncopation', *Musician*, 7 (1902): 341.

Gautier, Théophile, Histoire de l'art dramatique en France depuis vingt-cinq ans, vol. 1 (Paris: Édition Hetzel, 1858).

Grainger, Percy, 'Collecting with a Phonograph', in Teresa Balough (ed.), *A Musical Genius From Australia: Selected Writings By and About Percy Grainger* (Nedlands: Department of Music, University of Western Australia, 1982).

Grainger, Percy, 'The Impress of Personality in Unwritten Music', in Teresa Balough (ed.), *A Musical Genius From Australia: Selected Writings By and About Percy Grainger* (Nedlands: Department of Music, University of Western Australia, 1982).

Grant, Peter, 'A Package Deal', *Ethnic*, 1/4 (1959): 12.

Grant, Peter, 'The Pure Spring', *Ethnic*, 1/1 (1959): 10-11.

Grove, Lily, *Dancing* (London: Longmans, Green, 1907).

Hametab, Correspondence, *The Dancing Times* (January 1912): 120.

'Helps to Spread Civilization', *The Talking Machine World*, 2/7 (1906): 5.

'Herr Desider Gottlieb', *The Dancing Times* (July 1911): 230.

Humphrey, Walter, 'The Boston', *The Dancing Times* (March 1911): 144.

Humphrey, Walter, 'The 'Double Boston'', *The Dancing Times* (October 1911): 8-9.

Humphrey, Walter, Correspondence, *The Dancing Times* (December 1911): 78.

Hyatt-Woolf, Elizabeth, 'Passing of the Waltz', *The Dance Journal* (March 1910): 5-6.

Investigator, 'Will the Boston Live?', *The Dancing Times* (October 1910 and November 1910): 9-10, 33-4.

Israels, Mrs. Chas. H., 'The Dance Hall and the Amusement Resorts', *Transactions of the American Society of Sanitary and Moral Prophylaxis*, 3 (1910): 46-50.

Jenkins, William H., *The Romance of Victor* ([n.p.], 1927).

'Johnson's Resident Break', *Melody Maker*, 26 December 1936, p. 8.

'Ken Johnson has New Air Ideas', *Melody Maker*, 2 December 1939, p. 7.

Kennedy, Douglas, 'Editorial', *Folk*, 1 (1962): 1.

Kennedy, Douglas, 'A Fourth Folk Festival', *Sing*, 6/10 (1962): 107.
Kennedy, Peter, 'Harry Cox: English Folk Singer', *Journal of the English Folk Dance and Song Society*, 8.3, (1958): 142.
Kinney, Troy and Margaret West Kinney, *Social Dancing of Today* (New York: Frederick A. Stokes & Co., 1914).
Lennard, Janet, 'Ball-Room Dancing of To-day', *The Dancing Times*, April (1911): 164-5.
Le Semaine, 18 October 1829: 2.
Lloyd, A. L., 'So You Are Interested in Folk Music?', *Recorded Folk Music*, 1 (1958): 1-6.
Lloyd, A. L., 'Guest Spot', *Spin*, 1/6 (1962): 6, 8.
'London's New Ball-Room', *The Dancing Times* (January 1911): 82-4.
Luchet, Auguste, 'La Descente de la Courtille en 1833', in *Paris, ou le livre des cent-et-un* (Brussels: J.-P. Meline, 1833).
MacColl, Ewan, 'Why I Am Opening a New Club', *Sing*, 5/4 (1961): 65.
MacColl, Ewan, *Journeyman: An Autobiography* (London: Sidgwick & Jackson, 1990).
'Made in Britain', *Sing*, 4/4&5 (1957): 52.
'Making the Vacation 99 9/10% Fun', *The Voice of the Victor*, 10/8 (1915): 154.
Melrose, C. J, *Dancing up to Date* (London: Hart, 1892).
Mouvet, Maurice, *Art of Dancing* (New York: G. Schirmer, 1915).
'Much Perplexed', Correspondence, *The Dancing Times* (November 1911): 48.
Mumford, Ethel Watts, 'Where is Your Daughter this Afternoon?', *Harper's Weekly* (17 January 1914).
'Music at the North Pole', *The Talking Machine World*, 1/2 (1905): 10.
'Musical Impurity', *Etude*, 18 (January 1900): 16.
Nelson, Stanley, 'Swing – What are you teachers going to do about it?', *Dancing Times* (March 1938): 812-14.
'New British Coloured Band', *Melody Maker* (18 April 1936): 1.
Noël, François-Joseph-Michel, and M. Carpentier, 'Chahut et Cancans', in *Nouveau dictionnaire des origines, inventions et découvertes, dans les arts, les sciences, la géographie, le commerce, l'agriculture, etc.*, vol. 2 (Brussels: Librairie de Fréchet, 1828).
Northcote, Sydney, *Making Your Own Music* (London: Phoenix House, 1960).
Noverre, Jean Georges, *Letters on Dancing and Ballets*, translated by Cyril W. Beaumont (1803; reprint, Brooklyn, NY: Dance Horizons, 1966).
Østgaard, Nicolai R., *En Fjeldbygd: Billeder fra Østerdalen* (Christiania: Feilberg & Landmark, 1852).
Pierre, Monsieur, 'Dancing to "Swing Music"', *Dancing Times* (December 1939): 143-5.
'Policy', *Ethnic*, 1/2 (1959): 2.
'Policy Statement', *Ethnic*, 1/1 (1959): 2.
Robeson, Paul, 'Greetings', *Sing*, 2/2 (1955).

Sarcus, Charles Marie de, *Le Conservatoire de la Danse Moderne; charges Parisiennes* (Paris: A. de Vresse, 1845).

Scott, Edward, *The Art of Waltzing* (London: Hart, 1885).

Scott, Edward, *All About the Boston: A Critical & Practical Treatise on Modern Waltz Variations* (London: Geo. Routledge & Sons, 1913).

Sharp, Cecil J. (ed.), *Folk Songs of England Book 1: Folk Songs from Dorset Collected by H.E.D. Hammond* (London: Novello, 1908).

Sharp, Cecil J., *English Folk Songs, Vol. 1: Songs and Ballads* (London: Novello, [1921]).

Sheafe, Alfonso Joseph, *The Fascinating Boston* (Boston: The Boston Music Company, 1913).

Silvester, Victor and Philip J. S. Richardson, *The Art of the Ballroom* (London: Herbert Jenkins, 1936).

Smith, Paul, 'Danses prohibées', *Revue et Gazette Musicale de Paris*, 8/21 (February 1841): 113-14.

'Talking Machine a Civilizer: C. P. Sterns Tells of Trip Through the Philippine Islands in Which a Talking Machine Played a Star Part', *The Talking Machine World*, 1/8 (1905): 7. 'The British Association of Teachers of Dancing', *The Ball Room*, 16/206 (November 1912): 8-9.

'The Boston Dip', *The Director*, 1/1 (December 1897): 17-18.

The Edison Commercial System Conducted with the Business Phonograph (Orange, NJ: National Phonograph Company, 1907).

'The Most Popular Dance', *The Ball Room*, 16/197 (January 1912): 10.

The Phonograph and How to Use It (New York: National Phonograph Company, 1900).

'The Rise of English Waltz Composers', *The Dancing Times* (December 1910): 34-5.

'The Sitter Out' [P. J. S. Richardson], *The Dancing Times* (October 1910): 12-13.

'The "Talker" as an Educator', *The Talking Machine World*, 4/5 (1908): 3.

'The Talking Machine as a Musical Educator', *The Talking Machine World*, 4/5 (1908): 51.

The Talking Machine World.

The Voice of the Victor.

Three Modern Dances (Camden, NJ: Victor Talking Machine Co., 1914).

Un Vilain Masque, *Physiologie de l'opera, du carnaval, du cancan et de la cachucha* (Paris: Raymond-Bocquet, 1842).

Véron, Louis Désiré, *Mémoires d'un Bourgeois de Paris* (Paris: Librairie Nouvelle, 1856).

'Victor Letters to the Trade', *The Voice of the Victor*, 9/4 (1914): 76.

Index

References to figures are in **bold**.

0 1341 1464654 7

DATE DUE	RETURNED